MARCO POLO

IN DIA

CHINA
AFGHA-
NISTAN
NEPAL BHUTAN
PAKISTAN
IRAN New
Delhi
BANGLA-
Tropic of Cancer DESH
Kolkata
OMAN Mumbai MYAN-
MAR
INDIA
Arabian
Sea
Chennai
SRI LANKA
INDIAN OCEAN

www.marco-polo.com

THE TOURING APP

shows you the way...
including routes and offline maps!

FREE!

GET MORE OUT OF YOUR MARCO POLO GUIDE

IT'S AS SIMPLE AS THIS

1 go.marco-polo.com/ind

2 download and discover

GO!

WORKS OFFLINE!

SYMBOLS

INSIDER TIP Insider Tip

★ Highlight

●●●● Best of ...

 Scenic view

 Responsible travel: fair
trade principles and the
environment respected

PRICE CATEGORIES HOTELS

Expensive over 8,100 INR

Moderate 4,050–8,100 INR

Budget under 4,050 INR

Price for two people in a
double room, generally
excluding breakfast

**PRICE CATEGORIES
RESTAURANTS**

Expensive over 1,600 INR

Moderate 400–1,600 INR

Budget under 400 INR

Price of a meal comprising
three or four different dishes

CONTENTS

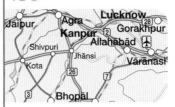

The best MARCO POLO Insider Tips

Our top 15 Insider Tips

INSIDER TIP **Hindustani-style design**

Nomen est omen – *Play Clan* design shops play on hackneyed Indian clichés. Very bright, very cool, very Indian → p. 126

INSIDER TIP **Beatle mania**

Relax like the Beatles: the Fab Four's best songs were created in a dilapidated *ashram* in Rishikesh → p. 59

INSIDER TIP **Exquisite jewellery**

Gleaming jewels fit for a king can be found in the *Bhuramal Rajmal Surana's* showroom in Jaipur. The descendants of jewellers who worked in the court of the Maharajas of Jaipur lack none of their ancestors' skills. → p. 76

INSIDER TIP **Sufi songs**

The air vibrates in *Hazrat Nizamuddin*! In the mausoleum of the Sufi saint Auliya people come together in the evening to sing trance-like chants. Ancient Islamic mysticism is more popular than ever in Delhi of the 21st century → p. 49

INSIDER TIP **Luxury in chaos**

The palatial *Dharampura* in Old Delhi will catapult you into the era of the Moguls. A unique experience: enjoying the view of the Jama Masjid while drinking a fresh lime soda on the roof terrace → p. 49

INSIDER TIP **Before sunrise**

Light a small oil lamp and float it down the Ganges like thousands of others and, from a boat, watch how the holy Hindu city of *Varanasi* becomes bathed in the gleaming golden yellow morning sun. This sight certainly makes up for having to get up early (photo above) → p. 62

INSIDER TIP **Oriental palace feel**

Step back to the days of great caravans: stay in the *Hotel Castle Mandawa* in Shekawati → p. 73

INSIDER TIP **Miles from anywhere**

Riding out into *Thar Desert* you will find nothing but sand, stones and sky (photo right) → p. 80

BEST OF ...

FOR FREE

● *Contemporary art*
Immerse yourself in the world of contemporary art when in India – and all for nothing. Stop by at *Jehangir Art Gallery* in Mumbai, probably the city's most famous gallery, or at *CIMA* in Kolkata, one of India's most renowned galleries with ever-changing exhibitions → p. 95, 117

● *Music and artistry on the beach*
In the finance metropolis of Mumbai there's not a lot free of charge. One of the few exceptions: *Chowpatty Beach*, where you can watch acrobats and musicians perform for free → p. 93

● *Tiffin delivery*
Around dabbawallas in Mumbai (photo) ensure that 200,000 commuters and schoolchildren are served their homemade meal every day. Watch how the dabbas – tiffin containers – are sorted and delivered in all directions: e.g. at lunchtime on the east side of *Churchgate Station* → p. 92

● *Light ceremony on the holy river*
Every evening, priests and Hindu believers celebrate *Maha Aarti Triveni Ghat* at on the banks of the Ganges in Rishikesh. Spiritual chants boom from loudspeakers and the priests hold up holy lights which are carried down the river after sunset. Nobody here asks for money as this is about something much more significant: the redemption from all sins → p. 59

● *Camel racing*
Have you ever had the chance of watching a camel race without paying anything? Not yet? Then head for the *Desert Fair Festival* in Jaisalmer → p. 170

● *Elephant polo*
It's not easy to grasp the rules of polo. So why not take up the offer made by most clubs and watch players training – for free? The oldest polo club in India, *The Rajasthan Polo Club* in Jaipur even offers free admission to matches → p. 77

●●●● Dots in guidebook refer to "Best of ..." tips

● *Sari Emporiums*

Every city has several emporiums full to the brim with fantastic sari material. These materials can be hemmed immediately or alternatively transformed into a blouse, for example in the *Vishvanath Gali* in Varanasi. The silk is more or less tightly woven depending on the region and the patterns also reveal where it has come from → p. 65

● *Open-air washing days*

There are laundries in every larger town in India. The biggest *open air laundry* is next to Mahalakshmi station in Mumbai (photo). The best place to watch the *dhobis* (laundry workers) doing the washing in stone troughs is from the road bridge → p. 95

● *Bazaars*

Immerse yourself in this sensual experience of intensive smells and brilliant colours to the confusing symphony of thousands of voices. Most of the colourful bazaars are divided into various sections for fruit, medicinal herbs, spices, jewellery, etc., such as in *Sardarpura Bazaar* in Jodhpur → p. 81

● *Ayurveda*

This ancient form of natural medical therapy is generally practiced largely in Rishikesh and Kerala. Many hotels and holiday resorts have picked up on the trend and Ayurveda can be found throughout India, e.g. in *Indeco Mahabalipuram* in Mamallapuram → p. 140

● *Auto rickshaws*

They clatter around everywhere in India, squeeze through the narrowest of alleyways and can transport a surprising number of people and items of baggage. The three-wheeled *auto rickshaws* can be found on every street corner and are one of the best ways to get around busy Chennai, for example → p. 124

● *Temple rituals*

Temple rituals in the morning and evenings with offerings, prayers and singing are fixtures in the everyday life of many Indians. Not everywhere is it forbidden for non-Hindus to go inside a temple or the sanctuary. In *Kalighat Kali Temple* in Kolkata, for instance, you can even allowed to be blessed with holy ash → p. 110

ONLY IN

BEST OF ...

PERFECT FOR ALL WEATHERS
Activities to brighten your day

● Barmy Bollywood
Don't be put off by Bollywood blockbusters in Hindi if you want to avoid the monsoon or the scorching heat. Much more interesting than the dialogue is the audience's reaction! In *Raj Mandir* in Jaipur, for instance, you can dance along with everyone else in the aisles → p. 77

● A day in a museum
Take an audio tour of the *National Museum* in New Delhi and find out about the fascinating wealth of 5,000 years of Indian cultural history. It comes as a bonus that the rooms are nice and cool → p. 47

● Off on a shopping spree
Huge shopping centres in the metropolises invite you to spend some time and money. The *Ambience Mall* and *Metropolitan Mall* (photo) in Delhi, for example, are quite an experience. Go for clothes, especially those made of cotton, silk or cashmere! → p. 44

● Kathakali – masks in Kochi
One of the fascinating things about the masks is how the make-up is put on beforehand. You can even take pictures of actors lying on the ground. If it rains, the performances are usually indoors or under trees → p. 136

● Hill Stations
The British colonial rulers planted these small towns as vanishing points for their heat-afflicted officers. One of them is *Mount Abu*, where in the hottest months, temperatures only reach a good 30 °C/86 ° F, whereas the nearby plains of Rajasthan heat up to more than 40 °C/104 °F → p. 82

● Dine in Style
Do what many Indians do when the weather is impossible – go out for a meal! Indian food, served as tasty titbits as starters, on a "sizzler" or in a clay pot, is celebrated with pleasure and is a nice pastime. Try, for example, *Dum Pukht* in Delhi → p. 48

RAIN

RELAX AND CHILL OUT
Take it easy and spoil yourself

● *Yoga in Sivananda Ashram*

If you fancy a bit of yoga and meditation to balance your body and mind, the *Sivananda Ashram* in picturesque Rishikesh at the foot of the Himalayas is a good place to forget the sometimes demanding pressures we have to face – emotional or otherwise → **p. 59**

● *Above the roofs of Ahmedabad*

The restaurant *Agashiye* has three terraces above the heritage hotel to which it belongs. After a day on the hectic streets of Ahmedabad you'll certainly appreciate the feeling of space, the peace and quiet and the excellent food → **p. 69**

● *The desert under a starry sky*

The expanse of Thar Desert (photo) is a relaxing sight. In a dip in the desert on your way to Fort Khimsar you can enjoy the wonderful silence of a moonlit evening and spend the night in *Khimsar Sand Dune Village* after sitting around the romantic campfire → **p. 80**

● *The botanic garden in Kolkata*

Havens of peace in a bustling megalopolis such as former Calcutta are priceless indeed. As such, the *botanic garden* in the city is a treasure to be cherished where you can forget the smog and noise outside its walls among the shade of the trees and water courses → **p. 110**

● *Beauty salons*

Let yourself be pampered for hours on end in *Noemi's Hair & Beauty Salon* in Panjim – just like the locals do. Traditional methods are used here by an experienced team → **p. 130**

● *Backwaters*

A tour lasting several hours or even days on a bamboo houseboat on the network of waterways called the *Backwaters* in Kerala is an experience not to be forgotten. In addition, a cook on board conjures up gourmet delights while you can watch the untouched scenery glide past in slow motion → **p. 135**

INTRODUCTION

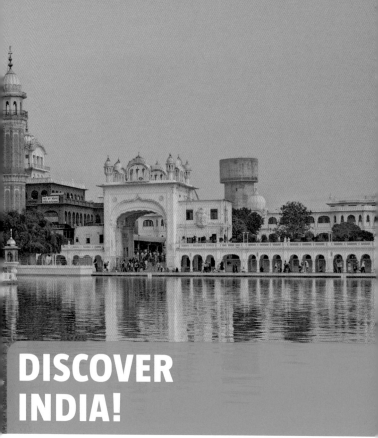

DISCOVER INDIA!

When you walk into the arrivals hall at Delhi Airport, you'll be automatically in for a big surprise! Designers have come up with an exotic, distinctly Indian style that is quite unmistakable. Two larger-than-life elephants on high plinths dominate the arrivals' experience here – encouraging after such a long flight. And this sets travellers in the mood for the country that has long since ceased being a poor nation.

For decades, the rest of the world felt sorry for India and dismissed it as backward and impoverished. Today, economics experts are discussing whether it will be China or India in top position in thirty years time as the fastest *booming nation*. The number of Indian millionaires runs into six figures. Mukesh Ambani, the richest of over 100 Indian billionaires and one of the richest men in the world, bought his wife an Airbus and built a private skyscraper in Mumbai just for his family and guests. The Indian steel millionaire, Lakshmi Mittal, reputedly the fourth wealthiest Indian man, acquired the European Arcelor concern and now owns the world's largest steel consortium. Narendra Modi, a former tea merchant and today Prime Minister of India, received compliments from the ex-President of the United Sates Obama: his meteoric career was a prime example of the *dynamics* and opportunities of progress in modern India.

India's high-tech future has long begun in megacities such as Bangalore

Although the indisputably gigantic economic leap forward has had little initial impact on the lives of the some 300 million Indians who live below the breadline, anyone who knows the India of five or ten years ago can sense a *difference* today. Many Indians are much more optimistic about the future and are enjoying the first signs of a new level of prosperity.

The boom is reflected in improved roads, well-constructed National Highways, new airports, exclusive hotels, *smart resorts* and well-equipped homestays. Today, tourism in India offers far more than just beach holidays with palm trees and excursions riding on camels: you now have an extensive choice of activities ranging from Ayurveda treatments, trekking tours and paragliding in the Himalayas to house-boat holidays in the backwaters of Kerala, rafting in the mountains, riding safaris in Rajasthan and journeys in historical luxury trains.

The *variety of scenery* is breathtaking – from the majestic peaks of the Himalayas to Thar Desert and mile-long, virtually untouched tropical beaches. It is also fascinating to see how many of the 1.3 billion Indians have retained their ancient cultural

Approx. 2800 BC
Indus Valley Harappan culture – writings, artificial irrigation

Approx. 1400 BC
Arrival of migrants from Afghanistan and the Persian territorries; emergence of Hinduism

Approx. 500 BC
Buddhism and Jainism oppose the caste system

Approx. 270–236 BC
Emperor Ashoka extends the first major Indian empire (Maurya) further south and promotes Buddhism

4th–8th centuries
Gupta dynasty; Indian culture flourishes once again

traditions while an enormous *shift into the modern age* has changed the whole country at the same time. You will find the original India in temples and palaces, villages and national parks – and the high-tech future in the booming megacities. The adventurous will find their eldorados somewhere, be it on the Lakshadweep Islands with their coral reefs or on the Andamans. The Indian tourist industry is promoting a new trend too – holidays in the countryside. There are after all more than 500,000 villages in India! Unmistakably Indian are meditation and *yoga courses* in an ashram. All in all, the country is now considered one of the most attractive tourist destinations in the world.

The economic boom has also enabled more and more Indians to explore their own country. However, for the majority of people, such luxuries are just a dream. In the state of Bihar, maladministration and corrupt governments have led to the number of poor people rising to 40 %. This is a striking contrast to the glittering shopping malls on the other side of the road and new palatial jewellers' *showrooms*, for example in southern Kerala. India is the country with the greatest quantities of gold still in private ownership anywhere in the world.

Despite all this, globetrotters do not need to worry that the old, adventurous and colourful India of old has disappeared. The expanses of farmland between the Himalayas and Kanyakumari

The multicoloured India of adventure has not disappeared

on the southern-most tip, are still unspoilt – as are the jungles and steppes, deserts and snowy mountains. *Shooting tigers, elephants and leopards* – with a camera of course – has survived to this day as has the India of magnificent religious sites carved out of stone, medieval forts and the palaces of the Maharajas, Hindu temples and Mughal mosques.

The year 1991 set the points for India's *economic boom*. The country was on the brink of national bankruptcy when a clever finance minister introduced crucial changes to commercial laws and reduced bureaucratic barriers: Manmohan Singh who was prime minister from 2010 to 2014. Since then, India's businesses and foreign investors have gained a certain freedom to operate while the market economy is still carefully monitored.

1192–93 Muslims sack Delhi (first Muslim attacks approx. 1000 AD)

1498 Vasco da Gama reaches India; start of European colonial rule

1526 Babur establishes the powerful Mughal Empire

1698 Foundation of Calcutta; initial claims by the British East India Company to make India a colony

1857–58 Mutiny against the British; the British Crown takes over rule from the East India Company

Covering an area of around 1.3 million mi² India may be smaller than Europe or the USA, but there are in excess of 1.3 billion more people living in India than in Europe and the USA combined. In a few years time, India will probably be the country with the biggest population in the world – ahead of China. Asian experts see the country as the most promising candidate for the number one slot – right after China, far ahead of Japan. India is second to none with regard to its wealth of new ideas, its flexibility and knowledge of languages, or so they believe. The growth rate of the Indian economy is already one of the fastest worldwide.

The economic boom, growth rate and *increasing population* – all these have their down sides too, for the countryside, people and animals. The water table in cities such as Delhi is constantly sinking and is also negatively impacted by environmental pollutants. The municipal water authority only turns on the mains for a few hours a day. The locals however have found a way to save water, at least in the rainy season. Rainwater is collected, filtered and then filtered again in the pipe system in each house.

How vitally important and yet how difficult the distribution of *water* is on a large scale, is reflected in negotiations with China and Pakistan on the waters of the Indus and Brahmaputra rivers. Such conflicts come on top of the age old ones that have been waged with both neighbours. Boundary disputes, for example, have caused many a war. Apart from these, democratic India has largely been able to avoid such global military conflicts. The country's domestic political stability

In no way are all Indians Hindus

is also greatly valued by the Indians. The Republic of India that was hastily created in 1947 is home to *people of different ancestry and skin colour*. The temples, mosques and churches make it plain to everyone that in no way are all Indians Hindus. And not only Hinduism but also Jainism and Sikhism evolved on Indian soil, as did Buddhism whose followers in India are largely to be found in Sikkim and Ladakh. Almost 1,000 years ago, Islam started to spread as a result of military conquests, bringing with it the arabic architectural language and its arts that reached its peak in the imperial mausoleum, the Taj Mahal. Saint Thomas Christians have been living in India since the 1st century AD and, through the colonial rule of the Portuguese, Dutch, French and British, the number of Christians and churches increased.

1911
Capital moved from Calcutta to New Delhi

1920
Mahatma Gandhi calls for non-violent resistance to the British

1947
Independence, separation of India and Pakistan; refugees and massacres

1962/1965–66
War with China; war with Pakistan over Kashmir

2014
Narendra Modi is appointed as Prime Minister

2018
Largest water shortage in the history of the country

Wild elephants can often be seen from a boat in Periyar National Park

The conflict in Kashmir is still on-going. It is as old as the foundation of the states of India and Pakistan. Mohammed Ali Jinnah, the long-serving president of the All-India Muslim League, politically pushed through the division of India. He gained the support of British diplomats in 1947 who released India from their colonial rule to create an *independent state*, but attempted to keep the future major power small. The intervention of the United Nations led to an evidently hopeless stalemate situation. The Kashmir question that has remained unsolved both politically and practically has led to war between India and Pakistan on several occasions.

Queen Victoria sits on her monumental throne in the centre of Kolkata

Despite the official truce between the two atomic powers, there is repeated unrest along the so-called control line dividing *Kashmir* into a Pakistani and an Indian side, although violations have become far less common in the recent past. The attacks in Mumbai in 2008 indirectly organised by backers in Pakistan disrupted the relationship between India and Pakistan, but the current government led by Prime Minister Modi appears to have upheld the policy of rapprochement initiated by the previous government.

Most Indians today who look at the bronze monument of Queen Victoria seated on the throne in Kolkata are much too young to have any personal memories of *colonial days*. The fact that the queen was once crowned Empress of India is, for the younger generation, something almost from pre-historical times. But even their parents did not regard the bronze statue as a provocation. Nor have they demolished the government buildings erected by the British in Delhi and Mumbai, or the old market halls and villas of the Portuguese in Goa. They have preserved them instead, just as they took over a great deal from the British administrative and legal systems and the railway network created by the British. More than seventy years after gaining independence, many families of *Portuguese origin* still live in India and for hundreds of thousands of British, India is a popular holiday destination.

> **Colourful festivals to honour the gods are celebrated loudly**

As a countermove, many Indian emigrant, who cannot find any work at home head for English-speaking countries. As a result, the percentage of Indian doctors working in the public health sector in the USA, for example, is extremely high, even reaching up to 40% in some regions. Young Indians have grown up in rural areas without any English and are unemployed, generally go to the Gulf States – and return as soon as possible. They benefit from the economic boom or find themselves back among their familiar *Hindu surroundings*, usually far from tourist centres. In the majority of private homes there are family altars with effigies of gods. In rural areas women often create *artistic patterns* on the road outside their front doors using powdered rice and bright colours – and that every morning. *Colourful festivals* to honour the Hindu gods are celebrated loudly – they are numerous and often last several days. Most people on holiday here however barely take any notice of these everyday occurrences.

The sheer dimensions of the subcontinent are enough of a challenge! From the Himalayas in the north to its southern-most tip, the country stretches 3,200 km/1,988 mi;

THE CASTE SYSTEM

Officially the caste system no longer exists. In cities, these old divisions are no longer observed (or else Indians would never shake hands with Europeans who do not belong to any caste). The castes established in the Vedic period (*Varna:* colour) – *Brahmim* (priests), *Kshatriyas* (warriors), *Vaishyas* (farmers and traders), *Shudras* (workmen) – play less of a role than the sub-castes (*Jati:* birth) which continue the hierarchical division of the *Varnas* downwards.

The caste system requires higher ranking groups to live separately from those in a lower caste – no inter-caste marriages, no eating together, no contact. But that is no longer the case everywhere today. The Indian government has set aside apprenticeships and jobs for members of the lower *Jatis* (scheduled castes) and the large number of Dalits, also known as untouchables. This category includes many tribal people descended from the original natives.

from west to east more than 3,000 km/1,864 mi. But that does not mean that there is anywhere with no people. Based on actual estimations (2017–2019), there are on average 1,057 people per mi², compared to 704 per mi² in the United Kingdom and 92 per mi² in the USA. The very different *standard of living* of many Indians, reflected in inadequate housing, a lack of hygiene and street beggars, never fails to shock visitors and frightens many from taking a trip to this exciting country. State-funded welfare programmes are in place, but most of the afflicted population is ignorant of these measures. Life-threatening conditions in cities primarily affect sick and disabled persons, the high rate of illiteracy (an estimated 30 per cent of the population) and other individuals in precarious situations. The vast majority of Indians however lives simply but has a modest livelihood, an intact social network and the firm will to improve things.

A Sadhu, a wandering Hindu ascetic

High hopes are being placed on *women*. Millions of well trained female Indians have qualified jobs, for example as teachers, journalists, business consultants in the IT branch or in the textile industry. Women in the country manage to earn a living thanks to their being able to take out a microloan for themselves and their families. There is however a clear economic difference between the northern and southern regions. The main reason for this is the better schooling in the south, especially in Kerala, which also benefits girls.

In the past, India was forced to endure foreign domination and has therefore suffered great adversity, but Indians today are mostly very friendly and interested in foreigners. *Hospitality* is a great priority, even among those who have little to offer. Tea or fruit is offered to guests as a friendly gesture to compensate for the language barrier which prevents a genuine conversation. Indian serenity and *cheerfulness* alone are reason enough to visit the country. On top of this there are the brilliant

> **Everything in India is completely unexpected**

colours, the palaces and ruins, the magnificent temples and *cheeky monkeys*, the jungle and the desert. India always has something surprising in store, something completely different. And India is changing every day – which makes it even more important to visit it now.

WHAT'S HOT

1 Intoxicating colours

Art on the street A larger-than-life Gandhi painted on the wall of the Delhi Police Headquarters, bright paintings in the Sassoon Docks in Mumbai – India's megacities are just discovering street art. While in the past, art was only shown in museums, up-and-coming artists are now decorating dull walls – supported by organisations such as *St+art India Foundation*. In India's capital city of art Mumbai, the place to view street art is in the Chapel Road in Bandra. Search there for the gigantic image of Bollywood's Amitabh Bachchan. The street-art hotspots in Delhi are Shahpur Jhat, Hauz Khas Village and the Lodhi Art District.

Hindi rap

Hip-Hop meets Bollywood Indian hip-hop is making its way into the charts. The Hindi rappers of the collective *Dharavi United (short.travel/ind13)* talk about their lives in the gullys of Mumbai. "Gully boy" is also the name of the film focused on the Indian hip-hop scene: in preparation, the Bollywood stars Alia Bhatt and Ranveer Singh took private dance and singing lessons from the rappers. A must-have for your Indian playlist: Divine, the founder of "Gully Gang", and Naezy.

3 Tea renaissance

The Chai café After the mushrooming of stylish coffee temples, there has now been a return to the Indian national drink: tea. Although chai wallahs still serve strong and sweet chai under every tree, there are also popular chai cafés where you can sit comfortably and chat with friends, particularly in Delhi, Mumbai and Bangalore, with names such as *Chaayos*, *Chai Point*, *Chai Story* and *Chai Stop*. At *Chaayos* you can even create your own personal chai.

Wine tasting

Indian wine Well-situated city dwellers are attracted to one of the 50 vineyards in the wine triangle between Mumbai, Pune and Bangalore. The most popular among them – *Sula Vineyards* – can be found in Nashik, the Indian equivalent of the Napa Valley. A great event is the *Sulafest* (*www.sulafest.com*) – where you can relax and enjoy wine, Electro, art and fashion for two days. Other top vineyards offering wine tasting are *Nine Hills* and *Fratelli*.

Cheese culture

Not just paneer If you think India's only type of cheese is paneer, a soft cheese deep-fried with curry, you are misinformed! India does have its own cheese tradition. In Kashmir there is a traditional snack called Kalari: small spherical cheeses made with goats' milk slightly reminiscent of mozzarella which are produced on a large scale by *Himalayan Cheese*, alongside chili Gouda. The recipe for Qudam from Kashmir invented by the Gujjar tribe remains a secret. The slightly salty Bandel from West Bengal is inspried by Portuguese cheeses and tastes really good with beer. *Mango Hill Cheese* in Pondicherry produces extravagant cheeses such as Pondicheeri which is ripened in curry leaves. *La Ferme Cheese* from Auroville has been a highlight of the Indian cheese culture since 1988. Camemberts and bries made by *The Spotted Cow* are ripened in a shop in Mumbai.

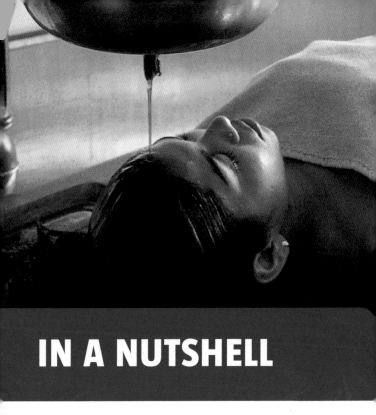

IN A NUTSHELL

ASTROLOGY: READING THE CARDS

Are you one of those people who read their daily horoscope? But do you also read cards before making investments or consult a fortune teller prior to a business decision? Most probably not. In India however, astrology is deeply rooted in its culture and remains popular even in the 21st century.

There are two million fortune-tellers in the country: advertising signs are omnipresent depicting bearded men offering their prophetic powers – now also online via apps such as Astrospeak. Here you can have your chances of marriage analysed or consult a numerologist on financial matters. Indian parents have a personal horoscope made for their children: the *janmakshar* foretells the entire life of the individual. In India everything from professions, illnesses and marriage partners is believed to be written in the stars.

AYURVEDA: INDIAN ANTI-AGEING

★ Warm sesame oil flows over your head and is gently massaged in – this is what being in heaven could feel like! Steaming bags of herbs are used stroke your painful back. Could this process be prolonged for ever? Admittedly, you could well do without the strong-smelling drink containing laxative powder, but our wish is to be rejuvenated and inner cleanliness is a vital element of ayurveda. The Sanskrit

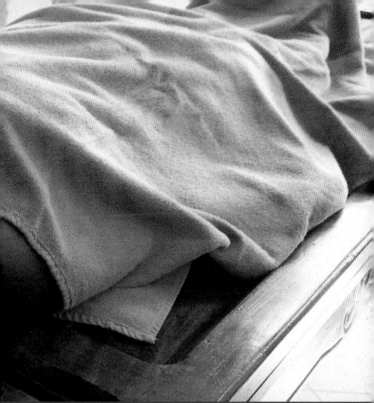

Holy cows, holy men and marriage according to horoscopes. Indians adhere to rules which appear foreign to us

term ayurveda can be translated as the "science of life": for over 3,000 years, illnesses have been prevented and body and soul brought into harmony with the aid of these holistic medical treatments.

If you are interested in taking an ayurvedic cure, you should allow at least one week for treatment, ideally a fortnight. Most ayurveda centres can be found in the south of India: in Kerala, numerous hotels advertise corresponding offers. At the beginning of the one-

to two-week cure, the doctor will first determine your type of constitution. Irrespective of whether you are a lively and breezy Vata, a fiery and sharp-witted Pitta or a gentle and well-earthed Kapha, you will unfortunately have to go without your usual stimulating hot drink in the morning and cool beer on the beach in the afternoon. Instead, your treatment will be punctuated by yoga sessions and meditation, such as on how to overcome your craving for sweets which are also forbidden.

WOMEN: WORSHIPPED AND ENSLAVED

On the one hand, Indian women are permitted to become doctors, manageresses and fighter pilots and on the other hand, Indian men fall to their knees before the power goddesses Durga and of women is also greatly dependent on regions, social class, individual castes and religion. One glimpse of hope is the advancement of the emancipation of women in the urban middle classes; in rural areas, only a higher level of education and enlightenment can improve the situation.

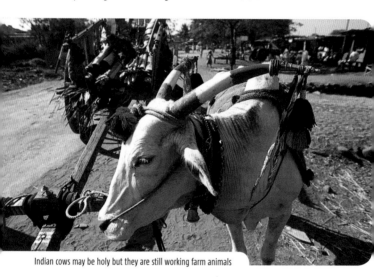

Indian cows may be holy but they are still working farm animals

Kali and idolise their mothers. This is something of a paradox, particularly when you read so many negative reports of girls and women who have suffered acid attacks carried out by men they have rejected, suffer burns after having reported a rape or die from a kerosine explosion in their kitchens because the family of her husband hoped for a larger dowry through a new marriage. The tougherning up of criminal law following the group rape of the student Jyoti Singh in Delhi in 2012 and the fact that these crimes can be punished by death is only a partial deterrent: unfortunately patriarchal concepts are too deeply entrenched. The treamtent

HOLY COWS: COWS' MILK AS A CURE FOR CANCER

In Britain, cows are kept in fields. In India, they sun themselves on the central lanes of multi-lane roads and trot through the middle of cities. If a cow eats a carrot from a market stall, it will receive a slap and then continue to be venerated. Cows are holy according to the Hindu religion and are considered a symbol of life. Any animals born with five legs are venerated as deities. Beauty contests for cows are shown on TV. Hard-core cow fanatics drink a glass of cows' urine every morning and believe that cancer can be healed by their milk.

You have a big problem if you dare to eat beef or are suspected of storing it in your freezer – even if it originates from the non-venerated buffalo; a Moslem man in Uttar Pradesh was lynched by a mob in 2015. Anyone found slaughtering a cow in the federal state of Haryana will receive a ten-year jail sentence. In the services of the holy animals, the *Gau Rakshaks* search for hidden cows which non-Hindus are planning to slaughter. A further aspect of the cult is the provision of care homes to nurse weak cows back to health.

HOLY MEN: ENLIGHTENMENT 3.0

You will not only encounter holy cows in India, but also holy men. Particularly in locations such as Rishikesh and Varanasi, the Sadhus, Nagas and Babas will emerge from their caves and pose for photos for cash. These orange-clothed individuals who can be recognised by the trident in their hands or ash markings on their faces have devoted their lives to asceticism and meditation – for most of the time. Today's Sadhus are however not disinclined to hitch a lift in an SUV, sit in the sun drinking coffee and reading the paper or fiddling with their smartphones. According to malicious gossip, some of them only became Sadus to be able to become high on ganja undisturbed. The herb of Shiva can be purchased legally in government bhang shops in the network of alleyways in the old town of Varanasi. It is also used in the innumerable lassi shops to pep up the Indian yoghurt drink. Returning to the subject of smartphones, modern Sadhus even have their own Facebook page. Lali, the "Facebook Baba" of Varanasi, spends half the day chatting with followers seeking advice from around the world. This is enlightenment 3.0.

MARRIAGE: LOVE ME TINDER

If you look through an Indian newspaper, you will be confronted by numerous pages devoted to personal ads on the subject of marriage. Parents are searching for a spouse for their children. Even in the age of Tinder & co, most marriages are still arranged by parents: only five per cent of Indian marriages are founded on love. Traditional marriage brokers are now also worried about their business as online-oriented parents are looking on the internet to discover the perfect son- or daugher-in-law. Matchmaking portals such as matrimony.com have flourished to become billion-dollar businesses. The search criteria include religion, caste, skin colour, language, salary and horoscope. The younger generation has in the meantime begun swiping to the right on their mobile phones – naturally in secret, as traditional parents still do not approve of free dating, even in the 21st century. Despite Tinder's boom, most young people must resign themselves to the fact that their parents will still have a large say in the selection of their marriage partner.

SELFIE MANIA: SAD RECORD

"One selfie please: one selfie!" You will hear this sentence constantly. Indians are the world champions of selfies and love including Western tourists in their photos of the Taj Mahal. Before taking the photo, the young man with Ray-Ban sunglasses will run his fingers through his gelled hair and then take up a Bollywood star pose. The selfie mania has unfortunately undergone a grotesque development: India is now the sad front runner before Pakistan, USA and Russia of so-called "killfies" – deaths caused by selfies. In one case in Rajasthan, a young

Waiting for the train: ten million Indians travel by train every day

man was lucky: the gigantic snake he had entwined round his neck "only" bit him on the shoulder. Things did not turn out so well for three students who were run over by a train while posing on the tracks or the young Punjabi who accidentally shot himself. The government has reacted by designating more and more "no-selfie" zones, including sixteen areas alone in Mumbai, particularly on bridges and on the coast. Anyone violating this prohibition will be fined.

LANGUAGES: AS ONCE IN BABYLON

The mixture of languages in the Tower of Babel was no comparison to India where an amazing 780 languages are spoken. If regional dialects are added and code languages such as the Koti of the transsexual Hijras, this total rises to 1,600, of which 22 are offically recognised. The most widely spread languages spoken in India after Hindi include Bengali, Telugu, Marathi, Tamil, Urdu, Gujarati and Punjabi. If a Tamil-speaking IT expert talks to his colleague from Kolkata, both will switch to English which is the second official language alongside Hindi. Anyone striving for professional success in this country must be fluent in English and things have gone so far that many families of the upper classes speak English all the time. You will also often hear "Hinglish", a type of hybrid language which is a colourful mixture of Hindi and English.

ENVIRONMENT: "CLEAN INDIA" NOT YET IN SIGHT

Does your throat feel scratchy after sightseeing in Delhi? You are most likely not catching a cold, but are suffering from the effects of smog. A day in Delhi is equivalent to smoking two packets of cigarettes and experts assert that you will lose two hours of your life. Coal-fired power stations, ancient diesel trucks and the immense volume of traffic In Delhi have earned the city the reputation of being "the dirtiest capital in the world". Environmental issues are not much better in the rest of the country. Especially in rural areas, drinking water is contaminated by pesticides; the Ganges only reaches bathing quality in two places; rubbish is piled up everywhere in great heaps and simply burned on the street due to the lack of an organised waste collection system. Despite numerous measures such as the cleaning up of the Ganges and projects including the recycling of sewage, the setting up of a workable waste collecting system and universal access to sanitary facilities for all Indians, it is a long way still to go until "clean India" as promised by the government is in sight. One ray of hope: an increasing number of locations are banning the use of single-use plastics.

YOGA: PRAYER TO THE SUN WITH PRIME MINISTER MODI

India is the cradle of yoga: 5,000 years ago, wise men recorded the method of achieving the unity of body, mind and soul through meditation, breathing exercises and body postures. You would however be misled if you thought that all Indians practise headstands before breakfast. Yoga has become marginalised in India. It is primarily young Indians who consider yoga to be old-fashioned and prefer dancing zumba. Things are however beginning to change, not least thanks to Prime Minister Modi who created a Ministry for Yoga and persuaded the UN to declare 21 June as International Yoga Day. The passionate practitioner of yoga has also practised in public – in front of a crowd of thousands on Connaught Place in New Delhi. It re-

mains to be seen whether his attempt to have yoga patented as an element of Indian culture will be successful. Modi continues to act as the nation's yoga instructor, presenting videos containing yoga exercises in 3D animation on his YouTube channel.

TRAIN TRAVEL: "CHAI, CHAI, CHAI ..."

"... coffee, coffee, coffee" – the monotone cries of the hawkers rushing through train compartments will remain a vivid memory long after you have left the train. Railway travel in India is a strenuous and challenging adventure, but equally cheap, comfortable and entertaining.

The Indian Railways business report reads like The Guiness Book of Records: up to 20 million passengers travel daily on a rail network with a length of 67,000 km/ 42,000 mi in 13,000 passenger trains stopping at 7,300 stations. The longest route is an astounding 4,273 km/ 2,655 mi travelled by the *Vivek Express* from Dibrugarh in Assam to Kanyakumari in the southernmost tip of the country. The least reliable train is the *Guwahati Trivandrum Express* which on good days takes 65 hours for the 3,552 km/2,207 mi route, but regularly achieves delays of up to 12 hours. Once you have succeeded in grappling with the incomprehensible reservation system, you can sit back and enjoy the landscape passing by while you are invited to try samosas by the family in your compartment.

You will have to pay an extortionate rate to travel in the five luxury trains travelling through India. The *Palace on Wheels* operating through Rajasthan is the most famous of these five-star luxury hotels on wheels and *The Golden Chariot* will take you from Bangalore via Mysore to Goa.

FOOD & DRINK

Are you not so keen on the Westernised cuisine in the large hotels? You don't have to go the whole hog and eat at a food stall on your very first day, but make sure you try tandoori chicken in a good local restaurant.

Indians like meeting up with friends in hotel restaurants – due to the quality of cooking and the often amazingly competititve prices – but the food in the superior Westernised hotels is often not really authentic. You can eat typical Indian food in a "normal" restaurant. Do not be afraid that they will expect you to eat here with your fingers from a banana leaf like native Indians in the south, forming compact balls of vegetables, sauce and rice which can then be eaten with elegance. You will be given a fork and knife and provided with a menu in English. If you would however like to try eating with your fingers – an art in itself – please do so with your right hand as the left hand is considered unclean. Good local restaurants are chiefly found in larger cities such as Delhi, Kolkata and Mumbai and tourist centres.

The Indian cuisine ranges from exquisite vegetarian food to fish and meat dishes – and countless varieties of desserts. It takes some getting used to how *hot* some dishes are due to the dozens of spices added, especially chili. Famed yellow curry powder is only produced for export in India and is hardly used on the subcontinent at all. *Curry* (Tamil: *kari*) in India is actually a sauce that is usually

Tandooris and *thalis*, curries and *idlis*: for the European palate India's food is a real explosion of different tastes

made with vegetables and spices, with every cook having his or her own recipe. Snacks prepared on the roadside are very spicy. The *dhabas*, as the stands are called on motorways, often have kebabs and rice *biryanis* like those cooked in the Punjab region.

Rice mixed with various vegetables is more frequently eaten in southern India than in the north. One exception is *Mughal* (or Muglai) fare which also includes recipes from Lucknow and Hyderabad with butter and almonds. *Dal*, the thick stew prepared with pulses, is served in a variety of degrees of spiciness. The *vegetarian dishes in southern India* are very hot. Fortunately, most waiters will understand what you mean when you say: "not spicy, not too hot, please". What is served is just about bearable for the more sensitive palate. The degree of spiciness can be reduced by adding yoghurt (not water!) that is provided with the food.

You won't need to worry about spiciness in the case of Indian bread! There are no

LOCAL SPECIALITIES

FOOD

alu matar – potatoes and peas in a sauce

biriyani – rice with spices, raisins, nuts or vegetables but also with meat – a Mughal speciality

chicken tikka – marinated, roast chicken pieces in a spicy sauce

dahi – yoghurt, also with pieces of fruit or vegetables as a raita (sauce or dip)

dal makhani – lentils, prepared in butter, served with rice or chapati (unleavened flatbread)

kebab – braised mutton or lamb in a sauce

kofta – meatballs with curry, rice and chutney

korma – gently stewed meat in a yoghurt sauce

murgh masala – chicken with yoghurt, spices and nuts

palak panir – diced cream cheese in spinach

pilau (pullao) – rice with spices and vegetables, sometimes with meat

roti – unleavened flatbreads made of unrefined flour (chapati), of fine wheat flour (naan) or as pancakes (parathas)

samosa – filled, fried, savoury, southern Indian patties (photo above right)

thali – titbits served in small dishes including curry, dal, rice, chapatti, chutney. Mostly vegetarian (photo above left)

DRINKS

beer – brewed in India, generally a light lager, popular brand: Kingfisher

coffee – southern Indian coffee served like a strong caffè mocha

lassi – yoghurt, thinned (ask for one without tap water!), sweet or savoury

lemon soda – refreshing but make sure the crown cap has not been tampered with

masala tea (tchai) – with spices, sugar and milk

loaves but chapati instead – a *flatbread* made of whole wheatmeal flour baked on a hotplate and served with every meal. Chapati is one of the staple foods in northern India. *Naan*, made of wheat flour with butter and baked in a clay oven is tasty. *Parathas* are light wholemeal flatbreads served at breakfast. The southern Indians love their staple foods – *idlis* (flat, round savoury cakes) made of cooked rice and *dosas* (thin, crispy pancakes) the size of a plate.

Not all Indians are vegetarians and there are also lots of *meat dishes* – except pork which is taboo for Muslims and is considered unclean by Hindus. Goa is an exception where numerous pork dishes such as the spicy sausage *chouriço* have survived from Portuguese traditions.

A thing of impossibility for Hindus is to eat the holy cow, so they stick to lamb and poultry instead. Marinated with yoghurt, ginger and pimentos, the meat is braised in a *tandoor* with clay-lined walls. Those who like fish and seafood can indulge themselves in Goa, in Kerala and in the Gulf of Bengal (e.g. *tiger prawns*). Fish cooked in a sour but spicy coconut sauce is popular in Goa as are crabs and vegetables.

You can recover from all the spiciness with a *sweet dessert* with rose water, saffron, cinnamon or cardamom. Some are dripping with honey, others with fat. Puddings made of condensed milk are also popular. You can eat peeled fruit without worrying.

Drinking is more important in a hot climate than eating. Indians are content with water that is always served without asking. But be careful! Buy still mineral water instead at all costs in bottles with original tops that have not been tampered with. Smaller villages often do not have any mineral water because it is too expensive for the locals. The milky liquid in freshly opened *coconuts* is healthy and thirst-quenching. Soft drinks of all sorts can be found everywhere, soda in bottles with crown tops and *lassi*, a yoghurt drink with spices and fruit juice.

Beer and spirits can be found in so-called wine shops (which sell virtually no wine) throughout India. The shops are usually uninviting places on the corners of busy streets. Restaurants

have to be licenced to serve alcohol. However, they sometimes serve beer – in coffee cups – if they are not licensed. Local spirits include *toddy* made from the sap of the coconut palm and *feni*, made

Chai is the most popular beverage in India

from the juice of the cashew apple and popular in Goa. The *national drink* is *chai*: strong Assam tea brewed with milk and lots of sugar. It tastes best at the INSIDER TIP roadside where it is poured by the chai wallah in a high arc from the kettle into a small cup, guaranteeing the correct drinking temperature. The spicy variant is called *masala chai* which also contains spices such as cardamon, cinnamon and cloves.

SHOPPING

The smell of cinnamon, cloves and incense lies in the air. Little mirrors catch the light, the gold glitters and brightly coloured saris shimmer. Bazaars and jewellery shops are enticing eye-openers. The times when India was a low-priced shopper's paradise have long gone but, nevertheless, lots of things are still relatively cheap because of low wages. Haggling is part of shopping and anyone buying more than one item has the best chances. But what is good value? There is no bartering in the state-run shopping centres, the "emporiums". Their prices may be generally higher than at a market, but comparing prices gives you some sort of orientation. Stroll through the *Central Cottage Industries* in Mumbai and Delhi, for example. Remember than anything more than 100 years old can only be exported with special permission – and it's bureaucratically complicated. Mega stores with countless shops inside are relatively new to India. The mixture of oriental bazaar and American shopping mall on several floors attracts those seeking both western and Indian up-market brand names, takeaways and leisure facilities ranging from cinemas to gyms.

CARPETS

More hand-knotted carpets are manufactured in India than in Iran. More than one month's work is needed for an average silk carpet which also make lovely wall hangings. The quality of a woollen carpet is measured by the number of knots per square inch. Some are mixed with silk which gives a carpet its gleam.

CRAFTS

Some streets have nothing but countless antique shops full of curios items. Handicrafts can be bought at every tourist destination – gods figures made of bronze, copper and brass or ceramics from small bowls to huge, colourfully painted elephants. Popular rustic-style pottery can be found in the country. The village of Molela, for example, near Jodhpur, is full of terracotta workshops. Metal handiwork with inlaid silver *(bidri)* can be very attractive, as are traditionally carved sandalwood sculptures of gods that are several feet high. Smaller sandalwood carvings are also highly appreciated but not cheap. Hindus consider leather unclean, but

In the past, everything was cheap. Nowadays you should follow this advice when shopping: first look, then select critically and barter.

Muslims manufacture items out of buffalo or camel skins. Then there are the pleasantly light, glossily varnished papier-mâché souvenirs such as boxes, writing sets and trays.

JEWELLERY

India mines rubies, sapphires and diamonds on its own territory and also imports on a large scale. Jewellers present their wares sometimes in palatial sales areas over several floors. Anyone interested in particularly beautiful pieces of the finest crafted jewellery should make enquiries at good hotels for trustworthy addresses. Jaipur is the main centre.

MINIATURE PAINTINGS

Thousands of artists work away at producing new versions of fairy tale-like scenes of gods and Maharajas, delicately applying extremely fine brush strokes to paper, silk or even palm leaves. You should pay special attention to the faces of the figures by which you can tell how well a painting has been executed. Crafts people in India normally do not mind people watching them work. Art schools are also often open to visitors.

SILK

Exquisite, lightweight Indian silks – are available in various qualities, ranging from gossamer to raw silks. In Varanasi you can find woven fabric with gold and silver threads. Other famous centres of the silk industry are Mysore and Hyderabad. Shirts, blouses and dressing gowns can be made to measure in lots of places, or plump for the 5.5 m/18 ft of silk needed for a sari. The sales assistants will happily show you the art of draping the silk around you and how to tuck it in.

DELHI AND THE NORTH

The fertile countryside of northern India between the light forests of Madhya Pradesh, "the heart of India" and the highest peaks in the world, spreads out like a huge bowl.

India's most sacred river, the Ganges, flows down from the Himalayas and sparkles in turquoise-green shades near its source. The winter in Srinagar in Kashmir and Leh in Ladakh with masses of snow, the rich harvest in the lush Punjab region and the debilitating heat in Delhi that starts at the end of April – these brief descriptions make the contrasts in northern India all that much clearer. India's most famous edifice, the Taj Mahal, is in northern India too – in Agra. The mausoleum reflects the glory of a time long past. A 1.5 hours journey away is the metropolis of New Delhi which is the capital of the largest democracy in the world. Mighty royal Hindu clans and Islamic conquerors ruled from here and many buildings from the British colonial period have been preserved.

The holiest site for Hindus and a place of pilgrimage for thousands of years is Varanasi on the banks of the Ganges. Hindus bathe here in the holy river to cleanse themselves of their sins and the deeply religious want to die and be cremated here. The honey-yellow temple sculptures of dancers and lovers in Khajuraho are world famous. They are a testimony to the seemingly taboo-free stand on eroticism of early Hindu rulers. In was not until 1838 that a British engineer discovered the temples of

Erotic scenes in Khajuraho, religious bathing in the Ganges and the magnificent Taj Mahal. The north offers a variety rich in contrast

Khajuraho which had become completely overrun by the jungle.

Anyone interested in Buddhist works of art will enjoy Sanchi, Sarnath and Bodh Gaya. Another highlight is the Sikh Golden Temple in Amritsar – a fairy-tale apparition floating above the "holy water".

For journeys to parts of Kashmir and to Darjeeling, as well as to the far north-east and the Chinese border, it is best to contact the Foreign Office for safety reasons before setting out, as it is advisable not to visit certain provinces in these regions.

AGRA

MAP ON P. 39
(186 A2) (*ⵍF–G6*) **The 220 km/ 137 mi trip Delhi–Agra (pop. approx. 1.7 million) and back again can in fact be done in one day with the express train.** However, the real beauty of the legendary Taj Mahal is best seen in the changing light during the course of a whole day. East of the city centre where the probably most photographed dome in the world

The Mughal emperor Akbar's 450-years-old Agra Fort that was never captured

with its four high minarets is situated on the banks of the Yamuna, you will find verdant gardens and shrubland.

Agra was designated a capital city several times during the 16th and 17th century, but the rulers subsequently relocated their centre of power back to Delhi. If it was not for the Taj Mahal, one of the seven wonders of the modern world, Agra would probably have sunk into insignificance for tourists. This would however have been an injustice for the industrial city as sultans and moguls such as Sikander Lodi, Akbar the Great and Shah Jahan have left behind an abundance of forts, palaces and mausoleums steeped in stories from the Tales of 1,001 Nights, far away from the white marble Taj Mahal.

SIGHTSEEING

INSIDER TIP ITMAD-UD-DAULA

If you ask someone the way to the Itmad-ud-daula in Agra, you only need to ask for the "baby taj". The monument directly on the Yamuna is a minitaure precursor of the Taj Mahal built a few years later. The similarity is genuinely striking: it is also built of marble and decorated all round with equally sparkling precious stone inlays. Look for the numerous images of wine caraffes with snake handles which are said to insinuate that the husband of the builder Nur Jahan was very fond of alcohol.

RED FORT

Have you ever read "The Sign of the Four"? The Red Fort in Agra is one of the settings in the Sherlock Holmes novel. For three generations of emperors, this was the seat of power until a red fort was also built in Delhi in 1640 which then became the capital city. The fort is much more than just a fortification: inside its red walls, you will find marble palaces, an elegant mosque and pavilions in which the imperial soldiers were able to relax in baths filled with rose petals and spa-like treatments. From the south entrance, you can see the Palace of the Emperor Akbar *(Jahangiri Mahal)* on the left, and on the south side directly behind the gardens, the Golden Pavilions from which however most of the gold has long peeled off. Take a look into the hall where the Emperor held private audiences and the mirror palace *(Sheesh Mahal)*. The view from the palaces of the Red Fort is one of the most romantic in the whole of India: Shah Jahan, imprisoned by his son Aurangzeb, is said to have constantly looked towards the monument of his wife. Open daily from 7am to 6pm.

TAJ MAHAL ⭐

On first sight, India's most famous building looms up magically as if in a dream. The white marble mausoleum placed between the two red sandstone buildings almost appears to float above its platform behind the elongated water basins in the garden designed according to a Persian model. The history of the Taj Mahal is full of romanticism: Mogul Shah Jahan encountered a young female jewellery seller in a bazaar whom he married and gave the name Mumtaz Mahal, pearl of the palace. She died in 1631 after the birth of her 14th child. The mogul had a mausoleum built as a sign of his love for her. The finest marble was brought from Rajasthan and precious and semi-precious jewels from Persia and Afghanistan. 20,000 stonemasons, calligraphers and artists worked for twenty years on its construction.

Get up closer to study the magnificnce in greater detail and marvel at the artistic jewellery inlays and flower motifs on the walls of the mausoleum. The Taj Mahal is at its most magnificent at sunrise when the onion-shaped cupola and minarets are steeped in a gentle pink light which slowly transforms itself into a golden hue and the entire building is illuminated. If you would like to see the

---

MARCO POLO HIGHLIGHTS

⭐ **Taj Mahal**
The magnificent mausoleum of Empress Mumtaz Mahal in Agra → p. 37

⭐ **Fatehpur Sikri**
Emperor Akbar's "Victory City" → p. 40

⭐ **Golden Temple**
Amritsar in Punjab is home to the most beautiful Sikh holy site → p. 41

⭐ **National Museum**
A must for all lovers of art when in Delhi → p. 47

⭐ **Capital Complex**
The functional government buildings in Chandigarh were designed by Le Corbusier → p. 43

⭐ **Red Fort (Lal Qila)**
The stronghold of the Mughal emperors in Delhi – once it was considered to be paradise on earth → p. 47

⭐ **Swaminarayan Akshardham**
Delhi's most modern and largest Hindu temple → p. 48

⭐ **Khajuraho**
Erotic temple sculptures that were spared destruction by the Muslims → p. 52

⭐ **Bara Imambara**
Huge mausoleum in Lucknow built for a Muslim saint → p. 57

⭐ **Stupa**
The stone hemisphere in Sanchi is surrounded by reliefs that relate the life of Buddha → p. 60

Taj Mahal from a different perspective, you can visit the park  INSIDER TIP *Mahtab Bagh* on the opposite side of the Yamuna. Over the course of time, the marble has taken on a yellowish tinge as a result of the polluted air and was subjected to a mud treatment. This is a technique derived from traditional Indian cosmetics and is termed *multani mitti*, involving the blending of rose water with calcareous clay and painting it onto the marble. The treatment has only been moderately successful. Open Sat–Thu from 30 mins. prior to sunrise to 30 mins. before sunset; you can also visit the Taj Mahal in the evning on nights with a full moon and the two previous and following evenings.

FOOD & DRINK

DASAPRAKASH RESTAURANT

This restaurant is also popular with locals because of its excellent South Indian cuisine. The North Indian tandooris and curries are equally delicious. *Gwalior Road | Meher Cinema Complex | Rakabganj | tel. 0562 2 46 35 35 | Moderate*

SHEROE'S HANGOUT

The café was opened during the campaign *Stop Acid Attacks* and helps the victims to find a new place in society. The resilient women conjure up dishes ranging from Indian dahl and Chinese noodles to vegetarian sandwiches. Self-designed clothing is on sale in the shop. *Fatehabad Road, opposite the Gateway Hotel | tel. 0562 4 00 04 01 | www. sheroeshangout.com/agra | Budget*

SHOPPING

You must decide yourself whether a mini Taj Mahal would really fit in your living room. Alongside handicrafted objects made of marble, Agra is famous for its leather goods. Shopping areas include

Not only precious stones make the Taj Mahal a perfect jewel

Munro Road, the Sadar Bazar, Raja-ki-Mandi and the Kinari Bazar.

WHERE TO STAY

THE CORAL TREE HOMESTAY
Here you can stay in lovingly decorated rooms in a bungalow with views of the greenery from the balconies. You can also have your meals cooked for you. *4 rooms | 4, Amarlok Colony | tel. 089 38 99 99 20 | www.thecoraltreehomestay.com | Budget*

HOWARD PLAZA – THE FERN ☘ ◉
Offers stylish modern rooms with an Indian touch. A great advantage: the hotel has devoted itself to environmental protection. A further advantage is that you can see the Taj Mahal from the roof terrace. With restaurant, bar and attractive pool. *86 rooms | Fatehabad Road | tel. 0562 4 04 86 00 | www.howardplazaagra. com | Moderate*

THE OBEROI AMARVILAS ☘
Noble luxury hotel with the finest Indian decorations. The hotel is situated in a grand setting with a view of the Taj Mahal. There is a highly exclusive spa. *112 rooms | Taj East Gate Road | tel. 0562 2 23 15 15 | www.oberoihotels.com | Expensive*

INFORMATION

UTTAR PRADESH TOURIST OFFICE
64, Taj Road | tel. 0562 2 22 64 31 | www. uptourism.gov.in

WHERE TO GO

AGRA BEAR RESCUE FACILITY
(186 A2) (⏛ F6)

These animals became separated from their parents while they were young and were trained with hot iron rods – India's countless dancing bears. Fortunately, this practice was outlawed a few years ago and 200 of these bears found a sanctuary here. During the guided tour (2 hr), you will find out more about the fate of these mistreated animals and the origins of this tradition dating back to the 13th century. *Tel. 096 90 01 18 26 | www.wildlifesos.org | 30 km/ 18.6 mi from the town | NH in the direction of Delhi*

KEOLADEO NATIONAL PARK
(186 A2) (⏛ F6)

The national park also known as *Bharatpur Bird Sanctuary* is a mecca for birdwatchers. More than 350 types of birds fly through the air here including rare cranes from Siberia and migrating birds from China and Turkmenistan. A long time ago, hunting-loving maharajahs and their illustrious guests used to shoot ducks in this park with an area of 11.2 mi2 containing dense forests and swamps. The park has been a bird protection zone since 1956. A commemorative plaque informs about the former passion for hunting.

In the park, you can stay overnight at the *Bharatpur Forest Lodge (17 rooms | tel. 092 12 77 72 23 | www.bharatpur forestlodge.in | Budget)*. Outside the park, the *Birders Inn (24 rooms | tel. 05644 22 73 46 | www.birdersinn.com | Moderate)* with generous-sized colonial style rooms can be recommended. You can look out over the lush landscape from reclining chairs under the arcades. *Approx. 55 km/34.2 mi west*

FATEHPUR SIKRI ★ (186 A2) (⏛ F6)

The settlement built from red sandstone seems to rise up out of nowhere like a fata morgana in the blistering desert heat. Emperor Akbar had this new residence built in 1569 after the prediction uttered by the holy Sufi Salim Chishti that Akbar would have a son had been fulfilled. Only fifteen years later, Fatehpur Sikri had turned into a ghost town, most probably due to the scarcity of water. You can walk through the palaces and pavilions of Sikri, the "residential area" of the twin town. Also take a look inside the large mosque and the tombs of the Sufis with walls of open-worked marble in Fatehpur. The architecture, a wild blend of elements from Islam, Hinduism and Christianity, reflects the religions of Akbar's three wives. *36 km/22.4 mi west*

SIKANDRA (186 A2) (⏛ F6)

The mausoleum of Akbar was erected in the celebratory Mughal architectural style and set in a spacious park. The lower levels are of red stone, the upper floor is however different from most other Mughal mausoleums. Instead of a dome, as at the Taj Mahal, the building is crowned by an additional floor of gleaming white marble – an architectural element more typical of a palace. Watch out for the cheeky monkeys! The huge mosaics inside are real eyecatchers. *10 km/6.2 mi north-west*

AMRITSAR

(182 C3) (⏛ E3) Amritsar (pop. 1.1 million) is relatively prosperous thanks to its fertile fields and gardens, and its wealth of fruit, wool and spices.

The city is first of all famous as the spiritual centre of the Sikhs who make up the majority of the population in Punjab. Their morale, commitment and organisational talent have brought wealth to the region. However, devoutness does not exclude enjoying life or displaying a love of beauty. This is reflected in the streets and houses, temples, mosques, parks and gardens in the city.

in the water course at the entrance, you will be faced by a sea of pilgrims with orange headscarves and turbans of all colours, a striking contrast to the cream-white palace buildings surrounding the lake, the "nectar of immortality". The temple *Hari Mandir* looking like an oversized treasure chest covered in sheets of

In the Golden Temple – a Sikh reading the holy scripture, the Granth Sahib, out loud

Every Sikh visits the Golden Temple at least once in a lifetime. Today, this temple has luckily once again become a place of heavenly peace. In 1984, however, militant Sikh separatists fighting for the autonomy of Punjab occupied the temple. The government ordered tanks to storm the temple area, leading to a bloodbath and nationwide unrest.

SIGHTSEEING

GOLDEN TEMPLE ★

Once you have handed in your socks and shoes and washed your hands and feet

gold is reflected in the blue-green water. A bridge leads into the most sacred building. The highlight is the holy book *Granth Sahib* placed on a platform decorated with paintings and valuable carpets. Every morning, this book is ceremoniously carried to this location from the Akhal Takht, seat of the temple administration. Every hour, there are recitations from the book accompanied by ceremonious music blaring from loudspeakers in all directions. The Golden Temple extends a welcome to all, regardless of religion and nationality. This is symbolised by the temple doors which open on all sides.

The temple kitchen, probably the largest canteen in the world, is also open to everyone. Every day, thousands of pilgrims are offered dahl and flatbreads free of charge. Go and join the queue to experience an unforgettable night under the arcades along the lake. The temple area is open 24 hours a day and the Golden Temple from sunrise until 10pm.

FOOD & DRINK

You will find good restaurants near the *Ram Bagh Garden*. There are a few smaller restaurants and food stalls (dhabas) in the vicinity of the Golden Temple which offer Punjab specialities including fried fish.

CRYSTAL

Amritsaris choose the Crystal for special occasions. You should definitely try the creamy curries! The menu also includes European and Chinese food. *Queens Road | Crystal Chowk | tel. 0183 22 55 55 | Moderate*

KESAR DA DHABA

In this inconspicuous restaurant hidden away in a small alleyway, you can enjoy chickpea curry, *paranthas and dahl. The spiciness of the food can be neutralised by drinking lassi. Chowk Passian | tel. 0183 2 55 21 03 | Budget*

WHERE TO STAY

Do as the Sikhs do and stay in one of the pilgrim guesthouses *(gurdwaras)*. You can stay overnight for up to three nights free of charge (by making a donation) near the Golden Temple in the *Sri Guru Ram Das Niwas, Sri Guru Nanak Niwas* and the *New Akal Rest House in dormitories or double rooms (shared bathrooms). Alcohol, nicotine and drugs are prohibited.*

INSIDER TIP ► **MRS. BHANDARI'S GUEST HOUSE**

This is a charming oasis amongst lush greenery. Staying here feels a little like holidays long ago with grandparents – lots of beautiful old furniture and the rooms have their own fireplaces. *12 rooms | 10, The Cantonment | tel. 09872 2 9 74 22 | www.bhandariguesthouse.wordpress.com | Budget*

RANJIT'S SVAASA ◉

The friendly and cosy heritage hotel in the centre near the shopping arcade is built with the use of lots of natural materials. Rooms in the courtyard and at the back are almost completely screened from the noise by the park. Restaurant and café. *21 rooms and suites | 47-A The Mall | tel. 0183 2 56 66 18 | www.svaasa.com | Moderate*

INFORMATION

INFORMATION OFFICE OF THE GOLDEN TEMPLE
At main entrance | tel. 0183 2 55 39 54 | www.goldentempleamritsar.org

CHANDIGARH

(183 D4) *(ᗰ F4)* **A mecca for fans of architecture: Chandigarh (pop. 960,000) is a very green city, very tidy, very un-Indian and the first city in the country to have been designed completely at the drawing board – by none other than the famous architect Le Corbusier.** Functional buildings erected in 1951–65 with clear geometrical lines and contours characterise the capital of the states Punjab and Haryana until today. The squares and roads in the residential areas, laid out at right angles, were landscaped at that time and now have

Rock Garden: monument and sculpture garden created by the artist Nek Chand Saini

a number of tall trees. Main attractions include the ★ *Capital Complex*, with government and parliament buildings, and the law courts with their shell and ramp-like structures. Here you will also find the emblem of the city – the *Open Hand Monument*, which was also designed by Le Corbusier.

The ⊕ INSIDER TIP *Rock Garden (open daily 8am–6pm | Sector 1)* is a good example of indvidualistic creativity. The artist Nek Chand Saini built up a bizarre fantasy land between 1965 and 1976 constructed from all possible types of waste and recycling materials with over 2,000 quirky sculptures which resemble goblins or mythical creatures.

Anyone seeking romanticism will also search for Suchna Lake for a magical sunset.

Alongside Pune and Delhi, Chandigarh is a hotspot for micro-breweries. In *Hops n Grains (SCO 358, Sector 9, Panchkula | tel. 0172 4 02 66 66 | Moderate)*, you will not

only find good beer, but also Indian-style pizzas and delicious mixed platters with all types of Indian delicacies from panner to tandoori chicken.

How about staying overnight on a farm rather than in Chandigarh's newest luxury hotel, the *Oberoi Sukhvilas Resort*? Just 15 km/9.3 mi out of the city, you will find the *Baans Bagh, (3 rooms | Old Parol Link Road, Village Siswan | tel. 09818 57 58 47 | www.baansbagh.com | Moderate)*, a homestay in a typical bungalow. The colonial style of the lounge and taking tea on the terrace gazing at the foothills of the Himalayas will make you feel you are living in a dream.

INFORAMTION

CHANDIGARH TOURIST CENTRE
Several information points, e.g. at the central bus station, at the Plaza in sector 17 and at Sushna Lake | tel. 0172 2 70 38 39 | www.chandigarhtourism.gov.in

DELHI

MAP INSIDE BACK COVER
(185 F1) (*ᗡ F5*) **India's capital with a population of almost 17 million has many different facets. People and vehicles continuously jostle for space in the narrow streets in the Old City, past bazaars, crumbling buildings and the Red Fort.**

To the south-west lies the colonial city of New Delhi with *Connaught Place* at its centre. Wide boulevards fan out from here in all directions. Glass and steel skyscrapers are now being built – this

> **WHERE TO START?**
> **Connaught Place:** This circular central hub (Rajiv Chowk) with three concentric rings of colonial arcades, can easily be reached on the Delhi Metro (lines 2 and 3). Janpath and its craft outlet stores starts at the southern-most point and intersects with Raj Path, the major boulevard in the government district which is best reached by auto rickshaw or taxi.

is where business is booming. To the south is the government district built in the Classicist style with *Rajpath*, which is regularly used for parades, and other wide boulevards lined with elegant villas, diplomatic buildings, museums, parks and luxury hotels.

Dilli Dilli, as the inhabitants (Dilli wallahs) affectionately call their town, is a city of eight separate cities. A host of different rulers have left their mark on Delhi including Hindus, Muslims, Persians, Afghanistanis and then the British colonial rulers over a period of more than

1,000 years. Only ruins of the formerly magnificent cities have survived. The derelict remains of Tughlaqabad, the third capital city, are now ruled by monkeys and snakes, whereas the oldest city Feroz Shah Kotla is now home to Djinns. Thousands of Dilli wallahs who believe in the power of these invisible spirits make pilgrimages to the crumbling fort next to the cricket grounds and write their prayers on scraps of paper to be read by the djinns.

Shahjahanabad, the capital of the Moghul emperor Shah Jahan during the 17th century, is a lively location. Here in Old Delhi you will discover the most magnificent Moghul buildings, the most colourful markets and the greaest degree of noise and chaos. In 1911, the British relocated their capital from Kolkata to Delhi and founded the city of New Delhi which was laid out very much in the style of a British garden town. India's political elite moved into the parliament buildings designed by British architects and partly inspired by the Mughal style. India gained independence in 1947.

Modern Delhi consists of a conglomerate of towns and villages, seamed by green residentail areas to the south such as Hauz Khas and Greater Kailash. Further out to the west, the business town ● Gurgaon shot up with its glittering office tower blocks and hyper-modern shopping centres such as *Ambience Mall* and *Metropolitan Mall*.

SIGHTSEEING

BAHAI HOUSE OF WORSHIP OF THE INDIAN SUBCONTINENT

The architectural model for this building was not the Sydney Opera House, but an unfolding lotus flower with 27 marble petals, symbolising a tribute to the beauty of creation. The interior contains no religious objects whatsoever, as

Chandni Chowk: battle your way through the colourful busy bazaar

Bahai teaching postulates the equality of all religions; the House of Worship with its idyllic garden is therefore more a site for inner reflection than a temple. Spectacular image at sunset. *Bahapur | 6, Canning Road*

CHANDNI CHOWK

Of all the colourful bazaars in Old Delhi, this is one of the most interesting. It's well worthwhile exploring the side alleys and simply soaking in the thousands of colours and smells in this world apart that invents itself anew every day. Take a walk through the *Kinari Bazar* where brides purchase their wedding jewellery. This is where sequins are manufactured which even grace western designed fashion. Allow yourself to be fascinated by the displays of goldsmiths and silversmiths in the *Dariba Kalan* and inhale the scents set out by perfume sellers at the *Attar Bazar: a true intoxication of the senses! In the north of the city*

GANDHI SMRITI MUSEUM AND LIBRARY

The spinning wheel, quill, sandals, the bloodstained loincloth he wore the day he died – all testify to the great preacher of peace who was shot here by a fanatical Hindu on 30 January, 1948, on his way to prayers. The house, garden, prayer room, collection of photos, Gandhi quotations and library that make up the *Eternal Gandhi Multimedia Museum* form a sheer inexhaustible memorial. *Tue–Sun 10am–5pm, closed every 2nd Sat in the month | 5, Tees January Marg*

HUMAYUN'S TOMB

The mausoleum was the first Moghul garden tomb in India. If you recognise a certain similarity with the Taj Mahal, you have guessed correctly: this was the predecessor of the marble wonder of Agra. The dome has a height of 43 m/141.1 ft and the quadratic building in the Persian style conceals an octagonal burial chamber. Take a closer look at the small towers with blue mosaics and delicate marble inlays on the façades. Additional mausoleums can be found in the extensive gardens with water channels. *Lodi Road*

INDIA GATE

Paris has the Champs-Elysées and the Arc de Triomphe and Delhi the glamour mile Raj Path and the India Gate. The inofficial symbol of Delhi was based on the Parisian model and designed by the British architect Edwin Lutyens. Just as interesting as the monument erected in memory of the Indian soldiers who lost their lives in the First World War, is the tumultuous life around the gate: picnicking families, cricket players and street vendors. A good evening programme: sit on a blanket, taste *garama garam bhutta*, buttered corn on the cob, and wait until the India Gate is illuminated in all its slendour.

JAMA MASJID

When you approach Old Delhi's main shopping street via the *Chawri Bazar*, you will soon catch sight of the white onion domes of the Jama Masjid which seems to blend into the milky white sky. The largest mosque in India is considered to be the most beautiful as well. Shah Jahan, who had the Taj Mahal built, commissioned this imposing mosque for Friday prayers in 1650 for his new capital Shahjanabad (now Old Delhi). Constructed of black and white marble as well as red sandstone it encloses a courtyard that hosts up to 25,000 people on Friday prayers, and has gates two-storeys high and a two-aisled prayer hall with eleven impressive pointed arches. Relics kept here include a hair from Mohammed's beard.

"The mosque that reflects the world", as Jama Masjid was originally called, offers magnificent views from one of its two 40 m/131.2 ft high ⚜ minarets. *Daily, 30 mins. after sunrise–12.15pm and 1.45pm–30 mins. before sunset | between Chwari Bazar and Netaj Subhash Marg*

NATIONAL GALLERY OF MODERN ART

The excellent collections rid anyone of the clichéd notion of India as a backward

In Jama Masjid, the largest and perhaps most beautiful mosque in India

country. The permanent exhibitions display the self-confident art of India in the 19th and 20th centuries, with an emphasis the time of the independence movement. *Tue–Sun 10am–5pm | Jaipur House, near India Gate*

NATIONAL MUSEUM ★ ●

Rich collections including masterpieces of Indian sculptures and paintings as well as native Indian art that is still very much alive today. The audio tour helps give you some sort of orientation in the face of 200,000 exhibits from 5,000 years. *Tue–Sun 10am–5pm | 10, Janpath*

QUTB MINAR

The name of the huge red sandstone tower with its elaborate ornamentation and verses from the Koran goes back to the time of Qutb-ud-Din Aibak who founded the first sultanate in Delhi in the 12th century, thereby ending the rule of the Hindus. It remains unknown whether this slim but giant tower was erected as a triumphal column or a minaret calling believers to prayer. It is without doubt the highest minaret in the whole of India with a height of 73 m/239.5 ft and definitely worth visiting. It used to be possible to give the rusting iron pillar in the courtyard a "back-to-front" hug to bring you luck, but unfortunately, the access has been stopped. *Sri Aurobindo Marg | 13 km/8.1 mi south of the centre*

RED FORT (LAL QILA) ★

The inscription over the entrance to the Hall of Private Audiences, means: "If there be a paradise on the earth, it is this." The words of its builder, Shah Jahan, were not too much of an exaggeration as even the stripped halls today are a marvel to look at. However, since the Mughal emperor built the fort in 1639–48 when the palaces inside were finished

with inlaid precious stones, silk hangings over the terraces and water basins to cool the air, times of war have wrought their havoc over this oriental wonder. Today, you have to use your imagination to conjure up their former magnificence. To the north is the *Hamam* (the royal baths) whose coloured glass windows produce a very special light inside and the elegant *Moti Masjid* (Peark Mosque). Don't forget to take a look round the *Museum of Independence* displaying objects relating to the fight for freedom from the colonial powers. *Daily from sunrise to sunset;*

LOW BUDGET

Delhi's *Metro* is way better organised than the buses. It is also safer, cleaner, more reliable – and incredibly cheap. Depending on the route, tickets cost 20–60 rupees. A trip on an auto-rickshaw will also get you through the chaotic traffic easily and cheaply – from around 15 rupees, depending on your negotiating skills.

Pretty and reasonably priced hand-crafted items, including paintings, are created in the *Crafts Museum* that has been constructed like a village. *Tue–Sun 10am–5pm | admission free | Bhairon Marg | north of Purana Quila, Delhi*

For less than 325 rupees in each case you can take a guided tour of the city – in the mornings around New Delhi (4 hours), afternoons around Old Delhi (3 hours). Tickets e.g. from the *India Tourist Office (88, Janpath)* or *Delhi Tourism (DTTDC) (Baba Kharak Singh Marg)*.

Agra Fort – private audiences were once held in the Diwan-i-Khas

museum daily 10am–5pm, Tue–Sun in the evenings sound and light show | between Yamuna and the Old City

SWAMINARAYAN AKSHARDHAM ★

One of the largest Hindu temples in India is located at the heart of a garden complex. Although the architecture displays the traditional playful domes and red sandstone façades, it is a modern multi-media temple. Films in an Imax cinema and a multi-media show showcase elements of the Hindu religion. This was set up by a guru named Pramukh Swami Maharaj. You can go for a walk or a boot trip in the *Garden of India*. *Tue–Sun 9.30am–6.30pm | NH 24, near Noida Mor | www.akshardham.com*

FOOD & DRINK

DUM PUKHT ●

Here you will be transported into a different time not only by the interior, but also the cuisine inspired by old recipes from the Nawabs of Lucknow. The special cooking pot (*Dum Pukht*) allows the aromas to develop in a slow oven. You will taste the difference! *ITC Maurya | Diplomatic Enclave | Sardar Patel Marg | tel. 011 26 11 22 33 | www.itchotels.in | Expensive*

PARIKRAMA REVOLVING RESTAURANT ✼

Dizzying! Tuck into Indian and western food as this restaurant on the top floor of this tower block turns slowly. *Antriksh*

Bhawan | Connaught Place | Kasturba Gandhi Marg | tel. 011 23 72 16 16 | Moderate–Expensive

STREET FOOD

Anyone not intimidated by the threat of "Delhi Belly" should certainly try food at the street food stalls in Chandni Chowk and the Chawri Bazar: sweet and sticky Jalebis at *Shiv Mishtan Bhandar* or faluda cooked with dried fruits in rosewater and milk at *Giani's di Hatti*. The signature dish at *Natraj Dahi Bhalle Wala* is spicy dough-nuts with creamy yoghurt and you can choose from 30 different types of bread at *Paratha World* in the "lane of fried bread" with fillings. *Kuremal Mahavir Prase* is considered as the master of Indian ice cream Kulfi. *Budget*

INSIDER TIP UNITED COFFEE HOUSE

This restaurant is the only one to have survived on the legendary address on Connaught Place. You can dine here under gigantic chandeliers as in the colonial period and round off the meal with a coffee! *Circle, E15 | Connaught Place | tel. 011 23 41 60 75 | www.unitedcoffeehouse.com | Expensive*

SHOPPING

KHAN MARKET

You would not guess from the crooked houses close to the India Gate that this is one of the trendiest shopping districts in Delhi. You can purchase attractive objects for the home, colourful tunics at *Anokhi and Fab India* and peruse the latest bestsellers of contemporary literature in *Bahri & Sons* and *Full Circle.*

SHAHPUR JHAT

Dusty alleyways at the edge of an old residential quarter conceal the most attractive boutiques in the city. Here you will find fine scarves and shawls, sparkling jewellry, cluch bags and T-shirts with cartoon prints, augmented by an infinite number of cafés and restaurants.

ENTERTAINMENT

INSIDER TIP HAZRAT NIZAMUDDIN

Twisting alleyways lead past stalls selling rose petals and joss sticks lead into the Muslim quarter Hazrat Nizamuddin. The air vibrates with ecstatic music – It is Qawwali time! The followers of the Sufi saint Auliya dance like dervishes to the trance-like poetic songs around his mausoleum. Enigmatic Islamic mysticism found its way from the deserts of Rajasthan to Delhi over 700 years ago and is now more popular than ever. *Close to the Police station Hazrat Nizamuddin | Fri–Wed 7.45pm–8.30pm | www.nizamuddinaulia.com*

HAUZ KHAS VILLAGE

When the sun sets behind the medieval ruins of Hauz Khas, bathing them in a reddish light, the alleyways near the park start filling up. People from all across Delhi flock to the popular Hauz Khas Village – come and join in the celebrations! The best bars include *Hauz Khas Social, Bulldogs, The Beer Café and Kaffeine and Capsule.*

WHERE TO STAY

INSIDER TIP HAVELI DHARAMPURA

Restored mansion with a touch of luxury. Decorated round archways, antique furniture and brightly coloured glass impress all visitors to this oasis. Let yourself be inspired by the sights of Old Delhi while drinking a fresh lime soda on the roof terrace before you enter the fray. *14 rooms | 2293 Gali Guliyan | Dharampura*

| tel. 011 23 26 10 00 | www.havelidharampura.com | Expensive

DHARAMSALA

INSIDER TIP MAIDENS

A historic gem from 1903. Garden with wonderful trees and large pool, dignified colonial style, north of Old Delhi. *55 rooms | 7, Sham Nath Marg | tel. 011 23 97 54 64 | www.maidenshotel.com | Expensive*

PRAKASH KUTIR B&B

You will wake up to the sound of twittering birds and the call of the water seller on the street: "pani, pani". Otherwise, all is peaceful. The brightly decorated, airy rooms lead to a large terrace close to the Khas Market. At breakfast time you will be served parathras and given plenty of insider tips. *4 rooms | A-34, Khash Marg, Hauz Khas | tel. 011 26 52 01 34 | www.besthomestaydelhi.com | Moderate*

TREE OF LIFE

The name says it all: this homestay is located in the quiet Saket district of the city on a tree-lined road. You can see Qutb Minar from the roof terrace. The rooms are furnished according to Vaastu, the Indian equivalent of Feng Shui. *3 rooms | 193 Saket | tel. 011 98 10 27 76 99 | www.tree-of-life.in | Moderate*

INFORMATION/CAR HIRE

GOV. OF INDIA TOURIST OFFICE

88, Janpath and at International Airport | tel. 011 23 32 03 42 | www.incredibleindia.org

INSIDER TIP METROPOLE TOURIST SERVICE

Arranges cars with drivers for tours of northern India and helps in planning trips and arranging packages. *244, Defence Colony Flyover Market | tel. 011 24 31 03 13 | www.metrovista.co.in*

(182 C3) (𝒲 F3) A long serpentine road leads up the mountain for 5 km/3.1 mi from Lower Dharamsala in the Himalayas up to the attractive McLeod Ganj. Originally a former hill station created by the British, this city district is now known as "Little Lhasa".

Since the 14th Dalai Lama Tenzin Gyatso was driven out of Tibet in 1960, this has been his base and the location of the Tibetan exile government. The district is characterised by Buddhist monks in red robes, restaurants with Tibetan pasties (momos) and stalls selling silver jewellery and Yak wool scarves. If you are lucky, the Dalai Lama will be holding one of his Public Teachings in the *Tsuglakhang Temple* next to his residence. Even more impressive than visiting the Dalai Lama Temple is a walk through the small forest surrounding the complex, taking you past brightly painted prayer wheels. You can find out more about the life of the Tibetan refugees by spending an afternoon teaching English as a volunteer, for example in the Tibetan Children's Village, or immerse yourself in the world of Buddhism in a meditation retreat at the *Tushita Meditation Centre* in Dharamkot. A must for mountain fans is a two-day trek to *Triund* and a hike to the *Guna-Devi Temple*. Other sites worth visiting in the reagion include the hill station *Palampur* surrounded by tea gardens and pine forests, the paragliding eldorado *Bir* and the scenic *Parvati Valley*. The best place to spend the evening is the roof terrace of the *McLlo Beer Bar & Restaurant* where Pierce Brosnan was once seen enjoying a sundowner. The *Chonor House* is surrounded by scented cedars and has a view of the Kangra Valley. *(Tekchen Choeling Road | tel. 09418 43 64 10 | www.*

norbulingka.org/chonor-house | Moderate, a genuine oasis. The house is built of stone and slate from the local region and three temples was once said to be the most spectacular and secure stronghold in the whole of India. The complex was

The prayer wheels in Dharamsala, where the exiled Dalai Lama lives, contain holy scriptures

each of the eleven rooms is individually decorated with wall murals, hand-knotted carpets and Tibetan-style wooden furniture. Further information: *Himachal Pradesh TDC | Kotwali Bazar McLeod Ganj | north of the Bank of Baroda | tel. 01892 22 42 12 | hptdc.in*

begun by a Maharajah suffering from leprosy. There is a sound and light show at the fort every evening at 8.30pm. If you happen to be visiting Gwalior at the end of December, make sure you don't miss the *Tansen Music Festival* with classical Indian music!

GWALIOR

(186 A2) (𝒲 G6) Gwalior is located slightly off the path of customary round-trip routes and takes at least 3 hours to reach by train from Agra (pop. 1 Mio.) in Madhya Pradesh.

The principle attraction of Gwalior is situated on a table mountain rising high above the old town: a 1,000-year-old fort in which several ruling dynasties have fulfilled their architectural dreams. The sandstone fort with six palaces and

SIGHTSEEING

INSIDER TIP JAIN SCULPTURES

You will perhaps feel that you are being observed on your way to the south-west entrance to the fort – by the over-dimensional sculptures hewn into the precipitous mountain. Most of these honey-hued statues with their benign features are standing with their hands on their hips and some are seated in the relaxing lotus position. These 1,000-year-old statues also represent the teachers and saviours of Jainism and are known as

Tirthankas, literally fordmakers. More of these figures can be found on the south-east side of the castle hill.

MAN SINGH PALACE

The most splendid palace of the fort was built around 1500. Once you have admired the blue and multi-coloured tiles depicting ducks, elephants and lions, you should follow the guide with a torch down into the cellar whichh was formerly the site of a prison. Also take a look at the other four palace ruins and climb up one of the fortified towers. The large pool in the Shah Jahan Palace was the site of the *Jauhar*. When the Sultan of Delhi conquered the fort in the 13th century, masses of women and children committed suicide through self-immolation.

SASBAHU TEMPLE

We no longer know why the larger and smaller pair of temples (11th century) standing opposite each other are called mother-in-law *(Sas)* and daughter-in-law *(Bahu),* but they are highly attractive with their stone elephants, dancers and floral ornamentation.

SCINDIA MUSEUM/JAIVILAS PALACE

In the 19th century, the ruling Maharajah ordered the huge prison to be built by prisoners from the fort. 35 rooms have been transformed into a museum. You can stroke stuffed tigers and marvel at the glittering chandeliers and silver miniature railway running round the table which was used to pass round cigars. *Tue–Sun 10am–5.30pm (separate entry than the palace entrance)*

FOOD & DRINK/ WHERE TO STAY

NEEMRANA'S DEO BAGH

The heritage hotel owns two temples dating from the 17th century, a pavilion in which Moguls formerly slept and a secluded garden. Very stylish rooms are divided among five wings as in a palace. *Jadhav Kothi | tel. 0751 2 82 03 57 | www. neemranahotels.com | Moderate*

TAJ USHA KIRAN PALACE

Walk in the steps of the Maharajah of Gwalior in his former guesthouse. If all the suites with four-poster beds are already occupied, the superior rooms with their view of the wonderful garden will be sufficient compensation. *40 rooms| Jayendraganj | tel. 0751 2 44 40 00 05 | www.taj.tajhotels.com | Expensive*

TANSEN RESIDENCY

The exterior of the hotel named after a musician from the 16th century displays similarities with the fort, but you will stay in comfortable modern rooms. Certainly try the Punjabi dishes offered in the restaurant! *36 rooms | 6A, Mahatma Gandhi Road | tel. 0742 8 84 44 40 | www.tansen-residency-gwalior-mptdc.hotelsgds.com | Budget*

KHAJURAHO

(186 B3) *(*🗺 *G–H7)* **Kamasutra, Tantra and wild orgies – the erotic temples of ★ Khajuraho (pop. 25,000) contain revealing images. Despite their remote location, they are well worth a visit.**

The main attractions in Khajuraho were created by stonemasons of the kings of Chandella, a martial dynasty with an apparently highly permissive philosophy of life. Eighty-five temples were created in the 10th century displaying a wealth of bare-breasted female dancers and brawny warriors, some of whom are depicted in unamiguous poses. The temples remained in a deep slumber for hundreds of years, swallowed up by the jungle, until an officer sent by Queen Victoria discovered the "Kamasutra Temple" in 1850, apparently blushing with shame at the images he found there.

SIGHTSEEING

WESTERN GROUP OF TEMPLES

Do not be surprised if the custodian of the *Kandariya-Mahadeva-Temple* asks if you have also seen the sculptures round the back – "they are making love!" Genuine orgies are celebrated in the Western group of temples in Khajuraho, including the *Vishvanatha* nd *Lakshmana Temples.* And this in such a conservative country! Indian tourists therefore frequently react to the question with bashful giggles. You have to take a closer look to see what is concealed among the scenes of daily life and images from Indian mythology. You discover elephants, horses, camels and gods from the Hindu pantheon accompanied by mythical creatures and demons – and then suddenly the figures leap out at you from the sandstone surface: scantily dressed female dancers with generous proportions, nymphs gazing at themselves in mirrors and the warriors who are also scantily clothed. The Maithunas, couples involved in sexual acts are somewhat concealed – pure eroticism. Legends have sprung up about their origins. Some maintain that the images are a symbol of the act of the creation of the world by the gods and others see them as an animation for the reproduction-shy subjects of the kings of Chandella. The oldest temple in Khajuraho is the *Chausath Yogini Temple*. The Tantric temple is dedicated to 64 goddesses who drank the blood of demons – cheers! The best time for a visit is at sunrise when the sandstone is alternatively bathed in a delicated pink, light

Khajuraho: an abundance of erotic sculptured decorations

beige and luminous ochre. The temples of the eastern and southern groups situated a few miles away are not quite as impressive as the western group, but is worth cycling to the site in the afternoon when the village children gather to play cricket.

FOOD & DRINK

There are several simple restaurants opposite the western group of temples, many of them with gardens and roof terraces.

WHERE TO STAY

HOTEL ISABEL PALACE

Situated 15 minutes from the centre on foot, the marble-white hotel has airy, clean rooms with a balcony and view of the garden and a wonderful roof terrace. *14 rooms | Airport Road | tel. 09981 29 57 38 | www.hotelisabelpalace.com | Budget*

RADISSON JASS HOTEL

After your trip to the temples, let yourself be pampered in the spa or relax at the pool in the extensive garden: stylish, modern and quiet. Bicycles for rent. *94 rooms | Bypass Road | tel. 1800 108 03 33 | www.radisson.com | Moderate–Expensive*

INFORMATION

MPTDC TOURIST OFFICE

Sevagram, near the western group of temples | tel. 01800 2 33 77 77 | www.mptourism.com

LEH

(183 D2) (*ɯ F2*) The peaks of the Himalayas tower above the twisty road that winds its way up from Manali to Leh at 3,500 m/11,483 ft.

For seven months of the year the Ladakh region and its capital Leh can only be reached by air – when the weather permits. Irrespective of whether you have flown here or travelled by bus, you will initially gasp for air and puff like a steam engine at every step due to the thin air at this altitude. For this reason, take things easy during the first few days and drink plenty of fluids. You will also catch your breath at the unique landscape: Leh is located in a wide, lush green valley basin surrounded by gigantic barren mountains. In the winter, Ladakh is paralysed by cold when the temperature can drop to −50 °C/−58 °F, but in summer it is a pleasant 25 °C/77 °F. The environ-ment is highly sensitive and single-use plastic is therefore prohibited.

In this isolated location in the Himalaya, a Buddhist culture has been preserved that was influenced by Tibet over a long period. There are several monasteries which make you think you are in Tibet. Once you have become acclimatised, you can wander through the Tibet-influenced market, drink butter tea, eat a few momos (steamed pasties filled with vegetables or meat), take a walk past the green and white mosque and ascend the steps in the old town leading to the palace hill.

SIGHTSEEING

LEH PALACE ☆

The nine-storey palace dates from the 17th century when Leh was still a royal seat. Since the royal family was sent into exile almost 200 years ago the building has been left to fall into decay, but the scenery is impressive. If you are not completely out of breath, take the narrow footpath up to the *Gonkhang-Temple* which sits majestically on the summit.

FOOD & DRINK

In *Changspa* and near the *Main Bazaar*, numerous cafés and restaurants on roof terraces offer everything from muesli and pizza to Tibetan noodle soup. Some good names to remember include *Open Hand Café*, *Lala's Art Café* and *Tibetan Kitchen*.

DREAMLAND ☆

One of the oldest restaurants in town. You can enjoy specialities from Ladakh, Kaschmir and Tibet on the roof terrace with a view. *Fort Road | tel. 09858 06 06 07 | Budget*

The Kings' Palace originates from the era when Ladakh was still a monarchy

WHERE TO STAY

HOTEL ORIENTAL ☽

You will be reluctant to get up in the mornings here as you already have such a grand view of the mountains from the rooms furnished in Ladakh style, but there is an equally good view during breakfast in the garden. *39 rooms | Below the Shanti Stupa in the district of Changspa | tel. 0962 2 22 92 96 | www. orientalhotel-ladakh.com | Budget*

OMASILA HOTEL ☽

A green oasis in Changspa with traditional architecture featuring plenty of light-toned wood and a huge roof terrace with a view of the Shanti Stupa. *27 rooms and 11 suites| Changspa Road | tel. 01982 25 17 89 | www.hotelomasila.com | Budget–Moderate*

SHAMBHALA ◉

The comfortable family-run hotel is located in the middle of an apple orchard in the Skara district. The attractive rooms are furnished in traditional style. Meals are prepared with vegetables from the hotel's own organic garden. *27 rooms | Skara, near Zorawor Fort Road | tel. 09810 03 51 45 | www.hotelshambhala. com | Budget*

INFORMATION

TOURIST RECEPTION CENTER

On road to airport | tel. 09560 78 88 84 | www.jktourism.org

WHERE TO GO

Walk through fields of barley, past prayer wheels and the ubiqutous white stupas and tschortens to *Sankar* where there is a small Tibetan monastery. Perhaps you will even meet the *Ringpoche*, the abbot of the monastery. The monks will greet you with a cheerful "Yullay". Do not forget to wear hiking boots, sunglasses and high-level UV protection: Ladakh is a paradise for trekkers. Leh is the ideal starting point for multi-day tours, for example through the lonely *Markha Valley*. You can take a jeep and drive over the highest navigable pass road in the world from Lehto to the *Nubra Valley* and the dazzling blue *Pangong Lake*, half of which is bordered by Tibet.

HEMIS GOMPA (183 D2) (*M F2*)

The seat of the red cap order is one of the largest monasteries and most frequently visited. Hemis not only possesses the largest prayer wheel in Ladakh, but also the largest *thangka*: the gigantic rolled-up painting on silk is however only opened out once every twelve years in honour of the famous mask festival. In the evening, you can listen to drumming music at the ⚲ INSIDER TIP Shanti Stupa and also stay overnight in the monastery. *45 km/28 mi south*

SHEY (183 D2) (*M F2*)

Queens lived in this royal summer palace after giving birth to their children. Have a look at the restored *thangkas* (Tibetan votive paintings) and the gilded Buddha statue that is 12 m/39.4 ft high. *17 km/10.6 mi south-east*

STOK ⚲ (183 D2) (*M F2*)

The Choglamsar suspension bridge leads to the village Stok and the semi-derelict Stok Palace. Some of its 80 rooms now form part of a museum; other parts are still lived in. Momentos of the royal family included *thangkas and* ancient hats covered in jewels *(peraks)*. *May–Oct 10am–5pm | 17 km/10.6 mi south-west*

TIKSE ⚲ (183 D2) (*M F2*)

The monastery of the yellow cap order has a slight resemblance to the Potala palace in Lhasa. Arrive as early as possible or stay overnight in the guesthouse so that you can take part in the monks' morning ritual in the main temple. Allow yourself to be lulled into a doze by the Buddhist chants while the child monks secretly attempt to catch up on some sleep. *19 km/11.8 mi south-east*

Drum-induced trance – a Buddhist monk of the "Red Hat" order in Hemis Gompa

LUCKNOW

(186 C2) *(∅ H6)* **The capital city (pop. 2.8 million) of the state of Uttar Pradesh comprises a daring mixture of beauty and business.**

Following the trail of the unbelievably rich Nawabs of Avadh (or Oudh), the Muslim monarch dynasty, which ruled this region over a long period, will lead you far away from the hectic city life to palaces, avenues of trees and gardens. At the end of the 18th century, music and architecture blossomed in Lucknow, as did the production of wonderful textiles and fabulous culinary art of the Nawabs.

SIGHTSEEING

BARA IMAMBARA ★

One of the mighty Nawabs, Asaf-du-Daulah, had his future final resting place erected as a job-creation process during the great famine of 1784. The building of the large mausoleum lasted 14 years. The main hall is up to 15 m/49.2 ft high and has no pillars – an architectural marvel at that time. A narrow staircase leads to the *bhuul bhulaiya*, a labyrinth of dimly lit passages and viewing galleries. Do not be worried that you could get lost even if the guides standing around everywhere will tell you otherwise. They will also show you the walls where a mysterious echo can be produced. Coins tossed into the 60 m/196.9 ft deep well allegedly reach Shiva directly! Adjoining *Asfi Mosque* can only be visited by Muslims. *Sunrise to sunset | Husainabad Road | Chowk*

CHOTA IMAMBARA

The *Little mausoleum (Husainabad Imambara)*, was built in 1817–42 and is crowned by a golden dome that is visible from afar. Inside, cut-glass chandeliers and regal kitsch abound. *Sunrise to sunset | west of Bara Imambara*

LA MARTINIÈRE

A romantic notion turned into stone or just iced-cake kitsch? When the French soldier, adventurer and bon vivant, Claude Martin, furnished this stately property on the River Gomti at the end of the 18th century, he combined oriental and European architectural styles which he considered the embodiment of grandeur and magnificence. As a result, one of the most unusual buildings in northern India was created. At Martin's request, the building was turned into a college where lessons are still taught today. In Rudyard Kipling's *Jungle Book*, Kim attends this school that is a popular set for Bollywood films today.

RESIDENCY

The Nawabs constructed a town within a town for the officers of the British administration and their local servants towards the end of the 18th century, including a school, a hospital and even Moslem shrines, but only a few ruins have survived. During the uprising of the Sepoys (Indian soldiers in the British Army) in 1857, the residence was occupied for almost six months, during which violent battles were fought. You can still see the bullet holes in the Residency. The cellar where the women and children held out among the 3,000 besieged, is accessible. The tomb of the Chief Commissioner Sir Henry Lawrence in the INSIDER**TIP** graveyard bears the epitaph: "Here lies Henry Lawrence who tried to do his duty." *Museum daily 10am–5pm | Mahatma Gandhi Road*

FOOD & DRINK

In Lucknow it is compulsory to feast on the lavish Mogul cuisine. The biryanis and pilafs prepared with dried fruits and subtle spices are a festival for the senses. The kebabs melt in your mouth after having been slowly steamed in enclosed clay pots. You will find an abundance of restaurants serving traditional *chaat*, tasty snacks, in *Mahatma Gandhi Road* in the district of Hazratganj.

FALAKNUMA ✨

Here, you get the best Nawab food in town, creamy curries and succulent kebabs, with the best view of the town. *In the luxury hotel Clarks Avadh | 8, MG Marg | tel. 0522 2 62 01 31 | Expensive*

SHOPPING

The Nawabs loved opulence and surrounded themselves with silver decorations, highly scented perfumes and richly embroidered cotton fabrics known as *chikan*. In the narrow alleyways of the *Hazratganj* district, once a meeting place for "Bohemians", you will find shops selling these fine goods. There must still be room in your case for a flask of perfume.

WHERE TO STAY

OYO HOTEL GOMTI

Large rooms (the better ones with AC), attentive service. The restaurant and bar have been here for decades. *65 rooms | 6, Sapru Marg | tel. 0522 2 61 14 63 | oyorooms.com | Budget*

VIVANTA BY TAJ GOMTI NAGAR

First-rate accommodation, quiet, slightly out of town, tropical garden with a beautiful pool, 2 restaurants. Indian musicians play in the bar. *110 rooms | Vipin Khand | Gomti Nagar | tel. 0522 6 71 10 00 | www.vivantabytaj.com | Expensive*

INFORMATION

In Hotel Gomti | 6, Sapru Marg | tel. 0522 2 61 50 05

RISHIKESH/ HARIDWAR

(183 D–E 4–5) (*ᗰ G4*) **Here, at the foot of the Himalaya, the Ganges is still in its infancy. It is clean and particularly holy. It comes out of a narrow valley in the self-appointed yoga capital of the world, Rishikesh (pop. 102,000), the river's green clear waters flowing past sandbanks on its journey.**
25 km/15.5 mi further on, in *Haridwar* (pop. 225,000), the river finally leaves the mountains behind.
Every twelve years, one of the largest religious festivals in India is celebrated in Haridwar, *Kumbh Mela*. On 55 days in that year, up to 90 million people come to take a ritual bath in the Ganges – the next occasion is 2022. Pilgrims and yoga fans from all round the world flock to Rishikesh, the location of seers (rishis). Dozens of ashrams and yoga schools are crammed in along the riverbanks where sadhus with coils of dreadlocks are sitting.
In addition, Rishikesh is the perfect gateway to the Himalayas if you are planning to visit elevated locations such as the source of the Ganges in Gangotri or the holy mountain sites of Badrinath and Kadarnath. Water sport lovers can also go wild-water rafting on the Ganges.

Bathing in the holy river – every twelve months the Kumbh Mela is held in Haridwar

SIGHTSEEING

INSIDER TIP ▶ BEATLES ASHRAM

Many legends have grown up around the period that the Beatles spent in the Ashram of Maharashi Mahesh Yogi whom they met in London in 1967. The Fab Four practised transcendental meditation in egg-shaped mud huts, intoxicating themselves with mind-enhancing drugs and writing many of their best songs. Many decades later, the slowly decaying ashram was becoming overgrown by an ever-increasing area of jungle, but now you are officially permitted to walk around. A group focused around the Canadian artist Pan Trinity transformed the Sat-sang hall into a sort of Beatles shrine with the aid of colourful graffiti. Below the ashram, there is a gluten-free café and a Beatles museum is planned – Beatlemania Indian style! *Rishikesh | Swarg Ashram*

SIVANANDA ASHRAM ●

This ashram belongs to the *Divine Life Society* established by Sri Swami Shiva-nanda in 1936. You can take up residence free of charge in the ashram and take part in yoga and meditation courses. There are also free meals. *Rishikesh | www.sivanandaonline.org*

SWARG ASHRAM

You have to cross the Ram Jhula Bridge to reach the Swarg Ashram. Pilgrims purchase plastic bottles on the *ghats* (steps) which they fill with water from the Ganges to take home. Hundreds of people sit every evening on the steps to experience the magical aarti, the traditional fire ceremony. Upstream from the Ram Jhula Bridge, you can bury your feet in the white sand or walk on further to Lakshman Jhula.

TRIVENI GHAT ●

Another perfect place for Ganga Aarti: after sunset priests place floating lanterns in the water at Triveni Ghat. *Near Rishikesh's oldest temple, Bharat Mandir*

FOOD & DRINK

DEVRAJ COFFEE CORNER ☭

You should definitely visit the German Bakery upstream from the Lakshman Jhula Bridge to taste yak cheese sandwiches and apple strudel with the added attraction of a view of the mountains and the river. *Laskhman Jhula | Budget*

THE OFFICE

Here you can drink the best chai in Rishikesh and eat delicious mango samosas: the view of the Ganges from the small terrace is included in the price. *Swarg Ashram | Budget*

WHERE TO STAY

ANANDA HOTEL ☭

Luxurious hotel high above the Ganges valley. Outdoor swimming pool, spa facilities, Ayurveda, yoga, squash and trekking. 70 modernly designed rooms, 5 suites, many with sweeping views over the plain. *The Palace Estate, Narendra Nagar Tehri | tel. 0124 4 5166 50 | www. anandaspa.com | Expensive*

HOTEL GANGA KINARE

Tranquillity and nature: the smart boutique hotel is situated on the riverside. Delicious food in two restaurants. *38 rooms | 237, Verbhadra Road | Rishikesh | tel. 09015 54 40 00 | www. gangakinare. com | Moderate*

RISHIKESH VALLEY ⚙

The ecological resort has used natural materials for the construction of its comfortable wooden cottages in its jungle-like grounds. Here you can use the spa facilities, take yoga courses and book trekking and rafting tours. *3 km/1.9 mi from the Tapovan Police Station | tel. 0941 0 7115 03 | www. rishikeshvalley.com | Budget*

INFORMATION

GARHWAL MANDAL VIKAS NIGAM

Information also includes expert advice on rafting and trekking tours in the Himalayas. *Shial Vihar | Haridwar By Pass Road | Rishikesh | tel. 0135 2 43 17 93 | www.gmvnl.in*

SANCHI

(186 A4) (⵿ F8) The small town (pop. 8,400), around 45 km/28 mi from Bhopal, was one of the largest spritual centres of Buddhism in India between the 3rd and 13th centuries. Its major attraction is the ★ *stupa* on the hill above the sleepy old town.

It is not a temple but a place where relics are kept. Their purpose however remains a mystery. The ocherous stupa was built by Emperor Ashoka in the 3rd century BC. What makes this one of the greatest works are the reliefs on the large, encircling, stone balustrade with its four 10 m/32.8 ft high gateways. Buddha's life is depicted on hundreds of panels. The ruins of temples and old monasteries are in the vicinity, as well as a modern monastery run by monks and a small *museum (Sat–Thu 10am–5pm)*.

There is little choice of places to stay around Sanchi. The *Gateway Retreat (16 rooms | NH 86, Vidisha Road | tel. 07482 26 67 23 | short.travel/ind16 | Budget)* is inviting. The garden has a pool, the rooms are simple, cosy and clean.

SIKKIM/ GANGTOK

(188 A–B2) (🗺 M5) Sikkim, the former kingdom between Tibet, Bhutan and Nepal is full of colour despite the grey of the mountains further up.

Sikkimese, Tibetan and Nepalese Buddhists decorate the façades of their temples and halls in brilliant natural colours. The mountain slopes are covered by dense forests and rhododendrons flower in the spring. Prayer flags of all colours flutter in all directions. The whitewashed temples are colourfully ornamented and the gold roofs glitter in the sun, as does the snow on the massive Kanchenjunga, the third-highest peak in the world. The previously independent kingdom Sikkim has only been part of India since 1975. Here you will discover signs of its Buddhist heritage all around you. Sikkim is considered as the last Shangri-La in the Himalayas due to its seclusion. Once you leave behind the noise of the principle town *Gangtok* (pop. 100,000), you will find peace and tranquillity on your hikes. Perhaps you are also planning a retreat in one of the Buddhist monasteries?

SIGHTSEEING

ENCHEY GOMPA

When you have crossed through the small coniferous forest, you will come to the 200-year-old monastery with colourfully ornamented windows and numerous statues of Tantric deities. The best time of year to visit is in January/February when the monks are preparing for the masked dances. *3 km/1.9 mi north*

NAMGYAL INSTITUTE OF TIBETOLOGY

The museum with Mahayana Buddhism artefacts has a nice collection of *thangkas*, sculptures and religious objects. *Mon–Sat 10am–4pm | on the southern edge of the town*

INSIDER TIP WHITE HALL FLOWER EXHIBITION CENTRE ☆

A wonderful display of flowers, the orchids that can be seen here in March are especially beautiful. These include local species and new ones cultivated

Stupa in Sanchi – this stone hemisphere is used to house relics

in Sikkim that are different every year. *In Ridge Park*

FOOD & DRINK/ WHERE TO STAY

ELGIN NOR-KHILL HOTEL
Former royal guesthouse near the Paljor stadium with luxurious rooms, a secluded garden with a mountain view and restaurant. *30 rooms | Paljore Stadium Road | tel. 03592 20 56 37 | www.elgin hotels.com | Moderate*

NETUK HOUSE
Comfortable Tibetan-style hotel with Sikkimese food. *8 rooms | Tibet Road | tel. 03592 20 47 66 www.netukhouse.com | Moderate*

TEEN TALEY ECO GARDEN RESORT 🌱
Pure nature accompanied by all comforts: the cottages and luxury rooms are situated within an extensive garden. The kitchen cooks with their own-grown organic vegetables. *12 rooms | Rumtek | tel. 0973 3 06 46 00 | www.sikkimresort. com | Moderate*

INFORMATION

SIKKIM TOURISM DEVELOPMENT CORPORATION
MG Marg | Gangtok | tel. 03592 20 90 90 | www.sikkimstdc.com. A permit is needed to enter the state and a permit is also needed to go trekking in the north of Sikkim. It is best to apply for permits when applying for a visa to India before setting off from home.

WHERE TO GO

PELLING ⚓ **(188 A2)** *(𝄞 M5)*
Pelling is visited for its excellent views of the snow-covered *Kanchenjunga* (8,586 m/28,169 ft). If you want to get even closer to the third-highest peak in the world, you can book a helicopter flight in Gangtok which starts in Pelling. *Pemayang-tse Monastery* (1705), one of the oldest and most important in Sikkim, towers above the mountain forests. A short hike will take you to the cleared *ruins of Rabentse* that was once the capital. Accommodation is available in ⚓ *The Elgin Mount Pandim Hotel (30 rooms | tel. 03593 5 07 56 | www. elginhotels.com | Moderate)* with a view of Kanchenjunga. *110 km/68 mi west (approx. 4 hours by car)*

RUMTEK (192 A2) *(𝄞 M5)*
There are more than 200 monasteries in Sikkim, the largest and most visited is *Rumtek Gompa*, the hillside monastery of the "Black Hat" monks who fled Tibet. It is a copy of the ancient sanctuary in their native country and was built in 1960. The most impressive among them is Rumtek if you are able to experience the ceremonial chants or the masked dances which take place annually every May/June and before the Tibetan new year. *24 km/14.9 mi south-west*

VARANASI

🗺️ **MAP ON P. 64**
(187 D3) *(𝄞 J7)* **Life and death, a golden temple roof, shimmering silk, sick and elderly people waiting to die in this holy city – all these are Varanasi (pop. 1.2 million): India at its most Indian and where it touches the heart most.**
The west bank of the Ganges is lined with broad steps, *ghats*, with the towers of temples, old palaces, cremation sites and galis, the labyrinthine alleyways of the old town, beyond. INSIDER TIP The hour before sunrise is magic – when the sky

above the undeveloped east bank turns red and hundreds of tiny vessels made of leaves are sent off down river with little oil lamps burning on them.

Varanasi was named after the two rivers, the Varuna and the Asi, which flow into the Ganges here. In the Vedas (ancient sacred texts), the city is called *Kashi*, the "place of light". The city is considered the oldest in the world, as ancient as time immemorial. Hindus see Varanasi as the laid out to dry at the most significant and holiest of the more than 100 ghats in Varanasi, the *Dasaswamedh Ghat (in the middle of the row of ghats). You will see babas and nagas, sitting half-naked under sunshades in prayer performing Hindu rituals. You should not miss coming down in the evening to the Ganga Aarti where the action is more highly choreographed than in Rishikesh. You can then wander downriver to Man Mandir Ghat*

Smoke rises from a cremation site on the banks of the Ganges in Varanasi

gateway to *moskha*, the liberation of the soul: every devout Hindu visits the city once in a lifetime. It is said that whoever dies in Kashi and is cremated here will avoid the cycle of reincarnation and arrive directly in Nirwana.

SIGHTSEEING

THE GHATS OF VARANASI

You will encounter a sea of pilgrims, priests, flower sellers and colourful saris until you reach the semi-ruined palace belonging to the Maharajah of the same name. A Nepalese temple with a golden roof is on *Lalita Ghat*. Shiva's footprint, a Ganesh temple and water basin formed from a bead of Shiva's sweat make *Manikarnika Ghat* a holy place. Smoke rises unceasingly from the wood stacks piled up at the largest cremation ghat, surrounded by remnants of the red-golden fabric in which the corpses are wound and cremated around the clock.

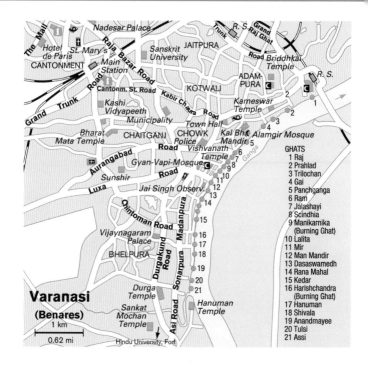

GHATS
1 Raj
2 Prahlad
3 Trilochan
4 Gai
5 Panchganga
6 Ram
7 Jalashayi
8 Scindhia
9 Manikarnika (Burning Ghat)
10 Lalita
11 Mir
12 Man Mandir
13 Dasaswamedh
14 Rana Mahal
15 Kedar
16 Harishchandra (Burning Ghat)
17 Hanuman
18 Shivala
19 Anandmayee
20 Tulsi
21 Assi

Varanasi (Benares)
1 km
0.62 mi

According to legend, the five holy rivers (Ganges, Yamuna, Kirana, Sarasvati and Dhutapapa) meet underground at *Panchaganga Ghat*, two ghats further downstream. The *Someswar Ghat* is upriver from the *Dasasvamedh Ghat*. People bathe here in the hope of being healed. At the *Tulsi Ghat*, ask for the way to the *Akhara* where Kushti is practised daily: an ancient traditional form of wrestling. Men with well-developd muscles dressed in loincloths train with antiquated dumbbells and wrestle in the sand.

FOOD & DRINK

BLUE LASSI SHOP
The creamiest and fruitiest lassi that you have ever tasted has been served here for the last 90 years. Do you prefer chocloate flavour or cardamon, pistachio or pomegranate? *CK 12/1 Kachowri Gali Chowk*

VEGAN & RAW RESTAURANT ⊘
Anyone who has had enough of Indian curry will be in seventh heaven in this small oasis run by the *Brown Bread Bakery*. Here you will be offered healthy, fresh and crunchy ingredients from the restaurant's own garden. *2 225-D-1 Shivala Road | Assi Road | Budget*

SHOPPING

Brocade and silk (saris, material sold by the yard) can be found for example on *Godoulia,* on *Maqbool Alam Road* and in the ● *Vishvanath Gali*. The shops in the alleyway lead down to the famous emporium Banarasi Sari – offering fine silks interlaced with golden threads. Good value: *Ali Handicrafts | C19/19A-5, Lallapura | near Varuna Hospital*

WHERE TO STAY

GANPATI GUESTHOUSE

You can take a break in the courtyard or on the roof terrace of this funky and colourful boutique guesthouse. You will find the entrance in a somewhat concealed alleyway in the old town. *20 rooms | Meer Ghat | tel. 0542 2 39 00 57 | www.ganpatiguesthouse.com | Budget*

NADESAR PALACE/THE GATEWAY HOTEL GANGES VARANASI

Five-star luxury well away from the hustle and bustle in the grounds of a palace dating from the colonial period offering modern rooms with old world charm. *10 or 130 rooms incl. 3 or 10 suites | Nadesar Palace Grounds | tel. 0542 6 66 00 01 | www.tajhotels.com | Expensive*

INFORMATION

GOVERNMENT OF INDIA TOURIST OFFICE
15B, The Mall | next to Hotel de Paris | tel. 0542 2 50 50 33 | www.uptourism.gov.in

WHERE TO GO

SARNATH (187 D3) (Ω J7)

In the afternoon, the large round *Dhamek Stupa* is bathed in a golden-red light, the gold leaf on the plinth reflects the sun. This is where Buddha held his first sermon after having found enlightenment in Bodh Gaya. In the *Museum (Sat–Thu, 10am–5pm),* look out for the pillar with the four lions erected by Emperor Ashoka whose capital has become the national coat of arms. *10 km/6.2 mi north*

This Sadhu is deeply immersed in silent prayer

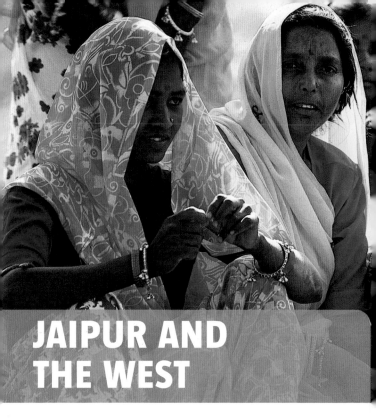

JAIPUR AND THE WEST

Rajasthan is often referred to as a desert state. Its name means "the land of kings". At one time there were twenty-three princely states competing against one another in this one region. The ruling Rajputs were proud warriors who made war against one another.

At that time a lot of rich merchants were living on the edge or in the middle of the desert. Palatial houses *(havelis)* with delicately carved stone façades often turned into hotels today. The Indira Gandhi Canal has transformed the desert in the west into a fertile country.

The *Palace on Wheels*, the refurbished, historical, luxury train of the Maharajas, now runs through Rajasthan and Gujarat, the most westerly state in India. The peninsula in Gujarat has beautiful beaches, wonderful temples and one of the world's biggest salt deserts. A small but influential religious minority group lives in Gujarat – the Jains. They built the temple city of Palitana, the "white wonder", and propagated vegetarianism and non-violence. These ideals also helped form the basis of Mahatma Ganhi's teachings. He was born in 1869 in Gujarat, in the port of Porbandar. The most beautiful palm beaches are on the southern-most tip of the peninsula. They are part of Diu, a small island that was a Portuguese colony until 1961.

AHMEDABAD

(184 C5) (ന D8) Magnificent buildings with a mixture of Hindu and Muslim

Photo: Women visiting a temple in Udaipur

A Thousand and One Nights in India – camp fires under a star-filled sky in desert, forts full of legends and incredible nature reserves

architecture testify to the complex history of Ahmedabad which was founded in 1411 by Sultan Ahmed Shah.
Today, the city (pop. 5.6 million) is a vibrant commercial metropolis. Unfortunately environmental pollution has taken its toll on many historical buildings erected by the Muslim founder.

In the late 19th century Ahmedabad experienced an economic boom as a centre of the cotton industry that led to it being nicknamed "the Manchester of the East". Gandhi lived here for several years. His commitment to the cotton workers influenced his ideas on civil disobedience. The cotton industry still plays an important role today. In 1960 Ahmedabad had to relinquish its status as the capital of Gujarat to Gandhinagar (25 km/15.5 mi north). In 2017, it was the first Indian state to be added to the Unesco list of World Heritage Sites. Prohibition still exists in the so-called "dry state", but you will still be served beer legally in most of the larger hotels.

SIGHTSEEING

INSIDER TIP CALICO MUSEUM OF TEXTILES

You can marvel at the traditional art of weaving here. It includes materials such as brocade and silk, embroidery and saris, wall-hangings and carpets. The textile museum is in the *Shahi Bagh*

Campus | L.D. Institute of Indology Campus | www.ldmuseum.co.in

SABARMATI ASHRAM

Mohandas Karamchand (Mahatma) Gandhi founded an ashram on the banks of the River Sabarmati in 1915 and lived here in accordance with the philosophy of *sathyagraha* – "insistence

A tailor at work: Ahmedabad is still the most important centre of the textile industry today

gardens. A visit is only possible as part of a (free) guided tour and booking in advance (Tue–Thu). *Tel. 079 22 86 81 72 | www.calicomuseum.com*

LALBHAI DALPATBHAI MUSEUM/ NC MEHTA GALLERY OF MINIATURES

A unique collection of miniatures and Indian crafts is exhibited in this building designed by Le Corbusier which has all the charm of a bunker. The Buddhist sculptures dating from the 2nd–5th centuries are a highlight. *Tue–Sat 10.30am–5.30pm | on Gujarat University*

on truth". It was here in 1930 that Gandhi's most famous campaign of civil disobedience began – the "Salt March", as a protest against the British colonial government. *Daily from sunrise to sunset | Ashram Road | 5 km/3.1 mi from the centre*

SIDI SAYET MOSQUE

The geometric patterns on the walls and the delicately ornamented windows are the striking features of the mosque which has virtually become the unofficial emblem of Ahmedabad. Look up and gaze in wonder at the vaulted ceiling. Situated between the *riverbank and the beginning of Relief Road*

FOOD & DRINK

AGASHIYE/GREENHOUSE ● ♨ ☯

Two gourmet oases under a single roof: in Agashiye on the roof terrace, you will be served at the table with vegetarian Gujarati Thali and in the Greenhouse you can enjoy healthy slow food. *In the MG-Hotel | Dr. Tankaria Road | tel. 079 25 50 69 46 | Moderate*

VISHALLA ☯

All the ingredients for the Gujarati Thalis are supplied by local farmers, the dishes are served on leaf plates for environmental reasons and you sit on the clay floor on bamboo mats just like in an Indian village. *Vasna Road | tel. 079 26 60 24 22 | www.vishalla.com | Moderate*

SHOPPING

For all shopaholics: make your way to the bazaar in the old town around *Relief Road* and *MG Road close to* the main mosque Jama Masjid to buy material, silver jewellery and heavenly confectionery. The modern shopping area can be found on *Ashram Road* on the west side of the river. In the state emporium *Gurjari*, you will discover handicraft objects from the whole of India and the cotton saris typical of Ahmedabad. *(Maheshwari).*

WHERE TO STAY

GOOD NIGHT

Well managed hotel serving Indian food. Opposite Sidi Sayet Mosque. *25 rooms | near Electricity House | Lal Darwaja | tel. 079 25 50 69 98 | www.hotelgoodnight. co.in | Budget*

THE HOUSE OF MG ★

This little, extremely well-run heritage hotel is also opposite Sidi Saiyyed Mosque. The roof-top restaurant is considered the best in town. *14 rooms | Dr. Tankaria Road | tel. 079 5 50 69 46 | www. houseofmg.com | Expensive*

INFORMATION

TOURISM CORPORATION OF GUJARAT LTD.

In the H.K. House, opposite the Bata showroom. *Ashram Road | tel. 079 26 58 91 72 | www.gujarattourism.com*

★ **The House of MG**
Heritage hotel with prize-winning roof-top restaurant
→ p. 69

★ **Junagarh Fort**
Magnificently opulent palace with gold, glass and mirror work in the city of Bikaner → p. 71

★ **Shekawati**
Desert settlements with artistically painted house façades
→ p. 73

★ **City Palace**
This palace of superlatives covers a huge area in Jaipur → p. 75

★ **Amber Palace**
Pure grandeur in Rajasthan's most famous palace complex
→ p. 78

★ **Havelis**
Impressively decorated houses in Jaisalmer that tell of the wealth of old → p. 79

MARCO POLO HIGHLIGHTS

Marble paving and elaborate carvings in the huge temple complex at Shatrunjaya

WHERE TO GO

MODHERA (184 C4) (*Ø C8*)
The probably finest sun temple in Gujarat is almost 1,000 years old and has survived earthquakes and hordes of Muslim conquerors. At both equinoxes, the rising sun first kisses the image of the sun deity Surya to whom the temple is dedicated. *102 km/63 mi north-west*

PALITANA ☀ (184 C6) (*Ø C9*)
The white shrines on the "temple mountain" at the Jain sacred site *Shatrunjaya* are enchanting. The mountain has been considered divine since the 4th century, the oldest temples still standing are from the 11th century. The walls are decorated with hundreds of intricately carved stone figures including buxom temple dancers. In the temple, you will come face to face with stone Jain saints whose poses almost look like yoga positions. There are purported to be 863 temples on the mountain that rises to a height of 600 m/1,969 ft. It takes around 1½ hours to climb the 3,300 wide steps to the top, INSIDER TIP the most beautiful time is at the first light of day. As leather is prohibited by the Jains, you should leave belts or watches with leather wristbands in your hotel. The holy mountain is left to the temple spirits in the evening light. *Daily 6am–6pm.*

In the little town of Palitana at the foot of the mountain, the GTDC *Hotel Sumeru (Station Road | tel. 02848 25 23 27 | booking.gujarattourism.com | Budget)* with 18 tiny, very clean rooms as well as *Vijay Vilas Palace (6 rooms | tel. 02848 28 2 63 02 02 | vishwa–adpur@yahoo.co.in | Moderate)*, a small heritage hotel some 4 km/2.5 mi from Palitana in the village of Gheti/Adpur-Palitana can be recommended. *217 km/135 mi south*

INSIDER TIP RANI-KI-VAV (184 C4) (*Ø C8*)
North of Modhera is a gem of artistic Hindu stonemasonry. *Vavs*, also called *Baori*,

are stepped wells that were built to provide people and animals with shade and water. They are typical for the states of Gujarat and Rajasthan which have little water. The *Rani-ki-Vav* is like an inverted temple with several pavilions and open areas. If you walk down the seven storeys, you can marvel at the hundreds of sculptures ornamenting the walls and pillars. *134 km/83 mi north*

BIKANER

(185 D1) (*ᗰ D5*) Bikaner (pop. 645,000) has entered the modern era more than 100 years ago.

At that time the Maharaja Dungar Singh had Rajasthan's first electricity power station built. His brother and successor, Ganga Singh, added to this later by constructing irrigation channels and hospitals.

The only camel research farm in India is not far from Bikaner and is open to visitors. The wind of the desert and reminiscences of the Arabian Nights make it a perfect base for camel safaris and excursions to the *shekawati (painted towns)* to the north-east. Even today Bikaner has all the magic of a bazaar and has a wealth of *havelis* – the mansion houses of wealthy merchants with ornamental carved stonework. Some of the most beautiful, like the Rampuria Haveli, are open to the public. The main attraction however is the Maharajas' Junagarh Fort.

SIGHTSEEING

GANGA GOVERNMENT MUSEUM
Built in 1937 to celebrate the Maharaja Ganga Singh's 50th year of rule, the museum includes archaeological exhibits, the Maharaja's collection of paintings, exquisite weapons and colourful folkloric items. *Mon–Sat 10am–5pm | Gandhi Park*

JUNAGARH FORT ★
This, the most primeval and biggest of all Rajasthan palaces, boasts an artistically decorated interior. The Maharaja spared no expense: gold leaf and cut glass, mirrors, Chinese wallpaper and Dutch tiles have all been added to this palace. Stroll through the *Karan Mahal* (audience chamber), *Chandra Mahal* (Moon Palace) and *Anup Mahal* (Cloud Palace) with displays of paintings and miniatures. A *palace museum* recalls the magnificent life of the Maharajas of Rathore. The *Prachina Museum (daily 9am–6pm | www.prachinamuseum.org),* which display some exquisite everyday items formerly used in the palace is also worth a visit. Small café adjoining. *Mon– Sat 10am–4.30pm*

LOW BUDGET

Admission to one of the most beautiful garden palaces in India costs less than 160 INR. This gem is in Deeg near Bharatpur and has also a museum. *Daily 8am–5pm | Deeg Palace*

You do not have to stay in the noble Lake Pichola Hotel to have a view of the "James Bond lake" in Udaipur. For only 1,377 INR, you can stay in a guesthouse owned by the Panorama Hotel on the Hanuman Ghat: simple but attractive rooms with a magnificent roof terrace. *18 rooms | tel. 02 94 2 43 10 27 | www.panoramaguest house.in*

FOOD & DRINK

AMBERWALLA

Delicious vegetarian Indian and continental food. If you have a sweet tooth, you have to try the dry fruit & mawa sweets! *Station Road | opposite Joshi Hotel | tel. 09829 06 99 33 | Moderate*

An abundance of gold: image of Krishna in Mandawa

SAFARIS & TOURS

RAJASTHAN SAFARIS & TREKS

The right address for camel and jeep tours through Thar Desert, including visits to villages and INSIDER TIP a stay with a local family. Ask *Birendra Singh Tanwar at the tourist reception centre or write an e-mail (*birendra@realbikaner.com).

WHERE TO STAY

BHAIRON VILAS

Historical haveli with garden west of Junagarh Fort. *18 rooms | near post office | tel. 09928 31 22 83 | www.bharionvilas. com | Budget*

INSIDER TIP BHANWAR NIWAS

The rooms in the heritage haveli of a traditional Marwari family in the Old City are divine. Mosaic and marble grounds, antique furniture and wallpapers with stencil paintings. *26 rooms | Rampuria Road | tel. 0151 2 20 10 43 | www.bhanwarniwas.com | Moderate*

INFORMATION

TOURIST RECEPTION CENTER

Assistance in finding private accommodation. *Goam Atithi | RTDC Hotel Dhola Maru Campus | Puran Singh Circle | tel. 0151 2 52 96 21 | www.realbikaner.com*

WHERE TO GO

CAMEL RESEARCH FARM
(185 D1) (*ω D5*)

Of the some five million camels in the world, around every seventh one is here in Rajasthan. The animals with their carers can be visited. *Mon–Sat 3pm–5pm | admission free | 10 km/6.2 mi south-east*

INSIDER TIP DESHNOK KARNI MATA
(185 D1) (*ω D5*)

Now even a rarity in India – the rat temple, the preserve of hundreds of rats, the incarnate form of writers and singers. For this reason there are often musicians outside the heavy silver doors to the temple. One strange thing is that the rats only breed slowly despite the fact that they are fed every day. *33 km/20.5 mi south*

SHEKAWATI ★ (185 D–E1) *(D–E5)*

If you find ruins romantic, love the picturesque and a quest for adventure then the north-eastern corner of Thar Desert is the right place for you. A round trip, for example from Mandawa to Bissau, Churu, Ratannagarh, Ramgarh and Fatehpur and back again to Mandawa is well worth the effort. The partly naïve, partly professional works of art from the 19th century can hardly be missed in this little town covered in sand. Paintings of dancers and gods, steam trains and even an early car adorn the façades of buildings and courtyards. INSIDERTIP *Hotel Castle Mandawa (51 rooms | Mandawa | District of Jhunjhunu | Shekawati | tel. 01592 22 31 24 | www.castlemandawa. com | Moderate)* has a palatial oriental atmosphere.

DIU

(184 B6) *(C10)* Sandy beaches and palm groves, the sound of crashing waves and the smell of salt in the air – the little island off the south coast of Gujarat is the right place for a few days' relaxing by the sea.

Like Goa, Diu (pop. 50,000, just under 15 mi²) was a Portuguese colony until 1961. Diu's harbour was important as maritime routes across the Arabian Sea – a territory disputed by the Ottoman dynasty, the Portuguese and the Muslim rulers of India – could be monitored from here. In 1535 the Portuguese succeeded in securing sovereignty over Diu for themselves. This remained unchanged for over 400 years. The reopening of the airport that was destroyed in 1961 during the Indian Invasion has fortunately not rid Diu of its dreamy atmosphere. While alcohol is prohibited in Gujarat, beer and spirits can be enjoyed legally just over the border in Diu – an opportunity of which many locals Gujaratis make regular use.

SIGHTSEEING

FORT

The Portuguese fort was completed in 1541. Surrounded by water on three sides and with walls surmounted by canons, the building makes a formidable impression. Part of the complex is used as a prison. *Daily 10am–5pm*

CHURCHES

Of the three churches, only one still retains its original function. *St Paul's*, inaugurated in 1610, is a brilliant white building with an artistically decorated façade and a lovely altar. *St Thomas' Church* not far away houses a museum with holy figures and ecclesiastic treasures. The neighbouring *St Francis of Assisi* church has been converted into a hospital.

FOOD & DRINK

SHRI RAM VIJAY REFRESHING

Delicious homemade treats have been made in this ice cream parlour for 70 years. The date and walnut ice cream can be especially recommended. *Town Square | diagonally opposite the post office*

BEACHES

Diu has six beaches suitable for swimming. a *Ghoghla Beach* is south of the area of Diu on the mainland. From here, the town of Diu with its floodlit churches on the east of the island is an attractive sight at dusk. *Jallandhar, Chakratirth Beach* and *Sunset Point* are to the south-

Innumerable steps lead down to the water – a water tank in Jaipur

west of Diu Town – but avoid hiking there in the heat of the day. The pearl among Diu's bays is *Nagoa Beach.* Remote is *Gomtimata Beach* on the west of the island. All beaches can be reached by auto-rickshaw or bus for just a few rupees. Most have neither restaurants nor snack-bars.

WHERE TO STAY

MAGICO DO MAR ☆
The resort is a nobleman's seat from the 1930s. 14 charming cottages, the more modern buildings are not so nice. Plus points include a lovely beach, palm trees and a view of the town about 3 km/1.9 mi away. When swimming, do not underestimate the power of the waves. *Diu Check Post, Ahmedpur Mandvi | tel. 02875 25 25 67 | www.magico domar.com | Moderate*

SAMRAT
The hotel is centrally located, very clean and has air-conditioned rooms. Good restaurant. *30 rooms | near the vegetable market | tel. 02875 25 23 54 | www. hotelsamratdiu.com | Budget*

UMASHAKTI
Hotel with a roof terrace, a cheap restaurant and a bar. *15 rooms | south of vegetable market | tel. 02875 25 21 50 | Budget*

INFORMATION

TOURISM OFFICE
On Diu Jetty diagonally opposite the post office | tel. 02875 25 26 53 | www.diu tourism.com and www.gujarattourism.com

WHERE TO GO

SOMNATH (184 B6) (⏷ C9)
The Temple of Somnath is one of the most important Shiva holy sites. It contains one of the twelve *Jyotirlinga* shrines (a *lingam* – representation of Shiva – formed by nature) and is a symbol of vitality. Its location on a headland above the sea is impressive. The temple was rebuilt several times after being destroyed by invading Muslims from the north. Before the first documented pillage in 1024 by Mahmud of Ghazni, the pilgrimage centre is reputed to have been able to feed 2,000 Brahmans, 300 musicians, 500 temple dancers

and 300 barbers. The present building dates from 1950. Remains of the old temple can be seen in the museum on the road to the temple. *Mon, Tue, Thu, Fri 10am–noon and 3pm–6pm)*. Sound-and-light show every evening from 8pm–9pm. *90 km/55.9 mi west*

JAIPUR

⚏⚏ MAP ON P. 77
(185 E2) (*∅ E6*) **Jaipur (pop. 3 million) is known as the "Pink City". Since the founding of the city in 1727 the palace and other official buildings were all built in the local reddish stone.**

The rest of the Old City was painted pink in 1883 as a traditional welcome to Prince Edward the Prince of Wales. In 1948 the old city walls and streets with their arcades were to make way for modern buildings. However Jawaharlal Nehru, the Prime Minister of India, stopped their demolition. Even in the narrowest alleys and passageways in Jaipur carpet dealers and jewellery sellers have made space for themselves. In the south-east of the walled city, well away from the tourist shopping areas, is the district where elephants are kept. The animals, accompanied by their *mahouts*, the keepers and drivers, carry tourists up to the Amber Palace every day. When you leave the pink old town, the capital of the state of Rajasthan boasts refreshingly open avenues and parks and museums. Jaipur is also well known for its palace hotels. You can reach the city from Delhi on the *Shatabdi Express* in just over four hours.

SIGHTSEEING

CENTRAL MUSEUM (ALBERT HALL)
Extensive collection of jewels, costumes, sculptures, music instruments and lovely

ⓒⓘⓣⓨ 🏴 **WHERE TO START?**
M. I. Road: The main artery Mirza Ismael (M.I.) is to the north-east and runs parallel to the "Pink City"; to the west are the station, tourist office and main post office. Parks and museums, hotels, cinemas and restaurants – all the most important places can be reached from here on foot. To visit the famous Amber Palace however you have to take a bus from Hawa Mahal (city centre–Amber).

miniatures. *Daily 9am–5pm and 7pm–10pm | Ram Niwas Garden | south of the Old City*

CITY PALACE ★
This is a genuine Maharaja's palace as the ruling family still lives in the seven-storey main building, the *Chandra Mahal*. The palace complex in the Old City covers 1.9 mi². The audience chambers, gateways with their ornamental peacock decoration and rooms full of the most beautiful miniature paintings are a marvel worth seeing – as are the two solid silver vessels the height of a grown man that show the opulent lifestyle of the Rajputs. In 1902, Sawai Madho Singh II took them with him on a trip to London filled with the holy water from the Ganges. *Palace museum daily 10am–5pm*

HAWA MAHAL ⚏⚏
Much-admired carved stone façade in ruddy sandstone. The so-called "Palace of Winds" was built in 1799 so that women who lived in the complex, strictly segregated from the outside world, were able to watch what was going on in the street from a multitude of windows without being seen themselves. Side

Silk or cotton, clothes or material – a visit to a bazaar in Jaipur is well worthwhile

alleyways lead to the rear entrance of the five-storey building which also includes a sculpture museum. *Daily 10am–4.30pm*

JANTAR MANTAR

Heading west from Tripolia Gate you will reach Jai Singh's open-air observatory (18th century). What look like abstract sculptures are precision measuring instruments when star gazing. For a knowledgeable guide ask at the tourist office. *Daily 9am–4.30pm*

FOOD & DRINK

GRAND CHANAKYA

Here you can enjoy the best vegetarian *thalis* in the city – in gaint-sized portions! *4, A. B. Kashi Bhawan | M. I. Road | tel. 0141 4 33 33 33 | Moderate*

NATRAJ

Small and cosy. Serves tasty, vegetarian multi-cuisine food. *M.I. Road, near Arvind Marg | tel. 0141 2 37 58 04 | Budget*

NIRO'S

Welcome to Jaipur's probably best-known restaurant: Bollywood star Amitabh Bachchan is a frequent guest here, as is supermodel Naomi Campbell. And not without reason: the tandoori dishes are especially mouth-watering. But international cuisine is also served at Niro's. *M. I. Road, near Arvind Marg | tel. 0141 2 37 44 93 | www.nirosindia. com | Expensive*

SHOPPING

You can browse endlessly in the bazaars in the Old City. Jewellers offer their wares in *Johari Bazaar*. Clothes, material and ceramics can also be recommended. Be careful when paying with credit card as card fraud is rife in Jaipur.

INSIDER TIP ▶ BHURAMAL RAJMAL SURANA

Top address for diamond, ruby and emerald jewellery, the showroom is quite an experience. *D-68 | J. Pragya L.N. Marg | www.suranas.com*

RAJASTHAN CRAFT INDUSTRIES

You can find here a large selection of carpets and handicrafts. *45, Haji Jumma Colony | Amber Road*

LEISURE & SPORTS

THE RAJASTHAN POLO CLUB

As visible from the photos in the polo bar in the oldest polo club in India (founded in 1918), the Maharajah of Jaipur entertained illustrious guests, even organising a tournament for Prince Charles in the grounds of Rambagh Palace. In addition to polo on horseback, polo with elephants can also be specially booked – unique across the world. Daily tournaments in January, March and September. ● Free entry for foreign visitors. *Ambedkar Circle | Bhawani Singh Marg | tel. 0141 2 22 73 75 | thejaipurpolo@gmail.com | rajasthanpoloclub.co.in*

ENTERTAINMENT

RAJ MANDIR ●

One of the most popular cinemas in India, seating 1,500. Art Deco lobby. This is where the public really let their hair down when classic Bollywood films are screened. *Bhagwan Das Road | near MI. Road | www.terajmandir.com*

WHERE TO STAY

ATITHI

One of the most popular guesthouses in Jaipur with unbeatably good service. Plus points include an attractive roof terrace and good vegetarian dishes. *22 rooms | 1, Park House Scheme | tel. 0141 2 37 86 79 | www.atithijaipur.com | Budget*

BISSAU PALACE

Heritage hotel in a former palace: you will be reluctant to leave the magnificent courtyard with the ornamented arcades. It has a pool and even its own museum. *52 rooms | Chandpol Gate | tel. 0141 2 30 43 71 | www. bissaupalace.com | Moderate*

MADHUBAN BANI PARK

Former family palace for a family of dukes; large rooms furnished in the Rajasthani style with a huge garden and

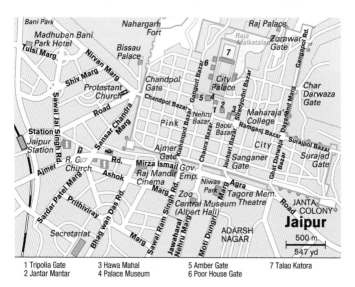

1 Tripolia Gate
2 Jantar Mantar
3 Hawa Mahal
4 Palace Museum
5 Amber Gate
6 Poor House Gate
7 Talao Katora

a lobby in the style of the sitting room of a Maharajah. *23 rooms | D-237, Bihari Marg | tel. 0141 20 54 27 | www.madhu ban.net | Moderate*

INSIDERTIP NARAIN NIWAS PALACE

One of the finest heritage hotels in Rajasthan, housed in a palace in the Victorian style. The rooms are amazing with high ceilings, four poster beds and chandeliers. The garden is a genuine oasis! *37 rooms | Kanota Bagh | Narain Singh Road | tel. 0141 2 56 12 91 | www.hotel narainniwas.com | Moderate*

RAMBAGH PALACE

Former summer palace of the Maharajas. Dine in a room decorated in gold, drink tea on the terrace. Golf, tennis, pool. *79 rooms and suites | Bhawani Singh Road | tel. 0141 2 38 57 00 | www.tajhotels. com | Expensive*

INFORMATION

GOVERNMENT OF INDIA TOURIST OFFICE
Hotel Khasa Kothi | M. I. Road | tel. 0141 2 37 22 00 | indtourjpr-rj@nic.in

WHERE TO GO

AMBER PALACE ★ ☆
(185 E2) (⊠ E6)
The contrast between the barren mountain ridges and the marble, mirrors and pillars in the palace could not be more obvious. You can travel to the palace in style on the back of an elephant. Even though official checks are made that the elephants are not overstrained, there have been reports of incidences of mishandling. For this reason, it is best to go on foot. Building first started in 1592 and has been added to since then. *Ganesh-Pol* (gateway), *Audience Hall, Sukh Niwas* (with an ingenious air-cooling system) and the *Shish Mahal* (Palace of Mirrors) are the main attractions. The deserted but forbidding *Fort Jaigarh* is on the top of the mountain. *Daily 9am–4.30pm | 11 km/6.8 mi north*

GALTA (185 E2) (⊠ E6)
This is a secret tip as these grounds including temples and palaces are primarily visited by Hindu pilgrims. Galta is also known as the Monkey Temple as hordes

Ornate columns up high – the Hall of Victory in the palace of Amber

of monkeys roam free around the area. The view of the steep valley with a natural swimming pool is best enjoyed at sunrise. *11 km/6.8 mi east*

SARISKA NATIONAL PARK
(185 E2) (*𝄞 F6*)
Let's get wild: antelopes, leopards, tigers and lots of different species of birds live in this park that covers 185 mi². Accommodation: *Sariska Tiger Heaven (tel. 09828 225163 | Moderate)*. 10 luxurious rooms, restaurant and tours. *110 km/68 mi north*

JAISALMER

(184 B2) (*𝄞 C6*) The "Golden City" is enchanting with its carved stone façades, vaulted shops seemingly straight out of the Arabian Nights and camel riders evoking dreams of riding with them across the extensive sand dunes into the sunset.

From Jodhpur, Jaisalmer is a 300 km/ 186 mi journey through Thar Desert with its sparse vegetation. But before you glimpse the town (Jaisalmer, pop. 89,000), enclosed by its sand-coloured defensive walls, you will see the mighty fort and former caravan station loom on a bluff. Wealthy merchants lived here in their town palaces *(havelis)* until goods started to be transported by other means such as ship and train. Since the division of India and Pakistan in 1947, Jaisalmer has gained a strategic military importance and desert safaris and excursions in Rajasthan often start here.

and Hindu temples as well as impressive stone carvings. *Palace: daily 8am–1pm and 3pm–5pm*

GARHISAR LAKE/GADI SAGAR
This artificial lake in the desert was created back in the 14th century and is surrounded by Hindu temples and pavilions. The magnificent gateway leading to the lake and temples was supposedly the gift of a courtesan. Puritanical dignitaries however did not dare demolish it as – in clever anticipation – a small temple shrine had been integrated in the structure. Adjoining is a private *folk museum (daily 8am–noon, 3pm–6pm). South-east of the town*

HAVELIS ★
The richly decorated merchants' houses are a testimony to the skill of the stone carvers and the wealth of those who commissioned the work. The larger Havelis are almost like a separate town within a town with massive gateways, a courtyard and a fountain. Building three or four-storey town houses was widespread throughout the whole of north-western India up until the 19th century. The majority however were built of wood. It was only in Jaisalmer that stone was cheaper and the town's architectural gems have survived the times and fashions in this dry desert climate. It is possible to visit some of the most beautiful havelis, e.g. *Patwon Ki Haveli* (in the north of the Old Town), *Salim Singh Ki Haveli* (near the entrance to the fort) and *Nathmalji Ki Haveli* (in the north).

SIGHTSEEING

FORT ⚜
The hill rises up 75 m/246.1 ft above the Old Town and is topped by the labyrinthine, seven-storey palace with its Jain

FOOD & DRINK

NARAYAN NIWAS PALACE
Multi-cuisine and Rajasthani food in an old caravanserai. *Malka Pol | tel. 02992 252408 | Expensive*

TRIO

You have a view over the old bazaar while you enjoy authentic Rajasthani cuisine. Built in the style of a desert tent, this has always been a popular location for the local inhabitants. *Amar Singh Pol | Gandhi Chowk | tel. 02992 25 27 33 | Moderate*

WHERE TO STAY

FORT RAJWADA ☼

Opulent new building in the traditional Rajasthani style. Enjoy the kebab barbecue at the pool or an Ayurvedic massage. *90 rooms, 9 suites | Jodhpur–Barmer link road | tel. 02992 25 46 08 | www.fortra jwada.com | Moderate*

HIMMATGARH PALACE ☼

Resembles the Fort of Jaisalmer from the outside. Nice rooms, with pool and garden. *40 rooms | 1, Ramgarh Road | 2.5 km/1.2 mi) from the Old Town | tel. 02992 25 20 02 | himmatgh@sancharnet.in | Moderate*

INFORMATION

TOURIST OFFICE

Station Road | Gadi Sagar Pol | tel. 02992 25 24 06 | www.rtdc.in

WHERE TO GO

INSIDER TIP ▶ THAR DESERT

(184 A–C 1–3) (ⓜ B–D 5–6)
Camel safaris through the desert, sleeping under the stars, are a real adventure. Make sure you take plenty of drinking water with you as well as a hat and warm clothing for the night. Your first ride on a camel can also take a bit of getting used to. Please take care when choosing your guide: do not simply accept the next best offer, although the most expensive one is also not necessarily the best. Ask in your hotel or other guests who have already been on a camel safari. The Oasis Camp, the Pal Raja Resort and the Damodra Desert Camp all offer glamping in the desert. Located in the dune landscape between Jodhpur and Bikaner is the ● *Khimsar Sand Dune Village (16 huts | 6 km/3.7 mi from Fort Khimsar | Ratanada | tel. 01585 26 23 45 | www.khimsar.com/dunes | Expensive)*. The beige round huts with thatched roofs are luxuriously furnished. End your day on a romantic note sitting by the campfire under the starry sky in the desert.

JODHPUR

(184 C2) (ⓜ D6) Rajasthan's second largest city (pop. 1 million) with lively bazaars, medieval gateways and a huge fort above vivid blue-painted houses, is a fascinating city.
These houses have given Jodhpur, located on the edge of Thar Desert, the nickname the "Blue City".

SIGHTSEEING

MANDORE GARDENS

Before Jodhpur was founded in 1459 by the Rathore Rajputs, they had their seat here in Mandore. Nowadays little remains, but the seemingly subtropical park is bewitchingly beautiful. The Hidhu gods and heroes carved out of the cliff face in the 18th century and now restored are also worth seeing. *Hall of Heroes | daily from sunrise to sunset | 8 km/5 mi north of the city*

MEHERANGARH FORT ☼

The Marwar rulers had the same status as Maharajas and undertook everything to hold their own against the Mughal emperors of Agra and Delhi. To do this

The exquisitely carved decorative stone work at the mighty Meherangarh Fort in Jodhpur

they turned the fort into one of the most formidable fortifications. Within its walls, the delicate stone carvings and the marmoreal coronation throne with its golden elephants come as a surprise. **INSIDER TIP** The more adventurous can experience the Fort from the air while ziplining. The circuit consists of six lines and takes approx. 1.5 hr.

FOOD & DRINK

OTA HERITAGE RESTAURANT ⬩⬩⬩
This restaurant is worth a special visit just for its view of the fort from the roof terrace. The six-course menu is somewhat pricey, but well worth ordering. *Gulab Sagar, near Mahila Bagh Zhalra | tel. 0911 6 08 20 20 | www.otajodhpur.in | Expensive*

SHOPPING

The emblem of the ● *Sardarpura Bazaar (east of the Fort)* is the conspicuous clock tower at its centre. You can try on a pair of jodhpurs at the bazaar: other special goods include copper and noble wood antiques, batik material and spices. You can buy strands of saffron and chili accompanied by a pinch of friendly advice at *Mohanlal Verhomal Spices (at the vegetable market | Shop 209 B)*.

WHERE TO STAY

INSIDER TIP KARNI BHAWAN
This hotel is a quiet oasis in a red sandstone colonial bungalow furnished in a tasteful Indian style with a garden and pool. *32 rooms | Defence Lab Road | Ratanada | tel. 02912 51 21 01 | www.karnihotels.com | Moderate*

BUNGALOW 2
This heritage boutique hotel combines Rajasthani design with modern features. You will stay in a bungalow belonging to the old Raikabagh palace which was passed down by the Maharajah to the owner's grandfather. Offers homemade local cuisine. *6 rooms | Bungalow 2, Raikabagh | tel. 09214 40 07 71 | www.bungalow2.in | Moderate*

UMAID BHAWAN

The Maharaja palace in the Art Deco style from the first half of the 20th century is located amongst extensive lawns. Golf, riding, indoor swimming pool, exclusive restaurant, museum and health club. *96 rooms and suites | tel. 02912 51 01 01 | www.tajhotels.com | Expensive*

In summer lots of Indians come up here to escape the heat down on the plain. They go rowing on Lake Nakki, celebrate weddings and enjoy the view.

Everyday life in Jodhpur: bustle including a holy cow

INFORMATION

TOURIST RECEPTION CENTRE

Here you will be provided with information including lists of selected private accommodation. *High Court Road | in the Ghoomar Hotel | tel. 02912 54 50 83*

MOUNT ABU

(184 C4) (*D7*) ● ↘↙ A twisty hairpin road up takes you up through a wonderful rocky landscape to Rajasthan's only hill station, Mount Abu (pop. 23,000), located in the Aravalli Range at an altitude of some 1,200 m/3,900 ft.

SEHENSWERTES

INSIDER TIP DILWARA-TEMPLE OF THE JAINS

The temple halls are marvels of marble carving (11th to 18th century, peak building phase during the 13th century) depicting hundreds of Jain saints and dancers, extravagant ornamental decoration and statues of elephants and Hindu deities. The Dilwara Temple is not only the most significant pilgrimage location for the Jains, but is also considered as one of the finest in the country. Photography and objects made of leather are prohibited. *5 km/3.1 mi from the town centre*

FOOD & DRINK

JAIPUR HOUSE ↘↙

Good food, magnificent view from the

terrace across the lake to the mountains. *Nakki Lake | tel. 02974 23 51 76 | Moderate*

WHERE TO STAY

PALACE HOTEL
Heritage hotel in former summer palace of the Maharajas of Bikaner, large park, nice rooms, pleasant restaurant. *33 rooms | Dilwara Road | tel. 02974 23 86 73 | www.palacehotelbikanerhouse. com | Expensive*

SHIKHAR HOTEL RTDC
You won't want to leave the cottages in a good location on the hill. *82 rooms | east of Tourist Reception Centre | tel. 02974 23 89 44 | www.rtdc.tourism.rajasthan. gov.in | Budget*

INFORMATION

RTDC TOURIST RECEPTION CENTRE
Arranges guided tours of temples. *Opposite bus stop | tel. 02974 23 51 51*

PUSHKAR

(185 D2) *(⚐ E6)* **A hill crowned by a temple dedicated to Brahma, a lake that has been considered holy since time immemorial with steps around its banks for the devout to pray, a white town all around and the whole surrounded by a stony desert.**

This is where Brahma reputedly dropped a lotus blossom while looking for a place to make an offering. Pushkar (pop. 21,000) exudes a hippie flair with its cafés and shops. This is a paradise for anyone keen on silver jewellery and leather goods. Please note: everything is fully booked up for the first full moon in November when the colourful Pushkar

Camel Fair, *Kartik Purnima*, is held. This is also true for the tented pilgrim camps and the Maharaja-style glamping tents.

FOOD & DRINK/ WHERE TO STAY

INN SEVENTH HEAVEN ✳
A 100-year-old resored haveli with charm. Each room has its own individual decoration. Seating areas lead into the airy courtyard where you can enjoy a cup of tea while admiring the view of the old town and the mountains. *15 rooms | Chotti Basti | tel. 0145 2 97 19 05 | www. inn-seventh-heaven.com | Budget*

NEW PARK ✳
Quietly located hotel with balconies and pool, roof-top restaurant and rose garden. INSIDER TIP View of Snake Mountains. *32 rooms and suites | Panchkund Road | tel. 0145 2 77 24 64 | www. newparkpushkar.com | Budget–Moderate*

INFORMATION

TOURIST INFORMATION CENTER
Near RTDC Hotel Sarovar, south-east of the lake

UDAIPUR

(185 D4) *(⚐ D7)* **The capital of the former principality of Mewar is one of the most beautiful cities in India. At 577 m/1,893 ft above sea level, it is located between the forested hills of the Aravalli Range around the banks of a number of lakes.**

The reflections of palaces shimmer in the water and the climate here is not that hot than in Rajasthan's desert regions. Udaipur (pop. 450,000) was founded in the 16th century. The romantically inclined can let themselves be rowed across *Lake Pichola* at sunset, the site where several wild pursuits with James Bond were filmed. Udaipar is a truly romantic location with its numerous fairytale palaces in which you can also stay overnight.

SIGHTSEEING

INSIDER TIP ▶ BHARATIYA LOK KALA MANDAL

This is a fantastic exhibition of Indian folk art including costumes, masks, innumerable puppets and – curiously enough – also marionettes from USA, Mexiko and Russia. Enjoy the puppet show with Rajasthani music and dance lasting one hour. *Daily 9am–5.30pm | north of the Chetak Circle*

CITY PALACE ◥◤

It took four hundred years to complete this palace, the largest in Rajasthan. The Sisodia family still lives in part of the palace complex. Another part was transformed into the luxurious *Shivniwas Hotel*, with an outstanding elegant restaurant. Take a look in the extensive *Museum (open daily 9.30am–5.30pm)* and the *Crystal Gallery (open daily 9am–7pm) containing the world's largest collection of crytal objects – including a bed. The exhibition of vintage cars is also interesting. Budget*

FOOD & DRINK

MILLETS OF MEWAR RESTAU-RANT ◥◤ ◉

Slow food and fusion cuisine from organically grown ingredients – here you will eat healthy and delicious food with a free view of the lake. *16, Bhim Parmeshwar Marg | www.milletsofmewar. org | Budget*

WHERE TO STAY

JAGAT NIWAS

Maharaja-style atmosphere at an affordable price. The inner courtyards of the house with its nooks and crannies and large window alcoves are perfect for relaxing: an oasis with a wealth of greenery. *21 rooms | 24–25, Lalghat | tel. 02942 42 28 60 | www.jagatcollection. com | Budget*

LAKE PALACE HOTEL

Lodge in luxury style like Octopussy in the James Bond film in the probably most famous hotel in India. The palace on the island of Lake Pichola slightly resembles the shape of a ship. *81 rooms | tel. 0294 2 52 88 00 | www.tajhotels.com | Expensive*

THE TIGER ◥◤

Individually furnished rooms at the heart of the old town with a roof terrace offering a wonderful view. *19 rooms | 33, Gangaur Ghat | near Bagore ki Haveli | tel. 02942 42 04 30 | www.hotelthetiger. com | Moderate*

INFORMATION

TOURIST RECEPTION CENTRE

Fateh Memorial Building, near Suraj Pol | tel. 02942 411535

WHERE TO GO

CHITTORGARH (185 D3) (*ω E7*)

High above steep cliffs, the ruins of the town abandoned in the 16th century reflect the faded glory of the Mewar rulers. Many of the inhabitants chose to commit suicide during the conquests of the Muslims rather than being taken into captivity. A 37 m/121.4 ft high Tower of Victory can still be seen. Good accommo-

A supreme example of artistic stone carving – the white Jain temple in Ranakpur

dation is available at *Hotel Padmini (120 rooms | tel. 01472 24 17 12 | www.hotel padmini.in | Moderate). 112 km/70 mi north-east*

The owner of the hotel *Bassi Fort Palace (tel. 01472 22 53 21)*, 24 km/14.9 mi north-east of Chittorgarh also organises boat trips and campfires in the Vindhya Range. In village of Bassi, you will walk past temples, step wells, pottery workshops and small kiosks in which bidis (Indian cigarettes) are manufactured.

KUMBHALGARH 〰️ (185 D3) (🗺 D7)

Well worth a visit for the endless views of the surrounding natural idyll alone. The fort with its bastion towers thrones above the landscape at an altitude of 1,000 m/3,281 ft. Seven gateways have to be climbed through on the way up. The dangerous-looking thick iron spikes at the gateways were intended as a defence against elephants. Incidentally, the wall surrounding the fort is known as the "Great Indian Wall" because it is reputed to be the second-longest of its type after the Chinese Wall. *80 km/49.7 mi north*

RANAKPUR (185 D3) (🗺 D7)

A further highlight of Indian architecture: the Jain temple of Ranakpur streaked with white marble *(open daily midday– 5pm)* which is among the most beautiful Jain temples in the whole of India alongside the temple on Mount Abu. It possesses 29 halls and 80 domes – it is amazing what huge dimensions were created in the 15th century! Each of the 1,444 pillars is unique in its artistic ornamentation. In the bungalow hotel *Maharani Bagh Orchard Retreat (16 rooms | Ranakpur | Sadri | tel. 02934 28 51 51 | www. maharanibagh.jodhanaheritage.com | Moderate),* you can stay in comfortable cottages located within a fruit plantation. *70 km/43.5 mi north*

MUMBAI AND CENTRAL INDIA

Since 1996 Bombay has officially been called Mumbai and, as such, now draws on its own tradition rather than on a name introduced by colonial rulers. However, regardless of the name, most first time visitors to the capital of the state of Maharashtra suffer from an initial bout of "culture shock". With its skyscrapers firmly in the hands of banks and industrial concerns, the Manhattan of India now has an American-style skyline. Apart from that, this megacity on the Arabian Sea displays a fascinating mixture of western and oriental lifestyles in the markets and squares, in the film studios (Bollywood) and exclusive hotels, in the architecture and in the saucepans of Indian kitchens.

Maharashtra is a little more than twice the size of England and Wales. While the narrow coastal strip along the Konkan Coast has now been discovered by international tourism, the higher regions are central to India's culture. The artistic heritage of Buddhism and early Hinduism can be seen in the cave temples of Aurangabad, Ellora and Ajanta. In the 17th century, the Hindus rose up against the Muslim Mughals in Maharashtra. The history of the some 350 forts is that much older. And in the 20th century, followers from all over the world of Bhagwan Shree Rajneesh (Osho) came to his ashram in Pune (Poona).

Andhra Pradesh is rich in religious sites and early testimonies to Buddhism, such as in Warangal, Amaravath, Nagarjuna-konda and Tirupati. The state also has

The Manhattan of India, Bollywood and temples more than a thousand years old. Central India is an intriguing blend of ancient and modern

many areas of natural beauty, never-ending beaches untouched by tourism, mountains and caves. The capital, Hyderabad, with its imposing Golconda Fort is the main tourist centre in the region.

AURANGABAD

(191 D2) (*∅ E10*) This spread-out city (pop. 1.2 million) was founded in 1610. The Mughal emperor Aurangzeb made it his capital in 1653.

Several historical buildings from that period and his tomb have survived. Day outings to the famous cave temples in Ajanta and Ellora can be made from this modern, industrial, university city.

SIGHTSEEING

AURANGABAD CAVES ★
In the middle of the table mountains north of Aurangabad are twelve caves with monumental sculptures and reliefs, the oldest dating from the 2nd century,

most however from the 7th century. The caves are in three groups. The depictions of dancers and musicians (cave 7) and "Buddha entering Nirvana"(cave 9) are exceptional. You will be rewarded after the journey over numerous potholes by grain mill. This idyllic spot is of historical importance as the flour ground here has been used to feed the streams of pilgrims since the 17th century and, in a feat of engineering, water to drive the millstones has been brought here from miles away.

Hardly carved out of the cliff – the temple and monastery of Ellora

the amazing panorama of Aurangabad and the surrounding area. *Sunrise to sunset | 7 km/4.4 mi north*

BIBI-KA-MAQBARA
The Mughal emperor Aurangzeb wanted to erect a more imposing mausoleum than his father Shah Jahan who built the Taj Mahal – and spend less money doing so. The mausoleum for his wife Rabia-ud-Daurani is a good example of Mughal architecture on the Deccan Plateau.

INSIDER TIP ▶ PAN CHAKKI
The tomb of the Sufi master Shah Muzafir revered by Aurangzeb lies on the river Khan next to the water-powered

FOOD & DRINK

D'CURRY HOUSE ⊛
Small restaurant in the *Hotel Green Olive* serving new interpretations of traditional Indian cuisine. Only the best vegetables from local farms are used for curries and the delicious Dal Bukhara: the dishes are all meticulously prepared and cooked slowly. *13/3, CBS Road |tel. 0240 2 32 94 90 | Moderate*

WHERE TO STAY

AMBASSADOR AJANTA
Comfortable hotel with lovely garden and pool. Traditional Indian décor with

some antiques. 4 km/2.5 mi from the city centre. *96 rooms | Jalna Road Chikalthana | tel. 0240 6 60 72 36 | www. ambassadorindia.com | Moderate*

TAJ RESIDENCY
Luxury hotel in palatial modern style with pool and well-tended gardens. *40 rooms and suites | 8-N-12, Cidco | tel. 0240 6 61 37 37 | www.vivantabytaj.com | Expensive*

WHERE TO GO

AJANTA (191 E1) (*∅ E10*)
Buddhist monks chose this horseshoe-shaped cliff site above the deep gorge of the river Waghora in the 2nd century BC for their monastery. In the course of a thousand years new caves were cut out of the volcanic rock wall from time to time. The site was rediscovered some 200 years ago. The 29 caves were declared a World Heritage Site in 1983 on account of their exceptional sculptures and wall paintings – whose colours are still strong – depicting scenes from legends about Buddha and court life during the Gupta dynasty. The sculptures in caves 1, 4, 17, 19 and 26 and the paintings in 1, 2, 16, 17 and 19 are particularly noteworthy. *Tue–Sun 9am–5pm | 100 km/62 mi north-east*

DAULATABAD (191 D2) (*∅ E10*)
Of all the Indian strongholds from the Middle Ages and the early modern era, that in Daulatabad (Town of Fortune) is one of the most sinister. Full of treacherous surprises to ward off enemies, from iron prongs and poisoned water to the dark, twisty underground passages leading up to the ⛰ upper fortress, from where there are wonderful views. *Daily 6am–6pm | 14 km/8.7 mi north-west*

ELLORA ★ (191 D2) (*∅ E10*)
Turning the building process on its head – not putting one stone on another but tackling a huge cliff area from above – is how monks created *Kailash Temple* and its artistically carved sculptures. They chipped everything away, bit by bit, leaving only the external walls, steps, roofs, etc. This is the largest monolithic structure (i.e. made from one single stone) anywhere in the world. Kailash Temple – Mount Kailash is the home of the gods in the distant Himalayas – comprises the shrine of Nandi, Shiva's bull, and the principal temple of the *lingam*, the representation of Shiva. The *Buddhist caves* nos. 1–12, the *Hindu caves* nos. 13–29 and the *Jain caves* nos. 30–34 are well worth seeing. Best time to visit: October

---

MARCO POLO HIGHLIGHTS

★ **Aurangabad Caves**
Buddhist shrines off the masses
→ p. 87

★ **Ellora**
The Kailash Temple is a monolith carved out of the cliff → p. 89

★ **Golconda Fort**
Gigantic walls and an acoustic marvel → p. 92

★ **Crawford Market**
The scents and colours of the Orient in the "belly of Bombay"
→ p. 94

★ **Taj Mahal Palace & Tower**
Simply one of the best hotels in the world → p. 97

★ **Elephanta**
Tropical lush island with cave temples → p. 98

to March, INSIDER TIP best time of day (for light): afternoon. *Wed–Mon 9am– 5.30pm | 30 km/18.6 mi north-west*

GANPATIPULE

(190 C4) *(ᗯ D12)* **If you go for the more than 700 km/435 mi long Maharashtra coast rather than one of the many beaches in the south, there is a lot that speaks in favour of Ganpatipule, the ancient pilgrim town (pop. 2,000) and its broad, white beach.**

Surrounded by palms Ganpatipule still has that village feel about it. Pilgrims make a beeline for the "made out of itself" temple for Ganesha – which is a stone that naturally looks a little like the elephant-headed god of prosperity and fortune.

One lovely place to stay is in the INSIDER TIP *MTDC Resort Ganpatipule (Ganpatipule | District Ratnagiri | tel. 02357 23 52 48 | www.maharashtra tourism.gov.in | Budget)*. 96 rooms and suites have been built recently on and above the beach. Information about sightseeing is provided and there is a rustic restaurant.

There are several worthwhile excursions to make in the area, such as to the imposing coastal fortress of *Jaigarh* (35 km/21.8 mi north) that has survived the centuries behind an 8 m/26.2 ft high wall. Much further north on the N17, boat trips on the river Vashisti are available in the little town of *Chiplun (around 100 km/62 mi)*. Nearby there is a valley of temples and the comfortable *Riverview Resort (37 rooms | village Dhamandivi | tel. 09820 33 88 20 | www. chiplunhotels.com | Moderate)*, which is situated in a garden on a hill. With infinity pool!

HYDERABAD

(192 A3) *(ᗯ G12)* **Along with Bangalore and Mumbai, Hyderabad is pushing itself into the front line as the third major centre for the computer and software industry.**

The ultramodern district *Hitec City* is growing and growing. The palaces and administrative buildings in the Victorian-Indian style in the centre of the city with a population of 7 million south of Hussain Sagar, the large lake with its statue of Buddha, recall the time under British rule. But Hyderabad was in fact founded in 1590 by Nawab Muhammed Quli. Because of its rulers' immense wealth, the sound of the city's name had a fairy-tale ring to it for many people at that time. Today, Hyderabad is a metropolis of contrasts. A multiplex cinema and shopping complex have been built between oriental mosques, elaborate tombs and colourful bazaars. It even has INSIDER TIP Snow World, which generates its own chilly alpine conditions *(www.snow worldindia.net)*. The megacity of Mumbai cannot even equal that. A cinema tycoon erected *Ramoji Film City (tel. no. for visitors: 0180 0 42 50 99 99 | www. ramojifilmcity.com)* in the middle of this landscape.

SIGHTSEEING

BAZAARS AND CHARMINAR

Narrow steets lined with shops tempt visitors with a range of excellent handcrafted items including inlaid silver work *(bidri)*, woven silks and pearl jewellery. Right in the middle is the *Charminar*, a monument with five towers erected in 1591. It boasts projecting windows, decorative work and a mosque on the second floor.

BIRLA MANDIR ✿

A Vishnu temple built in 1976 by the industrial Birla family. It reputedly took more than 2,000 t of white marble from Rajasthan to complete this structure. Perfect views of the city and lake.

BUDDHA PURNIMA

The monolithic statue has been standing in Lake Huseein Sagar since 1992. It is one of the world's tallest sculptures, 17.5 m/57 ft high, and best viewed from a boat or Lumbini Park.

SALAR JUNG MUSEUM

Works of art from around the world and mementoes of the Mughals. Salar Jung III, former prime minister of the Nizam of Hyderabad, collected unusual items up until his death in 1949. Whether it is more kitsch than art is up to the viewer to decide. *Sat–Thu 10am–5pm | 100 m/328 ft east of the southern end of Musi River Bridge*

FOOD & DRINK

PALACE HEIGHTS ✿

One of the best restaurants in the city – and definitely the one with the best views. It has even a good wine menu. Taste the dragon rolls and the chicken majestic. *Triveni Building, 8th floor, Abids | tel. 040 24 75 44 83 | Moderate*

PRASAD – FOOD COURTS

No one has to stay hungry – be it dining in style or fast food – in the super-modern multiplex and Imax cinema centre. *Off NTR Gardens | tel. 040 23 44 88 88 | www.prasadz.com | Budget–Moderate*

WHERE TO STAY

THE CENTRAL COURT

You cannot go wrong with this hotel: you will be very comfortable and well catered for on a three-star level. *77 rooms | Lakdi-ka-pul | tel. 0900 0 66 33 45 | www.the centralcourt.com | Moderate*

THE TAJ KRISHNA

A five-star jewel in the Banjara Hills. The lawn is meticulously trimmed, the rooms first class and the exclusive restaurant promises culinary delights. *261 rooms | Road No. 1 | Banjara Hills |*

The bazar streets of Hyderabad are a bustling shopping paradise

tel. 040 66 66 23 23 | www.tajhotels.com |
Expensive

INFORMATION

GOVERNMENT OF INDIA TOURIST OFFICE
Sandozi Building | Street No. 1 | Himayat-nagar | tel. 040 7 63 00 37

WHERE TO GO

GOLCONDA FORT ★ ☆
(192 A3) (*ш G12*)
This formidable fort with its huge defensive walls on a granite rock 150 m/492 ft high was one of the most impregnable in India. The stronghold reached its present dimensions in the 16th century under Sultan Quli Qutb Shah. His successor however moved the seat into the newly founded city of Hyderabad as early as in 1590. The acoustics are amazing – clapping your hands at Balahisar Gate can be heard way above in the Durbar (Court) Hall. INSIDER TIP Extremely dramatic sound and light show (*Nov–Feb, Tue–Sun 6.30pm, March–Oct, Tue–Sun 7pm. 13 km/8.1 mi west*

MUMBAI (BOMBAY)

MAP INSIDE BACK COVER
(190 C2) (*ш D11*) **Immerse yourself in the pulsating, colourful life of an Indian megacity. Nowhere else on the subcontinent are the contrasts as extreme as in Mumbai.**
The slums are among the worst in the country, but on *Malabar Hill* there are supposedly more millionaires than in Manhattan. The legacy of the British is like a backdrop for a film – stations, museums and post offices in the Victorian, Gothic Revival or Indo-Saracenic architectural mixture of styles. Traffic roars around the temples, mosques and markets and the city faces the increasing threat of suffocating in its own exhaust fumes.

Mumbai is the heart of India's economy. Almost half the country's taxes are reputedly paid here. Despite this, every city administration so far has failed miserably in their attempts to put an end to mass poverty and the housing shortage, prostitution and criminality effectively. Officially thirteen million people live in the most densely populated city in India. A further three million commute regularly from elsewhere. This results in a twice-daily "mass migration" through the two large railway stations in the city centre: the Victoria Terminus and ● Churchgate Station. Long ago, fishermen lived on the island of Kolis. Later, they had to scrape a living as unskilled workers known as *Kulis*.

In 1534 the Muslim princes handed over the island of Salsete and seven other unimportant islands made up of salt marshes to the Portuguese who called their new property *Bom Bahia* – "beautiful bay". By chance, this sounds not dissimilar

---

WHERE TO START?
Gateway of India: For a long time, the Gateway of India in Colaba was the first sight many visitors to India saw. From here the Prince of Wales Museum and other reminders of colonial days can be reached on foot. Other places, e.g. Malabar Hill or Chowpatty Beach, are easily accessible by bus (line 103 from Colaba Depot to Kamla Nehru Park) or in a black-and-yellow taxi.

Magnificent building, crowned by a white dome: the Prince of Wales Museum

to the Hindu goddess Mumba, who was worshipped on an island. Hence the "new" but ancient name Mumbai.

In 1661 Bombay became British. From that time onwards, landfill turned the islands into a large peninsula and even today, land is being wrought from the sea. Merchants and traders from many different parts of India as well as members of various religions – Parsis, Jains, Muslims and Sikhs – settled with the Hindus in the newly founded colony that King Charles II had leased to the *East India Company*. Trade and industry boomed after the first railway was built in 1853.

SIGHTSEEING

INSIDER TIP BANGANGA TANK

The large water tank surrounded by steps is a wonderful place to find a moment of peace. Rama is said once to have fallen to the ground here almost dead with thirst.According to the legend, water from the Ganges *(ganga)* bubbled up from the place where his brother Lakshman had shot an arrow

(baan) – this was how the Banganga tank was created.

The *Banganga Tank* is one of Mumbai's best kept secrets: even many residents of Mumbai are unaware of the small oasis with the *Walkeshwar* Temple, shrines and brightly painted pilgrim refuges. *On the promentory south of Malabar Hill*

CHHATRAPATI SHIVAJI MAHARAJ VASTU SANGRAHALAYA (PRINCE OF WALES MUSEUM)

Indian art from all past ages is exhibited here in this impressive late colonial building – one of the best museum collections in the whole of India. *Tue–Sat 10.15am–6pm | 159/61, MG Road | www.csmvs.in*

CHOWPATTY BEACH ●

The beach is too dirty for swimming, but when evening twilight comes over the large semicircle on Marine Drive, thousands of Mumbaikar congregate here, including jugglers, masseurs, street vendors and mobile food stalls. Try *Bhel Puri*, a sweet and sour delicacy made of rice, potatoes and tamarind chutney.

CRAWFORD MARKET ★

Officially the market in the south of Mumbai is called Mahatma Jyotiba Phule Market but lots of people do not know its new name. The "belly of Bombay", built in 1871, is full of fresh fruit, vegetables, spices and both live and just slaughtered animals every day. The mixture of colonial architecture and Indian bazaar amazing. If you happen to be here between April and June during the harvest season, don't miss the the complex structure of the area with companies such as Reality Tours *(www. realitytoursandtravel.com)*.

FILMCITY MUMBAI

In India and the dream factory Bollywood, more films are produced than anywhere else in the world – around 1,900 every year. A large proportion of these are made in Filmcity, a gigantic area in the suburb of Goregaon with 40 outdoor film sets and 20 studios. You

Crawford Market, the "belly of Bombay", is bursting with fruit, vegetables and spices

Alphonso mangos. One of the stands reputedly supplied fruit for the Queen's coronation in 1953. *Carnac Road/D. Naoroji Road*

INSIDER TIP DHARAVI

The largest slum in Mumbai is shaped like a heart and here is where the heartbeat of the city is located. Dharavi is not only home to at least 1 million inhabitants, but also houses around 15,000 small businesses such as potteries and leather workshops supplying their goods to the whole of the city. You can gain an authentic insight into

can watch filming during a guided tour. Perhaps you can even join in – in Colaba, trend scouts regularly search for western tourists as extras. *www.mumbaifilmcity tours.com*

GATEWAY OF INDIA

The gateway in the British-Indian style on the bank of the old port is a sign of welcome – from the point of view of the colonial power when westerners would have arrived by ship. Built in 1926, the gateway commemorates the visit of King George V when he was crowned Emperor of India. Today this is the first point of call for domestic tourists. The atmosphere is almost like a funfair with tea stalls and balloon sellers.

HANGING GARDENS ☼

The Hanging Gardens in the area of *Malabar Hill* are a work of art laid out by landscape architects and include topiary in the shape of monkeys, elephants and giraffes. There are lovely views of Marine Drive. From the neighbouring *Towers of Silence*, where entry is prohibited, you can only see a large platform with an opening in the middle. This is where vultures used to circle round, eating the corpses laid out on the grating of the tower. The Towers of Silence was used as a cemetary for the Parsis, a religious community who had emigrated from Persia to India. Today, the corpses rot through the heat of the sun.

JEHANGIR ART GALLERY ●

The street artists painting on the Khala Goda Pavement Gallery next to the real art gallery dream of being exhibited in the oldest and best-known collection of art in Mumbai as this is almost the equivalent of being knighted. The art gallery displays a selection of modern Indian art which can also be purchased here. *Open daily 11am–7pm | MG Road | Fort Mumbai*

COLONIAL BUILDINGS

The most impressive example of the wild mix of styles of colonial architecture in Mumbai is the *Chhatrapati Shivaj Terminus* which was designed in imitation of St. Pancras station in London. You can find an abundance of colonial buildings in the Indian-English Neo-Gothic style opposite the *Oval Maidan*. Look out for the *High Court* and the *Rajabai* Clock Tower which looks like a Gothic castle reminiscent of Big Ben and is part of the also at-

tractive University of Mumbai. The Flora Fountain amid dense traffic on MG Road is decorated with floral ornamentation. Another Victorian masterpiece is *Elphinstone College*.

MAHALAKSHMI DHOBI GHAT ●

Green hospital gowns and white sheets flutter on the clothesline. Even hospitals and hotels have their laundry washed in Mumbai's washing district. The laundry is soaked, scrubbed and shaken out by over 5,000 dhobis working at the 800 stone basins. The washing is then ironed in the old tradition with flat irons filled with coal. *Close to the Metro station Mahalakshmi*

FOOD & RRINK

BOMBAY CANTEEN

In the charming colonial bungalow, ancient recipes with influences from all round the world have been refined. The chef has travelled through almost every inch of India. The Sikkimese fish is as sumptuous as the shrimp momos. The bar serves classical cocktails with an Indian twist. *Process House, Kamala Mills, S.B. Marg, Lower Parel | tel. 022 49 66 66 66 | www.thebombaycanteen.com | Moderate*

BOMBAY VINTAGE

Intense azure-blue walls with retro decorations from the Choor Bazaar and vintage books where delicious, hot, creamy food is served. Try a Tamarind Sour before you feast your way through the menu. *Indian Mercantile Mansion, Regal Circle, Colaba | tel. 022 69 44 41 23 | Moderate*

BRITANNIA & COMPANY

A visit to the oldest of the remaining Parsi cafés opened in the 19th century by the Zoroastrian immigrants is like a travel through time. Try their signature dish: Persian chicken with cashew nuts and barberries. *Wakefield House, 11, Sport Rd, 16 Ballard Estate | tel. 022 22 61 52 64 | Moderate*

SWATI SNACKS

People queue up here although only street food is on offer. But perhaps that is the true reason why they come here, as classical snacks such as Pani Puri are also popular with higher earners. It is much preferable to consume the food here in cool, modern surroundings than on the street. *Karai Estate, Tardeo Road | tel. 022 65 80 84 06 | Moderate*

SHOPPING

ANTIQUE SHOPS

If you are keen on antiques, you can rummage through the shops in *Colaba* behind the Hotel Taj Mahal. You will not find any bargains, but everything is at least of good quality. You will require an

export permit for objects more than a hundred years old.

INSIDER TIP CENTRAL COTTAGE INDUSTRIES EMPORIUM

Whether it's a miniature painting from Rajasthan or a solid sandalwood chest of drawers from southern India that you are looking for, the chances are that you will find it here. Handicrafts, toys and saris— and everything at set prices. *34, Shivaji Marg | Colaba*

MARKETS AND BAZAARS

North of the fort there are markets selling everything conceivable. The *Mangaldas Market* is for silk, the *Zaveri Bazaar* for jewellery with hundreds of shops proffering generally ostentatious items as well as exquisite oriental jewellery, and the *Chor Bazaar* – literally meaning "thieves market" – is a flea market for anything old or unwanted *(Mohammed Ali Road/Abdul Rehman Street)*.

Queueing for candy-coloured love stories in Mumbai, the home of Bollywood

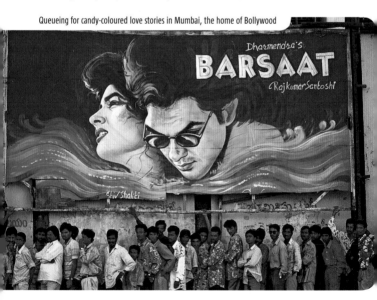

ENTERTAINMENT

BARS AND CLUBS
In Mumbai you can celebrate until you drop. Hipsters slurp cocktails in the futuristic *Aer* 🌿 in the *Four Seasons (1/136 Dr. E. Moses Road)* in Worli, Mumbai's highest roof terrace bar. For dancing go to *Trilogy (969, Juhu Tara Rd)* in Juhu or *Tryst (462, Senapati Bapat Marg)* in Lower Parel.

CINEMA
In the film city Mumbai, you must make at least one visit to the cinema! The best choice is *Regal*, the oldest Art-Deco cinema which showed a Laurel and Hardy film on its opening day in 1933. *Old Custom House Road, Apollo Bunder | www.regalcinema.in*

WHERE TO STAY

CHATEAU WINDSOR GUEST HOUSE
The hand-operaterd lift dates from pre-history, but the rooms are attractive in a good location close to Marine Drive: excellent cost-performance ratio. *50 rooms | 86, Vir Nariman Road Churchgate | tel. 022 66 22 44 55 | www.chateauwindsor.com | Budget–Moderate*

GODWIN 🌿
An evergreen in Coloba with new rooms on the upper floors. You can see the *Gateway of India* from rooms 805 and 806 as well as from the roof terrace. *52 rooms | 41, Garden Road Coloba | tel. 022 22 84 12 26 | www.hotelgodwin.co.in | Moderate*

RESIDENCY HOTEL
Have you ever slept in a former fire station? If not, take the opportunity to do so in this historical building close to the Fort. The rooms are small but smart and a delicious breakfast is served in the *Spice Lounge Café. 40 rooms | 26, D.N. Road, | el. 022 66 67 05 55 | www.residencyhotel.com | Moderate*

TAJ MAHAL PALACE & TOWER ⭐
This iconic hotel at the Gateway of India will be your choice if you would like to bask in pure luxury. Two years after the attacks in 2008, the historical jewel built by the industrialist Jamsetji Tata was returned to its former glory. You can also enjoy the tasteful ambience as a non-resident by taking afternoon tea in *The Sea Lounge*: very British! *582 rooms and suites | Apollo Bunder | tel. 022 66 65 33 66 | www.tajhotels.com | Expensive*

YWCA INTERNATIONAL CENTRE
Men are also permitted to stay here. This is a good alternative if you are eager to stay overnight in central and comfortable lodgings. A Bible is placed on your

LOW BUDGET

On first sight, the restaurant *Crystal* does not look very inviting, but inside you will be rewarded with the best Punjabi cuisine in the whole of Mumbai. You must definitely try *rajma*, red kidney beans in a mild tomato saouce. *19, Chowpatty Sea Face*

Anyone not put off by the slightly musty and dusty atmosphere will find high quality silk clothing at sensational prices in the *Khadi Village Industries Emporium* in Mumbai alongside clothes made of khadi, the handspun and woven material made famous by Ghandi. *286 Dadabhai Naorji Rd*

bedside table: half board is also available. *15 rooms | 18/II, Madame Cama Road | tel. 022 22 02 50 53 | www.ywcaic.info | Budget*

PUNE (POONA)

INFORMATION

GOVERNMENT OF INDIA TOURIST OFFICE
Tours to Filmcity and others can be booked here. Gateway of India | tel. 022 22 84 18 77 | www.maharasthratourism.gov.in

WHERE TO GO

ELEPHANTA ⭐ (190 C2) (*𝄞 D11*)
Whoever wants to have an authentic boat trip to the tropical island should not board the luxury launch but take a less touristy boat. You will pass stalls with colourful devotional kitsch on your way to the steep steps leading up to the cave temples. The main attraction is the *Mahesha temple* where you can marvel at an image of Shiva and a huge *lingam* or symbolic phallus. *Departure from the Gateway of India 9am–3.30pm) | 7 km/4.4 mi east*

(190 C3) (*𝄞 D11*) The "Queen of the Deccan Plateau" enjoys a refreshing climate all year round thanks to its location at an altitude of almost 600 m/1,969 ft.

As a result, Pune (pop. 3 million) was chosen by rulers as a suitable place to live from an early age. The British also left gardens, a golf course, horse racing tracks and bungalows, Bhagwan left followers from all over the world in his ashram, and now the IT sector is booming Furthermore, the best universities of the country are to be found here.

SIGHTSEEING

GANDHI NATIONAL MEMORIAL
Freedom fighters, among them Mahatma Gandhi and his wife Kasturba, were imprisoned in the former palace of the Aga Khan, built at the end of the 19th century. Kasturba died here. Photo-

The cave temple on Elephanta where Shiva was once worshipped is now a World Heritage Site

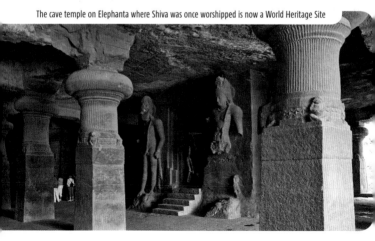

graphs and personal mementoes are on display. Large park. *Daily 10am–5pm*

OSHO INTERNATIONAL MEDITATION RESORT

Osho, formerly known as Bhagwan, used to preach the liberation of the soul through a blend of Tantric practices, Zen hypnosis and Tibetan pulsing. The ashram founded back in the 1980s is now more an all-inclusive resort with a spa, swimming pool, cafés and tennis courts. You can also pay a visit as a non-residential guest after undergoing a complicated procedure including an HIV test. *Open daily from 9am–4pm/ 17, Koregaon Park | www.osho.com*

PARVATI HILL ☆

Once you have climbed the 103 steps, you can enjoy one of the best panoramas of Pune, including temples devoted to Shiva's wife Parvati and other Hindu gods. The museum in the palace is dedicated to the Peshwas who once ruled Pune. This is the origin of the name of the local professional basketball team – the Pune Peshwas.

INSIDER TIP RAJA DINKAR KELKAR MUSEUM

Art and crafts from many eras assembled by a private collector. Many of the more than 20,000 exhibits seem rather bizarre such as the areca palm nutcrackers or antique musical instruments. *Daily 9.30am–5.30pm | 1377/78 Nastu Baugh | Off. Bajirao Road | Shukrawar Peth | tel. 020 24 48 21 01*

TRIBAL MUSEUM

Black magic – cult objects belonging to the original inhabitants of Maharashtra are exhibited here alongside jewellery, musical intruments and everyday objects in a fascinating display providing an insight into almost forgotten cultures. *Daily 10.30am–5.30pm | 28, Queens Garden*

FOOD & DRINK

GERMAN BAKERY

This is a good place to go if you fancy a change from all the curries you have eaten. The menu is a journey across the world with German sausages, Japanese omelettes and Lhasa chicken momos. *292, Koregaon Park, Road No. 1 | tel. 020 39 39 55 52 | www.germanbakerypune.in | Moderate*

MALAKA SPICE

The recipes with their unique touch have been compiled from the restaurant owners' trips round South-East Asia. One of the best slow food restaurants in Pune. *Koregaon Park, Lane No. 5 | tel. 07507 48 69 69 | www.malakaspice.com | Moderate*

WHERE TO STAY

BLUE DIAMOND HOTEL

Pure luxury with a pool and first-class restaurants. The rooms are as stylish as the hotel itself which has genuinely earned its five stars! *114 rooms | 11, Koregaon Road | tel. 020 66 02 55 55 | www.vivantahotels.com | Expensive*

HOTEL WOODLAND

Located in the urban Koregaon Park district not far from the station. With vegetarian restaurant. *87 rooms | Sadhu Vaswani Circle | tel. 020 26 21 21 21 | www.tghotels.com | Budget–Moderate*

INFORMATION

MAHARASHTRA TOURISM DEVELOPMENT CORPORATION (MTDC)

Booking service for MTDC hotels and tours. *Central Office Building | Sassoon Hospital Road | tel. 020 26 12 68 67 | www.maharashtratourism.gov.in*

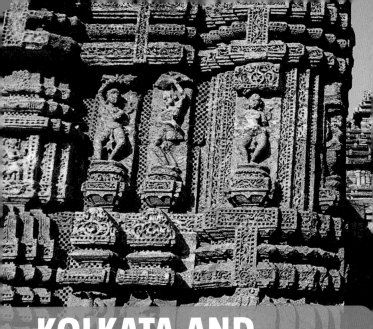

KOLKATA AND THE EAST

Bihar and West Bengal, two of the three large states in eastern India, are among the most densely populated on the subcontinent along with Kerala in the far south.

Odisha, or Oryia – previously known as Orissa – on the contrary, with its inviting wealth of palm groves and beaches, richly decorated temples and living works of art, is relatively sparsely populated by Indian standards. Sikkim and the states or territories in the far north-east – Assam, Meghalaya, Tripura, Mizoram, Manipur, Nagaland and Arunachal Pradesh – are special cases both from cultural and touristic points of view.

Until recently, Restricted Areas Permits (RAP) were needed to travel to the north-eastern states, also known as "The Seven Sister States". Now, you can visit Assam, Meghalaya and Tripura without any special formalities. The bus, train and air connections to and from Guwahati, the capital of Assam, and Shillong, have been improved. National parks such as Kaziranga in Assam, with rhinoceroses and herds of elephants, can once again be visited.

Kolkata (formerly known as Calcutta), the cultural centre of the east, forms a stark contrast to the green vegetation of the Himalayan territories. The great urban sprawl, with a population of more than 14 million, is for many the epitome of poverty and the demise of India. But that's no longer true. The streets are now cleaner than in many metropolises in the western world; investments are

The verdant Himalaya region, the megacity Kolkata and the cradle of Buddhism – this and more awaits visitors to the east of India

being made and the underground network is expanding steadily. Kolkata can now hold its head up high again.

Since Bengal was divided in 1947, with the eastern section first becoming part of Pakistan before being declared the independent state of Bangladesh, there has always been a certain tension here with an sheer endless stream of refugees flooding into the Indian state of West Bengal. India's earliest historical and mythological sites can be found in the state of Bihar, which, unfortunately, generally lags way

behind in social terms and is marked by violent exploitation and the perversion of justice. Bihar was the cradle of Buddhism. Later, Hindu Emperor Ashoka – perhaps the most important ruler in the history of India – had his seat of power here. He converted to Buddhism after fighting bloody battles against the Kalinga Empire and tried to establish peace. 800 years later Hindu dynasties won the upper hand over the Buddhists. The heritage of the Kesari dynasty was preserved until the present day: their magnificent temples survived the destructive Mughal invasion in the 16th century.

BHUBANESHWAR

(193 F2) (⚑ L10) Temples, temples and yet more temples – this is the capital city (pop. 840,000) of the state of Odisha. More than 7,000 temples were built here between the 8th and 12th century. Hundreds are still standing, many with their decorative sculptures intact, while others are ruins plundered for building

holy rivers of India are believed to join up beneath this point. Shiva is supposed to have created the lake to quench his companion's thirst. The most magnificent of Bhubaneshwar's temples were erected around Bindu Sagar. The *Shikaras*, the towers of the temples rising above the holiest of buildings looking almost like stacked up fancy cakes, are typical of Odisha's temple architecture.

LINGARAJA TEMPLES
Non-Hindus are forbidden from entering the temple complex, but the sculptures on the external walls – depicting deities, women and pairs of lovers – and the imposing temple tower are visible from

Ploughing with oxen – agriculture is still extremely important in India

material. Next to the expansive archaeological sites, there is a modern, spacious new city. The temples are spaced widely apart: it is best to take an auto rikshaw to get from A to B.

SIGHTSEEING

BINDU SAGAR
The water in the temple pool in the south of the city is highly revered as all

the outside. You will have the best view from the INSIDER TIP viewing terrace with the aid of binoculars. The almost one thousand-year-old temple is one of the most significant buildings of its time and is considered as a masterpiece of temple architecture in Odisha. The site contains a total of 60 small temples amd shrines with stone sculptures of female dancers, musicians and deities. *South of Bindu Sagar | Old Town*

MUKTESHWARA TEMPLE

Erotic sculptures full of a zest for life also decorate this small temple built in the 9th century, referred to as a "dream in sandstone". A *torana* (gateway) with a wonderful reliefs leads through to the temple. *East of Bindu Sagar*

MUSEUM OF TRIBAL ARTS & ARTEFACTS

Odisha is home to over 60 different tribes. Immerse yourself in the multi-faceted cultures and wander through the exhibition of musical instruments, jewellery, weapons and household objects. *Daily 10am–5pm | Gopabandhu Nagar, near Highway NH 5*

RAJARANI TEMPLE

The temple is also known as "Khajuraho of the East" for its erotic sculptures. Although many of the sculptures have suffered damage, the site is well worth a visit for its peaceful atmosphere amongst greenery. *East, on the far side of Lewis Road*

FOOD & DRINK

HARE KRISHNA

Here you will be offered vegetarian food, but without garlic and onions as the restaurant decorated with many images of deities adheres to the principles of Jain. This does not however spoil the tastiness of the food. *Lalchand Market Complex | Janpath | tel. 06742 53 41 88 | Budget–Moderate*

SHOPPING

BOYANIKA SHOWROOM

Odisha is not only well-known for delicate silver jewellery, but also for high-quality handwoven materials. Come here to buy amazing scarves and attractive bed throws and cushions with attractive embroidery. *Hall No. 11, Western Market Building, AG Square*

WHERE TO STAY

HOTEL DEEPALI INTERNATIONAL

This hotel should be your first choice if you are looking for a good place to stay which is both economical and close to the temples. *21 rooms | 54, Budhanagar/Kalpana Square | tel. 0674 2 31 07 84 | www.hoteldeepaliinternational.in | Budget*

MARCO POLO HIGHLIGHTS

⭐ **Bodh Gaya**
The site where Buddha found enlightenment under the Bodhi tree → p. 105

⭐ **Tiger Hill**
Breathtaking views of the highest peaks in the Himalayas, near Darjeeling → p. 107

⭐ **Indian Museum**
Resplendent mansion in Kolkata housing exquisite exhibits → p. 110

⭐ **Oberoi Grand Hotel**
Traditional hotel from the days of the British Raj in Kolkata: famous for its impeccable service → p. 114

⭐ **Sundarbans**
Impressive, untamed mangrove forest covering 2.5 million acres not far from Kolkata → p. 115

⭐ **The Sun Temple of Konark**
Temple complex with fascinating and intricate sculptural work with erotic scenes → p. 116

BHUBANESHWAR

The Buddhist pilgrim centre Bodh Gaya where Buddha attained Enlightenment

PANTHANIVAS TOURIST BUNGALOW
One of 20 *panthanivas* in Odisha: simply furnished state-run hotels with economic room rates and a pleasant atmosphere. *Close to the temples. 54 rooms | Lewis Road | tel. 0674 2 43 25 15 | www.pantha nivas.com | Budget*

INFORMATION

ODISHA TOURISM
At the station *(Old Block, Jayadev Marg | tel. 0674 24 31 2 99)*; at the airport *(tel. 0674 2 40 40 06 | www.odishatourism.gov.in)*

WHERE TO GO

CHILKA LAKE (193 E2) *(ฒ L10)*
This large lagoon covering some 425 mi² has numerous islands and is especially attractive for ornithologists. Many migratory birds spend the winter here. The best time to visit is in December. Siberian cranes can also be watched here. The little settlements of *Barkul*

and *Rambha* at the southern tip of the lagoon have some modest places to stay. *105 km/65 mi and 135 km/84 mi respectively, south-west*

NANDAN KANAN (193 F1) *(ฒ L10)*
Surrounded by forest is one of the few zoos in India worth visiting. White tigers can be found here (Lion and Tiger Safari) as well as Asian lions, rhinos, snakes and of course monkeys. The two-hour tour in an ⊙ electric bus and the aerial ropeway over the lake are both very popular. Boat trips also available. *Tue–Sun 7.30am–5.30pm (April–Sept), 8am–5pm (Oct–March) | some 20 km/12.4 mi from the city centre | bus from Kalpana Square | www.nandankanan.org*

PIPLI (193 F2) *(ฒ L10)*
You could be afflicted by a shopping frenzy: beautiful appliqué work is made in this small town (pop. 17,000) and used to decorate sunshades, bags and rugs. *20 km/12.4 mi south*

BODH GAYA

(187 E3) (*∅ K7*) ⭐ **Buddha found enlightenment under a INSIDER TIP Bodhi tree in this small town (pop. 38,500) located in the state of Bihar. The legendary sacred fig tree which has grown from the shoots of the original tree is now adjacent to the Mahabodhi Temple, one of the sacred sites of Buddhism. Thousands upon thousands of pilgrims from all over the world flock to this special location, following in the steps of Buddha.**

To witness the special magic of this site, you should visit in the morning or evening. Take a walk around the area and look at the huge stone slab with Buddha's footprint and the sculture of the snake god who protected him from a downpour. A further sacred site is the *Banyan tree* under which Buddha lectured a Brahman on the deficiencies of the caste concept. If you have more time, you can also watch the rituals of the Buddhist monks and nuns who walk round the temple and prostrate themselves. Alternatively, do as the pilgrims do and collect a leaf of the Bodhi tree which is said to bring good fortune.

SIGHTSEEING

INSIDER TIP MAHABODHI TEMPLE
The seven-storey temple tower is surrounded by sandstone pillars with lotus reliefs and exquisite depictions of scenes, made in the 2nd and 1st centuries BC and in the 4th and 5th centuries AD. The originals are in now Kolkata and London.

NEW TEMPLES
Surrounding the Mahabodhi complex, you will find temples constructed by other countries with Buddhist populations for their pilgrims. You can easily recognise the temple built by Thailand by its intensely ornamented entrance shining golden in the sun and the temple of Bhutan with its characteristic multi-level rooftop. The Japanese and Mongolian temples are much plainer. *Normally open from 8am–midday and 2pm–5pm*

FOOD & DRINK

TIBET OM CAFÉ
Popular Tibetan restaurant attached to a monastery. Here you will find the best momos in the town and can also try the tasty noodle soup. *Closed in the summer | close to Birladrhamsala | Budget*

WHERE TO STAY

TATHAGAT INTERNATIONAL
The rooms in this modern building are a little smaller than you would think looking at the balconies on the white-painted façade, but clean. The hotel and restaurant is opposite the entrance to the wildlife park and within walking distance of the temple complex. *33 rooms | tel. 0631 2 20 01 07 | www.hoteltathagatbodhgaya. com | Moderate*

INFORMATION

TOURIST COMPLEX
Bodhgaya Road | tel. 0631 2 20 06 72 | www.bstdc.bih.nic.in/BodhGaya.htm

WHERE TO GO

NALANDA (187 E3) (*∅ L7*)
Anyone interested in finding out more about Buddhism should visit Nalanda where Buddhist monks founded the then largest teaching institution in the world over 1,500 years ago. Buddha himself was among the 10,000 students who had

come from all over Asia. Although the university was destroyed by the Muslim conquerors in the 12th century, the ruins of the school, temple and monasteries have remained in good condition. It is also worth visiting the Archaeological Museum with its stone friezes and Buddha figures and the *Nalanda Multimedia Museum (both open Sat–Thu 10am–5pm). 100 km/62 mi north-east*

SASARAM (187 D3) (*📖 K7*)

The little trading centre of Sasaram (pop. approx. 147,000), almost exactly half way between Bodh Gaya and Varanasi, has an impressive mausoleum to Sher Shah, the founder of the short-lived Sur dynasty. He built the longest and oldest road in Asia, now called the *Grand Trunk Road* that links Amritsar with Kolkata. INSIDER TIP *Sher Shah's tomb rises* 46 m/151 ft above a square, artificial lake and has a dome spanning 22 m/72.2 ft that is bigger than that of the Taj Mahal. *140 km/87 mi west*

DARJEELING

(188 A2–3) (*📖 M6*) **A high-altitude eldorado for all tea-lovers! The terraces round about are covered in tea plantations.**

These were built from 1835 onwards after the British had been "lent" land by the Maharaja of neighbouring Sikkim, as it provided the right climatic conditions for a certain type of tea bush, grown originally from shoots imported from China. A road was built to transport the tea harvest, followed later by the daring construction of a railway line. Today, there is a *toy train (www.dhr.in.net)*, a narrow-gauge railway offering spectacular views and sometimes passing so close to the houses that you can see right into the residents' homes. During the days of the Raj, Darjeeling was a hill station for Europeans who came here to escape the searing heat of the lowland plains.

The town of 🌿 Darjeeling (*Dorje Ling* means "the land of the thunderbolt" in Tibetan) spreads out over a steep hillside at an altitude of more than 2,100 m/6,890 ft. It has a population of around 120,000 with many residents originally from Nepal, Bhutan and Tibet. Spectacular: on a clear day, you can see *Kanchenjunga* (8,586 m/28,169 ft), the third highest mountain in the world, and even *Mount Everest*, some 200 km/124 mi away. October and November is the time for the best views, although you have to wrap up warmly at this high altitude.

SIGHTSEEING

GHOOM BUDDHIST MONASTERY

Darjeeling is much influenced by Buddhism due to its proximity to Nepal, Sikkim and Bhutan. One of the most beautiful monasteries is the *Gompa* of the yellow-hat sect in Ghoom, particularly notable for its magnificent sculpture of the Buddha of the Future. *8 km/5 mi south | also reachable on the toy train (at the line's highest station)*

HAPPY VALLEY TEA ESTATE

The verdant tea plantations on the slopes below the town shimmer in all shades of green. You can watch how tea leaves are wilted, rolled and fermented at the Happy Valley Tea Estate and go for a walk through the plantations. You can buy tea on this plantation or at *Nathmull's (Laden-La Road | above the post office | www.nathmulltea.com)*, Darjeeling's oldest tea shop. *3 km/1.9 mi from the centre, at the end of TP Banerjee*

TIGER HILL ★

This means getting up early before heading off to Tiger Hill (2,590 m/ 8,497 ft) – mostly by jeep – to see the sun rise. The snow-covered peaks turn shades of pink and red set against a blue sky, assuming that the weather is right. Anyone not too exhausted after getting up so early can INSIDER TIP walk back to the town. *11 km/6.8 mi from the centre*

ZOO

Siberian tigers and black bears, with a breeding programme for snow leopards. The zoo also participates in the global project to save the red panda. *Fri–Wed 8.30am–4pm or 4.30pm in summer | near the Mountaineering Institute*

ESSEN & TRINKEN

THE ELGIN

Once the summer residence of a Maharajah, this building is now a heritage hotel with a tea lounge and restaurant serving both European and Indian food. *H. D. Lama Road | tel. 0354 2257226 | www.elginhotels.com | Expensive*

GLENARY'S

This is an institution in an old colonial house. On the ground floor, there is a *tea room* serving legendary fine bakery products, the bar *The Buzz* and a cosy old-style restaurant. *Nehru Road | tel. 0354 2254122 | Moderate*

SHOPPING

You will find numerous shops selling knitwear and craft objects along *Nehru Road* and the *Chowrasta*, the promenade square. You can also stock up on tea to take home with you.

Tea plantation in Darjeeling – the leaves are still picked by hand today

INSIDER TIP TIBETAN REFUGEE SELF HELP CENTRE

In 1910–12, the Dalai Lama at that time found refuge on this site. In 1959, as the Chinese army took control of Tibet, Tibetans in exile opened a self-help centre. The complex now includes a school, an orphanage, medical facilities, a print-shop, a temple and craft workshops. The centre is financed by donations and the sale of rugs, carvings, textiles and jewellery. *Mon–Sat | 65, Gandhi Road | tel. 0354 2255938 | www.tibetancentredarjeeling.com*

LEISURE & SPORTS

TREKKING

Darjeeling is a paradise for trekkers, for example the *Sandakphu trek* along the *Singalila mountain ridge* leading along the Nepalese border where at certain points you can even stand with one foot in Nepal! In *Nehru Road* and above the *Chowrasta,* you will find countless agencies where you can book a guided tour.

WHERE TO STAY

BROADWAY ANNEXE ぷ

In a central location close to the clock tower, this hotel is elegantly furnished with a profusion of pinewood. You can see the Kanchenjunga from the balcony. *14 rooms | Dr. Zakir Hussain Road 47 | tel. 0354 2 25 32 48 | www.broadwaydarjeeling.com | Budget*

DEKELING ぷ

Simple, cheap and good. You can relax in the library and feast on Tibetan specialities made by the friendly Tibetan owner. Another feature is the amazing view! *11 rooms | 51, Gandhi Road (The Mall) | tel. 0354 2 25 41 59 | www.dekeling.com | Budget*

SINCLAIRS

Furnished in the Victorian-British style with a slight modern touch. You can enjoy your Darjeeling tea on the sun terrace and have a drink in the colonial style bar in the evening. *46 rooms | 18/1, Gandhi Road | tel. 0354 2 25 64 31 | www.sinclairshotels.com | Budget*

INSIDER TIP WINDAMERE HOTEL

Wonderfully old fashioned – with an open fire, hot water bottles, tea time and enthusiastic staff. There are no telephones or TV; instead there is a piano and a garden in a beautiful location. British fare. *27 rooms | Observatory Hill | tel. 0354 2 25 40 41 | www.windamerehotel.com | Moderate*

INFORMATION & PERMITS

TOURIST OFFICE WEST BENGAL

1, Nehru Road (upper floor) | Belle Vue | tel. 0354 2 25 41 02

WHERE TO GO

INSIDER TIP KALIMPONG
(188 A2–3) (*ℳ M6*)

The trip to this market town (Wed and Sat), with its plethora of gardens and old Buddhist monasteries, will delight you. The quietly but centrally located heritage hotel *Himalayan (16 rooms and suites | Upper Cart Road | tel. 011 42 42 31 00 | www.heritagehotelsofindia.com/west-bengal/himalayan-hotel | Moderate)* with a garden in the extremely scenic Teesta Valley is the most beautiful accommodation. *50 km/31.1 mi east*

SANDAKPHU ぷ (188 A2) (*ℳ M5*)

The village situated on a mountain ridge at an altitude of 3,636 m/11,929 ft is worth visiting for its breathtaking views of the Himalayas. Rhododendrons flower among the pine forests in the spring. You can either walk up here on foot or take a jeep. *60 km/37.3 mi north-west*

KOLKATA (CALCUTTA)

MAP ON P. 113

(188 A6) (*ℳ M8*) **Screaming street vendors, hissing trains and bearers brutally elbowing a path through the crowds wherever one looks.**

CITY WHERE TO START?
Maidan Park: It's not far from here to the Indian Museum and Victoria Memorial *(Metro station: Maidan)*. To the east is Nehru Road with both luxury and low-budget hotels, unusual shops and numerous restaurants. Bus no. 212 links Nehru Road with the colonial BBD Bagh.

Just a few yards from *Howrah Station*, one of the two big stations in Kolkata, *Howrah Bridge* crosses the murky waters of Hooghly river, a wide tributary of the Ganges. Millions of people cross this bridge, day in, day out, on foot, by lorry, bike, bus or car, or pushing a cart. The result is a bustling, noisy traffic jam from dawn 'til dusk. Urban planners attempt to gain control of the chaotic traffic by building new elevated roads. An underground metro line running under the Hooghly and linking the two main stations of the city should also provide some relief. Within an Indian context, Kolkata, known as Calcutta prior to 2001, is a relatively young city. All that existed here 300 years ago were a few villages. In 1960, the British East India Company was searching for a location for their production sites and administration centres and built a branch in the small village of Sutanuti. Later, the village was combined with Gobindapur and Kalikata: the latter is named after the goddess Kali and is the origin of the modern name of Kolkata. A harbour was built and the town developed into the largest trading metropolis in Asia – thanks also to the thriving opium trade with China – and became the capital of British India.

The Malik Ghat Flower Market in Kolkata is the largest of its kind in India

Kolkata was dethroned in 1911 and the capital moved to Delhi. Kolkata's glory faded simultaneously with the palatial residences of rich Bengal families dating back to the 19th century. The city collapsed under the burden of the explosive growth in its population after Indian Partition. The former jewel of the British crown was transformed into the poorhouse of India with uncountable shanty towns, the so-called *bustees*.

SIGHTSEEING

ACADEMY OF FINE ARTS

Anyone interested in Bengali art should head straight for the museum in the *Academy of Arts* which offers a series of temporary exhibitions, a sculpture garden and an attractive film programme *Tue–Sat noon–7pm, Sun 3pm–7pm | Cathedral Road | www.academyoffinearts.in*

BBD BAGH

The initial letters of the names of three Bengali independence activists gave this square in the old centre of the British city its new name (called Dalhousie Square until 1947). The administrative centre of Bengal is located here. On the northern side is the *Writers' Building* with its red and white columns. At one time this was where employees of the East India Company – so-called writers – lived and worked. The *High Court*, modelled on the town hall in Ypres in Flanders, is opposite. The *Raj Bhavan* is, as in the past, still a government building. Previously the official residence of the Viceroy of India, it is now used by the Governor of West Bengal.

INSIDER TIP ▶ BOTANIC GARDEN ●

The park on the west bank of the Hooghly is a pleasantly peaceful and relaxing place in this megacity during the week. The more than 230-year-old Great Banyan that, with is aerial roots, forms what looks like a whole forest of trees with a circumference of more than 400 m/1,312 ft, is little short of a wonder. *Daily sunrise to sunset*

HOWRAH BRIDGE

The best view of the bridge without piers is to be had from the ☼ *Millenium Park (Strand Road South)* near the Hooghly. The bridge with a span of almost 460 m/1,509 ft is the symbol of Kolkata and one of the largest suspension bridges in the world. It is officially known as *Rabindra Setu*, named after the poet Rabindranath Tagore.

INDIAN MUSEUM ★

This, the largest and oldest museum in India, is housed in a pompously designed building from 1875. Its exhibits include superb highlights of Indian art, such as Buddhist sculptures from a stone peripheral wall with larger-than-life female figures, paintings and miniatures, folk art, zoological and botanical collections. *Tue–Sun 10am–5pm | 27, Jawaharlal Nehru Road | cp.indianmuseumkolkata.org*

KALIGHAT KALI TEMPLE ●

Blaring temple music, crowds of people with their sacrificial offerings squeezed together, the floor slippery from all the butter fat and bits of flowers. The temple is dedicated to Kali, the patroness of Kolkata and the goddess of wrath and anger who also offers maternal protection. You are permitted to witness the rituals: sometimes goats are sacrificed – not for anyone of a nervous disposition. *Kalighat | in the south of the city*

MAIDAN

The park is a popular place for picnics, gymnastics, jogging and boating. The

The mighty structure of Howrah Bridge is crossed by millions of people every day

area includes the *Calcutta Cricket Ground*, other sports fields and *Eden Garden* in the north with a Burmese pagoda. *East of the Hooghly*

MALIK GHAT FLOWER MARKET

If you walk over the Howrah Bridge in the morning towards the city, you should not miss taking a look at the many-coloured sea of flowers and orange and yellow garlands on the right hand side. This is the Malik Ghat Flower Market which has existed for 125 years and is the largest flower market in India. *South-eastern end of the Howrah Bridge*

MOTHER HOUSE

There is hardly another individual so closely connected with Kolkata than *Mother Teresa*, recipient of the Nobel Peace Prize, who went to Kolkata as a young nun to help the poor and sick. Dozens of people make pilgrimages to her grave in the Mother House of the Missionaries of Charity. A small museum provides an insight into her work. Anyone interested in helping in one of the missionary's homes should allow at least one week's stay. (*Sr. Mercy-Maria, Missionaries of Charity, Sister in Charge of Volunteers*). *Fri–Wed 8am–midday, 3pm–6pm | www.motherteresa.org | 54/A AJC Bose Road*

PARSHWANATH JAIN TEMPLE

The temple hidden amongst the narrow alleyways of North Kolkata was founded by the court jeweller of the Viceroy in 1867. This is a blend of playful Rococo and pagoda styles full of glittering mirrors surrounded by a symmetrical garden. *Open daily 7am–midday and 3pm–6pm | Badri Temple Street*

ST PAUL'S CATHEDRAL

The brilliant white neo-Gothic church completed in 1847 is reminiscent of Canterbury Cathedral and the interior is also more British than Indian. The best time to visit is in the afternoon when the elaborate coloured stained glass windows are illuminated by the sun.

Legacy from the colonial era: the Victoria Memorial is a memorial to the former British Queen

VICTORIA MEMORIAL

This massive building, a blend of British and Mughal architectural styles, was dedicated to Victoria, Empress of India, and inaugurated in 1921. Lord Curzon, Viceroy of India from 1899–1905, arranged the funding of the splendid building with the support of prominent Indians. Early photographs of Indian towns and the country are well worth seeing. *Garden daily 5.30am–6.30pm, museum Tue–Sun 10am–6pm | www.victoriamemorial-cal. org | at the southern end of the Maidan*

FOOD & DRINK

There are lots of restaurants in *Park Street* and round New Market to suit all budgets.

AMBER

One of the oldest restaurants in the city, visited for many decades by the ancient families of Kolkata. Special tip: try the *Tandoor dishes! 11, Waterloo Street | tel. 033 22 48 67 46 | Moderate*

BLUE & BEYOND ⚜

The restaurant is well worth a visit just to see Kolkata by night from the stylish roof terrace. Enjoy a sophisticated cocktail and feast on north Indian cuisine. *Hotel The Lindsay Kolkata | Lindsay Street | tel. 033 22 52 22 37 | Moderate*

PETER CAT

A great institution, especially the mouthwatering kebabs. Incidentally, the chef of this popular restaurant learned his skills in Salzburg! *18A, Park Street/Middleton Row | tel. 033 22 29 88 41 | Moderate*

SHOPPING

Shopping in Kolkata starts with the *New Market*. It was formerly the British upper class who went shopping in this striking neo-Gothic location, but nowadays the whole city comes to barter at its 2,000 stalls. You can find absolutely everything here. Curiosities and rarities can be discovered in the traditional *Chorbazaar. The Chandni Chowk Market is located slightly*

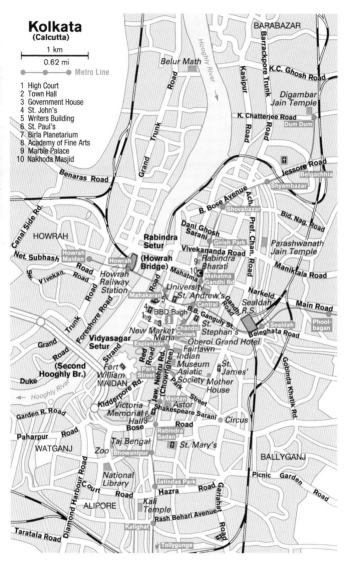

Kolkata
(Calcutta)

1 km

0.62 mi

Metro Line

1 High Court
2 Town Hall
3 Government House
4 St. John's
5 Writers Building
6 St. Paul's
7 Birla Planetarium
8 Academy of Fine Arts
9 Marble Palace
10 Nakhoda Masjid

further east of Jawarhal Nehru Road and the Indian Museum and is also known as the *Hardware Bazaar*: computer freaks can purchase equipment here at rock-bottom prices. Kolkata is also a paradise for book lovers: there is nowhere else you can find such a wide selection of second-hand books with the

If you look hard, you may find a good read in these piles of books

possigble exception of the Bouquinistes in Paris. Particularly in the university quarter, multitudes of books are piled up on innumerable stalls. If you would like to order clothes made to measure, you should head to one of the Chinese tailors on *Bentinck Street (close to BBD Bagh)* where you can select your material, have your measurements taken and come back in a few days to pick up the finished garments perfectly designed according to your wishes.

WHERE TO STAY

You will find most hotels in within the area between *Shakespeare Sarani Street* to the south and *Sudder Street* to the north up to the *New Market*. Alongside British-style B&Bs, an increasing

number of boutique hotels are being opened in restored colonial buildings, for example in north Kolkata and the Bengali city district.

THE ASTOR HOTEL

Colonial heritage meets modern luxury in the Victorian red brick house dating from 1905. The *Restaurant Kebab-e-Que* is one of the best in the city and the outdoor café and bar are real eye-catchers. *33 rooms | 15, Shakespeare Sarani | tel. 033 22 82 99 50 | www.astorkolkata.com | Moderate*

THE CALCUTTA BUNGALOW

A beautifully restored townhouse dating from the 1920s which you feel you could move straight into. The rooms spread around an open-air inner courtyard are all wonderfully decorated, featuring photographs from the various districts of Kolkata. This is a true feel-good oasis. *5 Radha Kanta Jeu Street | tel. 09830 18 40 30 | www.calcuttabungalow.com | Moderate*

INSIDER TIP THE ELGIN FAIRLAWN

The eccentric spirit of the long-standing proprietor Violet who died at the ripe age of 94 is still present in the legendary hotel dating from the era of British India which has seen guests such as Sting and Patrick Swayze. There is a British touch to the décor, pictures and old memorabilia and also a lush garden. *21 rooms | 13 A, Sudder Street | tel. 033 22 52 15 10 | www. elginhotels.com/fairlawn | Moderate*

OBEROI GRAND HOTEL ★

The hotel is housed in a Victorian building that, in 1938, was converted into a virtually perfect, elegant luxury hotel. An oasis of peace and quiet in the shade of palm trees with a large pool. *250 rooms | 15, J. Nehru Road | Chowringhee | tel. 033*

22 49 23 23 | www.oberoihotels.com | Expensive

THE CORNER COURTYARD
Attractive boutique hotel with colonial charm, south of the city. The décor of the individual rooms tells the story of the fascinating city of Kolkata. Fantastic food! *7 rooms | 92 B Sarat Bose Road | tel. 09903 99 95 67 | www.thecornercourtyard.com | Moderate*

INFORMATION

Government of India Tourist Office | 4, Shakespeare Sarani | tel. 033 22 82 14 75; counter at airport arrivals: *West Bengal Tourism | BBD Bagh | tel. 033 22 48 82 71 | www.wbtourism.gov.in*

WHERE TO GO

SUNDARBANS ★
(188 A–B6) (ɷ M–N9)
The Sundarbans is a huge national park with mangrove forests and Bengal tigers, crocodiles and dolphins. Enjoy a leisurely boat trip and marvel at the seemingly endless "beautiful forest" – as the name means – and the wetlands. You can then stay overnight in solid accommodation such as the *Sajnekhali Tourist Lodge (30 rooms | Sundarban's National Park | close to Gosaba | tel. 09732 50 99 25 | short.travel/ind17 | Budget)*. If you want to be gently rocked to sleep, you can book a houseboat trip lasting several days, e.g. at *Tour de Sundarbans (www.tourdesundarbans.com)* or *Sundarban Houseboat (www.sundarbanhouseboat.com)*. Approx. 100 km/62 mi south-west

KONARK (KONARAK)

(193 F2) (ɷ L10) The god of the sun is worshipped in Konark (pop. 16,700): the temple dating from the 13th century in the form of a chariot on wheels is considered an architectural masterwork

---

FOR BOOKWORMS AND FILM BUFFS

The God of Small Things (1997) – Arundati Roy's debut novel about childhood. Set in Kerala it provides an authentic insight into everyday life in the country, including the problems of the caste system.

The White Tiger (2008) – Aravind Adiga was transformed overnight into a best-selling author thanks to his prize-winning debut novel. He tells the bizarre story of a taxi driver from Bangalore involving murder, advancement, a mysterious white tiger and the abyss of corruption and caste differences.

NH10 (2015) – After a young couple witness an honour killing, they are pursued by a gang. This thriller with the heroine in the principal role was a box-office success and would have been unthinkable in Indian cinemas a few years ago prior to the debate on the rights of women.

Slumdog Millionaire (2008) – The story of Jamal Malik who grew up in a slum only to win millions in a TV quiz show. Romantic, thrilling and humorous without being implausible. 8 Oscars!

The Sun Temple in Konark with its marvellous ornamental sculptures

and is the largest and most significant temple to the sun in India.

The ★ *Sun Temple of Konark* was also known as *Black Pagoda* because the sandstone walls looked so dark from a distance. The 70 m/229.7 ft high temple tower which is now a partial ruin served as a landmark for European mariners. Numerous legends have evolved about this temple: it is said that built-in magnets were the cause for many shipwrecks on the coast. The temple dedicated to the sun god Surya subsequently lay buried under a huge sand dune for an extended period of time. When the sand was cleared away, the former glory of the temple was revealed once more: an oversized chariot symbolising the vehicle of the sun god pulled by seven horses of which only one has remained intact. You can still marvel at the walls with the 24 chariot wheels with a height of 3 m/9.8 ft. Thousands of sculptures have been worked into the temple walls – gods, birds, animals, mythological figures, dancers and numerous erotic representations with sensuous nymphs and pairs of lovers. A special tip: early risers will be rewarded with a wonderful light and the sight is equally impressive at sunset. First take a walk around the walls to get a sense of perspective. *Open from sunrise to sunset.*

In the *Archaeological Museum (Sat–Thu, 10am–5pm)* you will find more erotic sculptures. *Chandrabhaga Beach* is only 3 km/1.9 mi away if you fancy a swim after visiting the temple. The *Hotel Yatrinivas* with a restaurant and garden can be recommended for an overnight stay *(46 rooms | tel. 06758 23 68 20 | Moderate)*. The hotel also houses the *OTD Tourist Office (tel. 06758 23 68 21)*.

PURI

(193 F2) (⤢ L10) This is where surfers meet pilgrims: perfect waves crash onto the fine sandy beaches and the famous

Jagannath temple has transformed Puri (pop. 201,000) into one of the major pilgrimage sites in India.

Although the beaches in Puri cannot be compared to those in Goa, it is much quieter here. You can also go surfing as Puri is gradually becoming a favourite surfing centre. Alternatively, join the crowds of pilgrims who have come to worship the god Jagannath. Puri is one of the holiest sites in India and the so-called chariot festival *Rathjatra* one of the largest summer festivals acrioss the whole country.

SIGHTSEEING

JAGANNATH TEMPLE

Lord Jagannath is considered a form of Vishnu, the "Lord of the Universe", was ahead of his time: he refused the caste system. Only Hindus however are allowed inside his temple. For a donation, other people are allowed to look across from the roof of the library opposite into the 200 × 200 m/656 × 656 ft square temple site. However you can only see roofs and the 59 m/193.6 ft high temple tower. From this view, you will find it hard to imagine that over 10,000 people come to the temple every day, 6,000 of which are temple servants.

FOOD & DRINK

WILDGRASS RESTAURANT

The quiet garden restaurant should be your fist choice if you are keen to try specialities from Odisha. The tandoori dishes are also delicious. *VIP Road | tel. 09437 02 36 56 | Moderate*

WHERE TO STAY

NILANCHAL ASHOK HOTEL

The hotel with a garden and swimming pool is a little distance from the beach. *34 rooms | Swargadwar Road | tel. 06752 22 33 87 | www.hotelnilachal.com | Moderate*

TOSHALI SANDS

The bungalow resort is a real paradise under palm trees with a garden and swimming pool. It is laid out in the form of a small village and decorated with ceramic deities and animals and folk-style textiles. Shuttle service to the beach, boat trips on the river Nuanai available. There is also an apartment hotel building. *54 rooms and 50 villas/cottages | Konark Marine Drive | 8 km/5 mi from Puri towards Konark | tel. 09937 00 32 23 | www.toshalisands.com | Moderate*

INFORMATION

OTDC OFFICE

CT Road, near Banki Muhana | tel. 06752 22 26 64

LOW BUDGET

The proprietor of *Dolly's Tea Shop* in Kolkata writes books about tea and has some 24 different teas at incredibly low prices. *Approx. 2 km/1.2 mi east of Kalighat Temple | between the Metro station Rabindra Sarovar and Dhakuna station*

The ● *Centre of International Modern Art (CIMA)* in Kolkata has become one of the leading galleries in India for contemporary art. International artists display their works for free in a stylish exhibition space. *Sunny Towers | 43 Ashutosh Chowdhury Avenue | www.cimaartindia.com*

CHENNAI AND THE SOUTH

For many people only the south is the "real" India: jungles, green mountains and endless beaches. Temple towers stretching skywards above coconut palm groves are characteristic features, and this is where Ayurveda has its roots. Unlike in the north of India, the winters here are pleasantly warm by European standards. Hindi is not spoken here, but Kannada, Telugu, Tamil and Malayalam – all languages of Dravidian origin. But despite their many similarities the four southern states Karnataka, Kerala, Tamil Nadu and little Goa are very different. Traditionally a region of spices and silk, Karnataka's capital, Bangalore, has developed into an important centre of India's high-tech industry. Goa did not become part of the Republic of India until 1961 and, in 1987, the area became a state of its own. Magnificent beaches and a Portuguese-influenced culture have attracted sun-seeking hedonists since the hippie era. Kerala, where you can enjoy a relaxing holiday on a house boat in the backwaters, offers miles of sandy beaches, the highest rate of alphabetisation in India and the lowest unemployment figures and is most progressive on the topic of equality for women. Tamil Nadu, Kerala's neighbouring state, is famous for its Dravidian temple architecture which can be marvelled at in particular in Kanchipuram, Mahabalipuram, Madurai and Thanjavur.

You can learn a lot more about this region from the MARCO POLO "India South".

India's south offers a mixture of spices and silk, high-tech and Dravidian temples, the Backwaters and the beaches of Goa

BANGALORE

(194 C2) (*F14*) **The capital of South West India, Karnataka (pop. 8.5 million), is now a symbol of India's entry into the high-tech sector, spearheaded by the computer and software industry as well as space exploration.**

Some areas however still have the charm of a garden city. In the 19th century the British colonial government chose to make Bangalore its administrative

CITY **WHERE TO START?**
Mahatma Gandhi Road (MG Road): Start exploring Bangalore by taking a stroll down MG Road towards Cubbon Park. The old part of the city south of the station is best reached by Metro or by auto rickshaw along with the botanical garden Lalbagh, from which you have a good view of the city.

Call centre in Bangalore – this city symbolises India's high-tech boom

centre on account of its pleasant climate at an altitude of 1,000 m/3,281 ft. What is left of the old fort can be seen in the *market area*. This is where there are narrow alleyways, noisy bazaars full of different smells, and countless shop signs written in the curly Urdu and Kannada script. *MG Road* with its deafening traffic and the slightly quieter roads off it, on the other hand, are dominated by neon adverts, pizzerias, elegant restaurants, bars and shops. In the near future, it should be possiuble to avoid the chaotic traffic conditions on the streets of Bangalore: the long-awaited extension of the metro system is planned to be completed by 2021.

SIGHTSEEING

INSIDER TIP LALBAGH

Hyder Ali, the infamous former ruler of Mysore, a warrior and scourge of the British, commissioned *The Red Garden* at the end of the 18th century. The name is a reference to Hyder's love of roses. The park includes a beautiful botanical collection and a glasshouse.

NANDI TEMPLE

A green mountain ridge rises up at the edge of the city – the *Nandi Hills*. The journey to the hills is an experience in itself. On arrival you are rewarded not only by magnificent views and fresh mountain air but also by the impressive Nandi Temple. The impressive, huge, monolithic, granite sculpture of a Nandi bull, the riding animal of Shiva, stands outside the 16th-century Dravidian temple.

INSIDER TIP TIPU SULTAN'S PALACE

In the 18th century Hyder Ali and his son Tipu Sultan had a beautifully proportioned palace built within the fort from 1537 that they had had restored, complete with teak columns and pretty decoration. Also the little museum is worth seeing. *Daily 8.30am–5.30pm | Albert Victor Road | Tipu Nagar*

VIDHANA SOUDHA

The seat of the state legislature of Karnataka is India's largest government building. The foundation stone was

CHENNAI AND THE SOUTH

laid in 1951 by none other than Prime Minister Jawaharlal Nehru. With its idiosyncratic architectural style that can best be described as Neo-Dravidian or Indo-Saracenic, the building is a highly visible statement of the self-assuredness demonstrated by the young republic at that time. You are not permitted to enter the building to take a look around, but it is attractively illuminated after dark. *Next to Cubbon Park | diagonally opposite the main post office*

FOOD & DRINK

CAFE MAX

The roof restaurant of the *Max Mueller Bhavan* – the local name for the Goethe Institute – offers a culinary version of its German courses: Jägerschnitzel [escapole chasseur] and fried sausages. The restaurant has been a hit with local inhabitants for many years. *716, CMH Road | Indiranagar | tel. 080 41 20 04 69 | Moderate*

HARD ROCK CAFÉ BENGALURU

Although you have not come to India to go to an American restaurant chain, this café is well worth a visit just for its historical building which formerly housed the Tract and Book Society. In the evening, you can eat burgers to the accompaniment of live music. *40 St. Marks Road/ MG Road | tel. 080 41 24 22 22 | Moderate*

MAVALLI TIFFIN ROOMS

In 1924, this location was still known as the Brahmin Coffee Club serving only filter coffee and south Indian idlis (fluffy pastry balls with cashew nuts and coriander). The latter are still popular here alongside the spicy masala dosas. *14 Lalbagh Road | tel. 080 22 22 00 22 | www. mavallitiffinrooms.com | Moderate*

KARAVILLI RESTAURANT

The popular restaurant is well-known for its delicious seafood cooked according to south-west Indian recipes. The antique furniture is a striking feature. *In The Gate-*

MARCO POLO HIGHLIGHTS

BANGALORE

way Hotel Residency Road | 66 Residency Road | tel. 080 66 60 45 45 | *Moderate*

SHOPPING

Shopaholics will find paradise in *Commercial Road* and the districts *Chikpet* and *Indiranagar*. The malls such as *UB City* offer more luxury and air-conditioning.

CAUVERY ARTS AND CRAFTS EMPORIUM

Offers typical silks and regional items made of sandalwood, as well as crafts from all over India. *49, MG Road*

WHERE TO STAY

HIGHGATES

A heritage hotel from the colonial period which has enhanced its original charm with modern luxury. It is one of the oldest hotels in Bangalore.
40 rooms | 33, Church Street | tel. 080 40 22 29 99 | www.highgateshotel.com | Budget–Moderate

INSIDER TIP LEELA PALACE BANGALORE

Elaborate Indian workmanship, the charm of the Orient, the abundance of flowers and the creature comforts of the 21st century all make this heritage-style hotel one of the best in India. *252 rooms | 23, Kodihalli, Old Airport Road | tel. 080 25 21 12 34 | www.theleela.com | Expensive*

VILLA POTTIPATI

A boutique hotel in a villa dating from the 19th century with matching furniture and décor. Located slightly out of town, it is blissfully peaceful. With swimming pool. *8 rooms | 21, 4th Main Rd, Malleshwaram West | tel. 080 23 36 07 77 | www. neemranahotels.com | Moderate*

INFORMATION

GOVERNMENT OF INDIA TOURIST OFFICE

48, Church Street | tel. 080 25 58 30 30

KARNATAKA STATE TOURISM DEVELOPMENT CORPORATION

The day-trips to Mysore, Belur, Halebidu and Shravanabelagola can be recommended. Trips to Hampi can also be booked here. *Badami House/NR Square | facing BBMPI | tel. 080 43 34 43 34 | www. karnatakatourism.org*

WHERE TO GO

BELUR (194 B2) (ΩΩ E14)

The numerous friezes of reliefs, large sculptures and exquisite decoration make the temples of Belur among the artistically most important in India. Created during the Hoysala dynasty (11th–14th centuries), the sheer number of figures and the precision of their execution are fascinating.

The building of the big Vishnu temple *Channeskeshava* took 100 years. It was erected to commemorate a victory by the Hoysala army over the Chola rulers. The temple is completely covered with figures. Its star-shaped plan includes lots of niches and large areas on the façade for depictions of around 650 elephants (a symbol of the power of the monarch), gracious women and erotic games. Even the king and queen are shown naked. *215 km/134 mi west*

HALEBID ★ (194 B1–2) (ΩΩ E14)

In 1311, Halebid – the capital of the Hoysala Empire – was sacked by the Muslim troops of the Sultan of Delhi. The temple complexes however survived. The main temple Hoysaleshvara has several depictions of sexual acts.

The smaller Vijayanatha temple was built by the Jains in the 16th century and includes the tall sculpture of a naked Shantinatha, the "ford maker". Do not miss the small but exquisite collection of sculptures in the *Archaeological Museum (Sat–Thu 10am–5pm)*. The best place to stay is *The Gateway Hotel Chikmagalur (29 rooms and cottages | tel. 08262 66 06 60 | www.gateway.tajhotels.com | Expensive)*, near Chikmagalur and surrounded by beautiful countryside; with pool. *230 km/143 mi west*

SHRAVANABELAGOLA ⭐
(194 C2) (*ⁿ F14*)

Here you have to take off your shoes and climb the 614 stone steps up Indragiri, just like pilgrims have done for more than a thousand years. The 17 m/55.8 ft high monolithic statue of the naked ascetic and meditating Jain saint, Gomateshwara, carved out of the rocky peak is entwined by greenery. Every twelve years thousands of clay pots filled with liquid ghee (butter fat) and milk are doused on the statue – even from a helicopter – as well as flowers and paint, during a huge festival. The next time will be in 2029. *125 km/78 mi west*

CHENNAI (MADRAS)

⬚ MAP ON P. 125
(195 E2) (*ⁿ H14*) **The sixth-largest Indian metropolis (pop. 4.7 million, with its conurbations, almost 9 million) is primarily the location of multinational businesses. The cityscape of business highrises conceals a number of small jewels from the colonial era. The former Madras is also a good base for trips to the Coromandel Coast and**

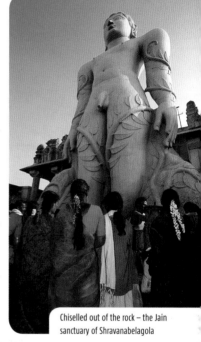

Chiselled out of the rock – the Jain sanctuary of Shravanabelagola

other destinations in the eastern part of southern India.

Chennai, that was ruled by the Portuguese in the 16th century and the British from the 18th–20th centuries, still boasts several buildings from the 17th century.

> ### 🏙 WHERE TO START?
> **Fort St. George:** the centrally located iconic administration building is the perfect starting point for a walk through the old business district *George Town* north of the Central Station. The main arterial road *Anna Salai* running south-west from the Fort leads to the modern part of Chennai.

It enjoys a pleasant tropical climate and has a 13 km/8.1 mi long beach, Marina Beach. The proud residents of Tamil Nadu's capital city speak Tamil and do not like being told what to do by a central government in the north.

● Auto rickshaws are ideal for a sightseeing trip. The three-wheeled vehicles will get you everywhere quickly and are

century). *Sat–Thu 9.30am–5pm | Pantheon Road*

FILM CITY CHENNAI

You can walk at your leisure around the props in the AVM Studios and watch films being made. Check first by phone to see if the studios are open. There is also a go-cart track on the site. *Mon–Sat 9am–9pm |*

Riding a scooter in a sari is an everyday occurence in Chennai

unbeatably cheap. You can even sweep up outside luxury hotels in a rickshaw too – many wealthy Indians do.

SIGHTSEEING

CHENNAI GOVERNMENT MUSEUM

A skeleton of an elephant, botanical exhibits, contemporary art – there's lots to see here. The Archaeological Museum boasts one of the best collections of ancient Indian bronze sculptures (11th

38, Arcot Road | Vadapalani | 10 km/6.2 mi from Chennai | tel. 044 42 13 67 00

FORT ST GEORGE

Prior to the completion of this building in 1644, the British East India Company had only operated from trading posts and St George was their first stronghold. Now the government utilises the buildings that do not look anything like a real fort: the *Fort House* is for example painted white and slate grey. There is a memo-

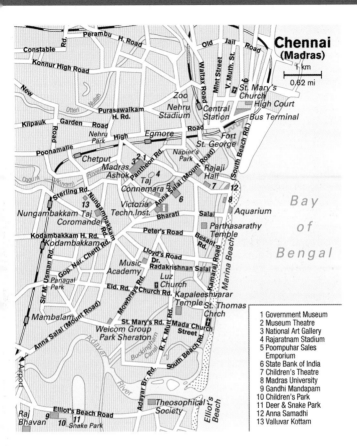

Chennai (Madras)

1 km
0.62 mi

Bay
of
Bengal

1 Government Museum
2 Museum Theatre
3 National Art Gallery
4 Rajaratnam Stadium
5 Poompuhar Sales
   Emporium
6 State Bank of India
7 Children's Theatre
8 Madras University
9 Gandhi Mandapam
10 Children's Park
11 Deer & Snake Park
12 Anna Samadhi
13 Valluvar Kottam

rial plaque in *St Mary's Church* (1680) to the English Governor of Bengal, Robert Clive – Clive of India – who got married here, and to Elihu Yale, the founder of the American university of the same name. The *High Court* (1892), to the north of the fort, is a typical building of the colonial period with domes, arched windows and a red and white façade. The *Fort Museum* (Sat–Thu 10am–5pm) is a treasure trove of items related to India's history.

GUINDY NATIONAL PARK

Covering an area of just 1.2 mi² this na-tional park is the only one in the coun-try that is near a major metropolis. By changing the status of the former hunt-ing ground into a national park in the year 1978, the tropical dry forest has been preserved. *From sunrise to sunset | Sardar Vallabhai Patel Road | short.travel/ind12*

ST THOMAS CHURCH

The Roman-Catholic church in the south of *Kamarajar Salai* was only built around 1890, although many seem to think it is the tomb of St Thomas, who allegedly came to India in 52 AD.

CHENNAI (MADRAS)

KAPALEESWARAR TEMPLE
The 300-year-old Shiva temple with its steep-sided tower covered with sculptures is in the southern part of Mylapore. Only Hindus may go inside.

FOOD & DRINK

ANNALAKSHMI
Mouthwatering south Indian cuisine in a restaurant with a special concept: the profits are donated to charitable organisations. *804, Anna Salai Road | tel. 044 28 52 51 09 | Moderate*

DYNASTY
This restaurant serves good Chinese and southern Indian dishes and is popular among the locals. It has a good reputation for its quick and friendly service. In *Harrisons Hotel | 315, Valluvar Kottam High Road | Anna Nagar | tel. 044 42 22 27 77 | Moderate*

PREMS GRAAMA BHOJANAM
Simple but colourful: here you can eat basic food in rural home cooking style with both north and south Indian recipes. *19, Sardar Patel Road | 1st floor | next to GRT Jewellers | Adyar | tel. 09840 06 27 72 | Budget*

INSIDER TIP RAINTREE
This restaurant in the traditional Vivanta Connemara hotel also sets up a buffet in the garden in the evening to accompany dancing and folk music performances. *Binny Road | tel. 044 66 00 00 00 | Moderate–Expensive*

UDIPI HOME MATHYSA
It is said that the best vegetarian curries in the city are served here. There is certainly an amazingly wide choice and a cosy atmosphere. *1, Hall's Road | Egmore | tel. 044 28 19 20 30 | Budget*

SHOPPING
You can buy good-quality, multicoloured, checked cotton material in Chennai which is actually woven here. The silks and hand-woven silk saris from the temple city of *Kanchipuram*, 70 km/43.5 mi away, are famous. Bespoke tailoring can be found on *Anna Salai Road* in particular. Head for the same road for trendy design articles from India: the shop INSIDER TIP *Play Clan (Teynampet | 044 28 30 99 99 | www.theplayclan.com)* is part of the Rain Tree Hotel and sells colourful accessories, designed with a lot of Indian aplomb and a healthy dollop of irony. Funny artworks that tell stories of Indian everyday life decorate iPhone covers, traditional wedding trumpeters or boxer shorts. There are other branches in Delhi, Mumbai, Goa, Kochi, Pune and Pondicherry.

ENTERTAINMENT
In Chennai you have the choice between classical Indian music played on traditional instruments and *Bharata Natyam* – classical Indian dancing. You'll find bars and clubs especially in luxury hotels. Check out *The Leather Bar* and *The B Bar*.

WHERE TO STAY

NEW WOODLANDS
With a garden, restaurant, small pool. *172 rooms | 72–75, Dr. Radhakrishnan Road | tel. 044 28 11 31 11 | www.new woodlands.com | Budget*

NILGIRI'S NEST
A hotel close to Marina Beach wth a good restaurant. *38 rooms| 105, Dr. Radhakrishnan Salai | tel. 044 28 11 51 11 | nilgirisnest@sify.com | Budget*

RESIDENCY ☼

There is a good view from the upper floors of this hotel. It has a popular restaurant. Advance reservation essential! *112 rooms | 49, GN Chetty Road | tel. 044 28 25 34 34 | www.theresidency.com |* *Moderate*

VIVANTA CONNEMARA

The most traditional hotel in Chennai, partly Victorian, partly Art Deco. *Pool. 150 rooms and suites | Binny Road | tel. 044 66 00 00 00 | www.vivantabytaj. com | Expensive*

INFORMATION

GOVERNMENT OF INDIA TOURIST OFFICE
154, Anna Salai | tel. 044 28 46 14 59 | www.incredibleindia.org | information counter also at the airport

WHERE TO GO

KANCHIPURAM (195 E2) (*Ⓜ H14*)
The former capital of the Kingdom of Pallava, now called Kanchi for short (pop. 165,000), is one of the seven holy cities of India. In addition, the INSIDER TIP best silk weaving is done here – and was first woven for the kings of Pallava in the 6th–9th centuries. There were reputedly more than 1,000 temples in Kanchipuram; today, 124 remain. The *gopurams*, typical southern Indian temple towers, stand out from afar. There are always crowds of pilgrims in Kanchi who come to worship Vishnu and Shiva.

Shri Ekambaranathar Temple, a Shiva temple with a 59 m/193.6 ft high *gopuram*, dates from the 16th century and is one of the most important temples. Non-Hindus are not allowed inside but are welcome to go to the temple pond which is full of holy fish and to the holy mango tree which bears four different types of mango on four branches, symbolising the four *Vedas* (religious texts).

Kailasanatha Temple (7th century) is a good example of early Dravidian art. Although the ornamental sandstone work has weathered, the painting inside gives an idea of its former glory.

Kanchipuram is still a much-visited pilgrim centre even today

Old Goa – white Baroque churches above the trees on the banks of the Mandovi

The monumental temple *Dewarajas-wami (Varadaraja)* is a masterpiece of Vijayanagara architecture from around 1500. Lions and other impressive stone sculptures decorate the hall with 96 pillars (called the "Thousand Pillar Hall"). *The temples are generally closed from noon–4pm.*

Comfort at favourable prices which is also "eco friendly" can be found at *Pinetree* 🌿 *(New No. 20, Old No. 73c/1a, Mettu Street | tel. 083 00 04 72 72 | www. pinetree.co.in | Budget). 70 km/43.5 mi south-west*

GOA

(190–191 C–D5) *(🕮 D13)* **"The Pearl of the Orient" is what the Portuguese called Goa and held onto the territory as a colony for 450 years.**

This little state covering a mere 1,429 mi² has only been part of the Republic of India since 1961. Goa (pop. 1.5 million) is – unlike other regions in India – not too densely populated, nor does it have any large conurbations. Most of all, however, it boasts a cultural heritage from two different worlds – the old Indian one that was not suppressed despite centuries of being a colony, and the Iberian-Portuguese culture. Apart from the 100 km/62 mi long coastal strip of beaches lined with wonderful palm trees and bays, some of which are romantic while others were ruined in the hotel boom, you can also visit churches, temples and markets.

The hippies first came to Goa more than forty years ago. They made it well known in Europe and the USA and the craving for sun and sea led to mass tourism, much to the dislike of some locals. Not least because of the environmental problems – the water supply for example could not cope and in several places far too many buildings shot up too quickly. Newer hotels are no longer being built right on the sandy beaches now, but behind a belt of palm trees, some 200 m/650 ft from the crashing waves.

Lots of little shops selling all sorts of bits and bobs have set themselves up in the towns. Further inland from Goa, the area has not been spoilt by tourism. Even the capital *Panjim (Panaji)*, with a population of around 100,000, has retained something of its provincial charm.

Goa's coastal plain rises to the east across forested slopes up to the Deccan Plateau. From here, rivers make their way down to the sea where they form wide bay-like estuaries – divine for secluded boat trips through the mangrooves.

SIGHTSEEING

SHREE BRAHMA TEMPLE

Rare Brahma temple, the idol probably dates from the 5th century *7 km/4.4 mi east of Valpoi in north-east Goa | near Karnataka*

SHREE MANGESHI TEMPLE

Typical Goa temple architecture with a seven-storey lantern tower in the courtyard. *Priol | 22 km/13.7 mi east of Panjim*

VELHA GOA (OLD GOA)

White Baroque churches gleam from among their seemingly endless green on the bank of the wide Mandovi River. This was once the capital of Portuguese India. What remain are the churches and church ruins surrounded by large areas of lawn. One is dedicated to Saint Francis Xavier (1506–52), the patron saint of Goa. Silver reliquaries and the saint's sarcophagus are housed in the *Basilica of Bom Jesus*.

The *Sé (cathedral)* with its high nave and gilded altars (1562–1619) is in the centre of Old Goa. Just a short walk away is the almost empty *Church of St Francis of Assisi* (1661) with murals depicting scenes from the saint's life. The *Archaeological Museum (Sat–Thu 10am–5pm)* in the

monastery has a portrait collection and items from the days before Goa became a Portuguese colony. The *Church of St Cajetan* which contains the tombs of the archbishops and viceroys is a copy in miniature of St Peter's in Rome. Barbaric trials were held here by the Inquisition. *10 km/6.2 mi east of Panaji*

FOOD & DRINK

Local specialities include pork dishes, often with the fiery *vindaloo* sauce, lamb or fish, marinated to make a spicy *xacuti* curry, as well as sausages and food cooked in coconut milk *(foogaths)*. *Bebinca* (made of flour, eggs and coconut milk) *or dodol,* a sweet delicacy made with cashew nuts, can be recommended as desserts.

MUSTARD

"France embraces Bengal" is the motto of this restaurant situated 15 km/9.3 mi from Panaji and beach locations such as Baga, Calangute and Anjuna. The décor is in fact just as reminiscent of a French cottage as the menu.You must try the *Chingri Maacher Malaikari* – golden-yellow giant king prawns cooked in coconut milk and fine spices. *House No. 78 Mae dey Deus Vaddo, Chogm Road, Sangolda | tel. 09823 43 61 20 | www.mustardrestau rants.in | Moderate*

BEACHES & ACTIVITIES

When people talk about "the beaches", they are usually referring to *Calangute* north of the capital Panjim and *Colva* towards the south. Each beach has its own special features. To the west of Panjim you will find *Dona Paula* and *Miramar*, lined by palm trees. North of Calangute is *Baga* – although the beach here is not so inviting. This is made up for by the popular clubs such as stylish *Tito's* and the slightly wilder *Café Mambo (tel. for both 0982276 50 02)* right next door. Lots of people visit *Anjuna* especially for its hippie flea market, which is held every Wednesday on the red cliffs. Hire a scooter and combine shopping in Anjuna with a tour along the coast.

In small *Arambol*, you will encounter hedonists and old and new hippies: here various activities are on offer ranging from Yoga and Tantra courses to Russian vodka parties. *Majorda* marks the start of lovely beaches south of the capital Panjim. You can hire bicycles in *Benaulim*

LOW BUDGET

The colourful Indian temple festivals are all free of charge. If you happen to be in Kerala in the spring, check the dates for Pooram. The elephant festival around Thrissur is particularly spectacular. *www.keralatourism.org/festivalcalendar*

On the beaches in the north of Goa, many tailors have set up stands and specialise in T-shirts with designs ranging from hip logos to classic sunsets. You can ask for whatever motif you want. Price: 240–400 rupees. Masses of stands can also be found in *Anjuna* and on the road to Mapusa.

Locals come to paddle or to picnic to *Veli Tourist Village* near Kerala's capital *Thiruvananthapuram*. The entrance fee costs just 5 rupees. On the edge of the picturesque lake you can see several modern sculptures. *Daily 8am–7.30pm | tel. 0471 250 0785*

to visit the restaurants on the beaches and take advantage of the many water-sports activities on offer – from a brief jump with a paraglide to jet-skiing over the waves. Especially romantic sunsets and live music can be enjoyed in *Palolem* with its characteristic cliffs and sandy beach. INSIDERTIP Silent Noise Parties *(every Sat evening except during the monsoon period | www.silentnoise.in)* at Neptune Point use a technical trick to get round the ban on parties under the stars with loud music after 10pm that applies to Goa. Wireless headphones enable raves to be held just like in the good old days of the legendary "full moon parties". If you find Palolem located in a crescent-shaped bay too overrun with tourists, you can stay in the neighbouring *Patnem* or *Agonda*. No shoes, no shows – things are much quieter on the two beaches with powdery sand.

In ● *Neomi's Hair & Beauty Salon (Navelkar Legend | Dhempe College Road | Miramar | Panjim | tel. 077 74 00 65 91 | www.neomissalonandspa.com)* Neomi and Mario Barneto have been offering beauty, spa and wellness treatments for over 20 years. In addition to the main branch in Panjim, the couple have additional salons in Ponda and Calangute.

WHERE TO STAY IN AND NEAR PANJIM

You can find attractive and favourably priced B&Bs and guesthouses primarily in the *Fontainhas* district. There are several comfortable hotels around *Church Square*.

CIDADE DE GOA
The brilliant colours and alcoves are highly reminiscent of Portugal. After dining in one of the five restaurants, you can work off the calories on the tennis court and in

the pool. *210 rooms | Vainguinim Beach | Dona Paula | 7 km/4.4 mi from Panjim | tel. 0832 2 45 45 45 | www.cidadedegoa. com | Expensive*

HOTEL MANVIN'S ☆

Spacious rooms, many with a view of the garden and river. Located on the 4th and 5th floors of a high-rise. *45 rooms | Municipal Gardens/Church Square | tel. 0832 2 22 83 05 | www.goamanvins.com | Budget*

INSIDER TIP ▶ PANJIM INN/POUSADA/PEOPLES

These three buildings in the picturesque historical district of Fontainhas have all been lovingly restored. Antique furniture and courteous service. *13 rooms | tel. 0832 2 22 11 22 | www.panjiminn.com | Moderate–Expensive*

WHERE TO STAY NEAR THE BEACHES TO THE NORTH

It is a great advantage to be able to leap out of the bamboo hut on the beach straight into the sea. An equally charming district features brightly painted Goan houses amidst the green jungle of the hinterland. Some of these houses can be rented complete on a weekly basis. Simply ask at cafés in your choice of location to find out which are still unoccupied. Many families have transformed their Portuguese-style villas into smart boutique homestays.

COCO BANANA

Everyone enjoys staying with Walter. No wonder, as the pretty house with a garden is simply charming: bright, clean and realtively quiet for Calangute. The beach is just round the corner. *6 rooms | Golden Beach Street | tel. 0832 2 27 90 68 | short. travel/ind9 | Budget*

Crafts for sale on the beach of Anjuna

HOLIDAY VILLAGE/FORT AGUADA BEACH RESORT

If you are travelling with children, the *Holiday Village* on the beach of Sinquerim is the perfect address. The *Fort Aguada Beach Resort* is located close by on the cliffs of the old Portuguese fort. If you want to give yourself a special treat, you can rent one of the Goan-style villas in the garden on the ramparts. *143 rooms, suites and villas | Sinquerim, Bardez | tel. 0832 6 64 58 58 | www.vivantahotels. com | Moderate–Expensive*

THE TAMARIND HOTEL

A boutique hotel with individually furnished rooms ranging from hyper-modern to Portuguese-Mediterranean in a central location in Anjuna: 4 km/2.5 mi to the beach and with a pool. *26 rooms | Kumar Vaddo | Anjuna, Bardez | tel. 09810 80 40 63 | www. thetamarind.com | Moderate*

WHERE TO STAY NEAR THE BEACHES TO THE SOUTH

BHAKTI KUTIR 🌀

Nice and cozy cabanas made of straw and bamboo and a stone hut surrounded by coconut palm trees on the cliff above the beach. Health food restaurant, great breakfast menu, yoga courses. *22 rooms | at south end of Palolem beach | tel. 0832 2 64 34 72 | www.bhaktikutir. com | Budget–Moderate*

COCONUT CREEK

Luxury cottages of elegant design around a pool. 20 minutes on foot to the beach and a short ride in a taxi to Dabolim Airport. The more basic *Joet's Guest House (7 rooms | Moderate)* is right on the beach and run by the same family. *20 rooms | Bimmut Ward, Bogmalo | tel. 0832 2 53 80 90 | www. coconutcreekgoa.com | Expensive*

THE LEELA PALACE ☼

This is pure luxury! The lobby is resplendent in the style of the "City of Victory" – *Vijayanagara* in Karnataka. The pink villas have a view of canals, bridges and gardens. Several bars and restaurants, games and gym club, golf course. *204 rooms, villa and suites | Mobor | Cavelossim/Salcete | tel. 0832 6 62 12 34 | www. theleela.com | Expensive*

PALM GROVE COTTAGES

The friendly proprietors have simple rooms in the old main house and bet-ter equipped rooms in modern auxiliary buildings – all set in a garden full of butterflies. *15 rooms | 1 km/0.6 mi from the beach | H.No 149 | Tambdi Mati | Vaswado, Benaulim | tel. 0832 2 77 00 59 | www. palmgrovegoa.com | Budget*

TURTLE HILL

This is a perfect place for anyone keen on stylish design. The bungalows on the hill above Patnem offer some peace and quiet. Near the beach you wake up to the sounds of the sea. The exterior is made of bamboo and the elegant interior designed by Bernd Slotta. *10 bungalows | Patnem Beach, Palolem | tel. 09421 25 71 64 | www.turtlehillgoa.com | Moderate–Expensive*

INFORMATION

GOA TOURISM DEVELOPMENT CORPORATION LTD.

Offering lots of things for tourists to do. *Paryatan Bhavan, 3rd floor, Patto, Panjim | tel. 0832 2 43 71 32 | www.goa-tourism.com*

GOVERNMENT OF INDIA TOURIST OFFICE

On the 1st floor of the blue-painted *Communidade Building* opposite the *Immaculate Conception Church. Church Square Panjim | tel. 0832 2 22 34 12 | www. tourism.gov.in*

HAMPI

(191 E5) *(𝑚 F13)* **It is the ruins of the now abandoned imperial city of** ★ *Vijayanagara* **that make this remote place (pop. 2,700) so magical.**

The landscape unfurling at the foot of Matanga Hill is almost surreal: a gigantic formation of reddish-brown rocks interspersed by small, graceful stone pavilions. These so-called *Mantapas* are the remains of Vijayanagara, the "city of victory". This was the realm of the Hindu kings of Vijayanagara who reigned over much of southern India with great wealth and pomp from 1336 until their violent demise in 1565. Even the stables for the elephants were more elegant than some of the guesthouses today in Hampi Bazaar. You can access some of the palace and temple ruins within the extensive location

they must have been. *Hazara Rama temple* is nearby with more than 100 scenes from the Indian heroic epic "Ramayana", carved as reliefs around the outer walls. The interior boasts beautifully decorated pillars of black granite.

VIRUPAKSHA TEMPLE

This temple must have attracted pilgrims long before the founding of Vijayanagara in the 14th century. Today, a stream of pilgrims worshipping the Hindu god

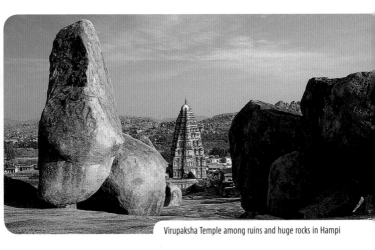
Virupaksha Temple among ruins and huge rocks in Hampi

with an area of 10 mi² by walking along the grey-blue river Tungabhadra (reddish brown during the monsoon) snaking its way across the landscape. Alternatively you can hire a bicycle or rickshaw. Hampi is magical at sunrise and sunset: the *Hanuman Temple* in Anegondi is the most perfect location for great views.

SIGHTSEEING

ROYAL ENCLOSURE

Even though only the foundations of the palaces still exist, with a little imagination you can envisage how magnificent

Shiva, venerated here in his incarnation Virupaksha, continues to make its way here from across southern India. The 56 m/183.7 ft high *gopuram* (temple tower) can be seen from afar rising above the complex which encloses several shrines. The *Ranga Mantapa* (Red Pavilion) of 1510 in particular is well worth seeing. Half of the 38 pillars depict Yali, a mythical lion-like figure. *Sunrise to sunset / at the western end of Hampi Bazaar*

VITTALA TEMPLE

Why didn't the Muslim conquerors destroy this temple too? The 56 fragile pillars, carved from one single block and hollow inside, would have been an easy target for the aggressors. Nowadays, the custodians make desperate attempts at stopping coach loads of tourists from touching these delicate works of art. The richly decorated stone chariot in the courtyard is one of Hampi's emblems. *At the northern end of the ruins, near the river bank*

INSIDER TIP ZENANA ENCLOSURE

Once reserved for the queen and her ladies-in-waiting, this is where you can stroll through Vijayanagara's most exquisite monument, the *Lotus Mahal*, that fuses elements of Indian and Muslim architecture. The name refers to its lotos blossom-shaped plan. *Beyond Hazara Rama temple*

FOOD & DRINK

In the Hampi Bazaar, you will find numerous street food stalls and small restaurants such as *Mango Tree* and *Funky Monkey*. In the *Laughing Buddha* in Virupapur Gaddi, you have a marvellous view on the other side of the river.

WHERE TO STAY

HOTEL MALLIGI
If you find the guesthouses in Hampi too basic, you can book a hotel room in Hospet, 13 km/8.1 mi away. One of the best is the *Malligi* with stylish amenities, a spa and a large pool. *116 rooms | Jabunatha Road | tel. 08394 22 81 01 | www.malligi hotels.com | Budget*

INFORMATION

TOURIST INFORMATION COUNTER
Hampi Bazaar | tel. 08394 24 13 39

KOCHI (COCHIN)

(194 B–C4) (∅ E16) The city that straggles several islands (pop. 2.1 million, including Ernakulam on the mainland) has been heralded the "Queen of the Arabian Sea" for centuries.

Its wealth came from spices that were sent by ship to the Arabian Peninsula and on to Europe.

The oldest part of Kochi, the fort district on the island of Mattancherry, can be reached from *Ernakulam* by taxi or by ferry from the *main boat jetty*. This picturesque area has always been a melting point between the West and the East. Jews and the Portuguese settled here in the 16th century, the Dutch captured the harbour in 1663, the British arrived in 1796. And the Arabs and Chinese were here much earlier.

Surrounded by sea like in a fantasy world, Fort Kochi – with its historical buildings and spice warehouses, gardens and

old trees – one of the cosiest places in southern India. Chinese fishermen's nets hung on hoists next to the promenade along the shore make a perfect holiday shot. Up to six fishermen are needed to operate these wooden constructions that are up to 10 m/32.8 ft high. The day's catch is sold fresh and then grilled on the beach – don't miss trying it.

SIGHTSEEING

BACKWATERS ★ ●

Kochi is one of the best places to access the backwaters, a picturesque network of canals edged with tropical scenery. The best way to explore is to sail on one of the *Kettuvalams,* rice barges transformed into houseboats. Whether you spend a week or only a day slowly drifting past small villages, temples, churches and lush banana plantations, you will lose all sense of time.

DUTCH PALACE ★

The Dutch Palace is one to the oldest buildings still standing constructed by Europeans in India. The old wall paint-ings (including scenes with the Hindu gods Krishna and Rama) are famous, but it is worth visiting for its architecture too. Erected by the Portuguese in 1557 for the Raja of Cochin in exchange for trading privileges, Mattancherry Palace (as it was originally called) was renovated and expanded 100 years later by Dutch conquerors. *Mattancherry | Sat–Thu 10am–5pm*

ST FRANCIS CHURCH

The oldest church has been standing in the fort district since 1503. In 1524 the explorer and later viceroy Vasco da Gama was initially buried here. His mortal remains were later transferred to Portugal in 1538; the tombstone still exists.

SYNAGOGUE

The Jewish quarter is south of *Mattancherry Jetty*. It is now an attractive place to explore simply because of all the different things to be found in the ancient alleyways and old vaulted spice storerooms. The Jewish community built its synagogue in 1568. It was rebuilt in

Near Kottayam – enjoying a relaxing boat trip on the Backwaters

1662 after being destroyed by the Portuguese. In 1760, a rich benefactor, Ezekiel Rahabi, had this house of god decorated

Colourful Kathakali dancer

with blue and white Chinese tiles. Apart from the bright synagogue itself with cut-glass chandeliers, there is an exhibition on the history of the Jewish congregation, which is dwindling in number due to emigration. *Fri–Sun 10am–noon and 3pm–5pm*

FOOD & DRINK

Kerala is the spice garden of India. Fans of cardamom, chilli and ginger will be in seventh heaven. You will be served fish and dishes prepared with coconut milk.

GINGER HOUSE RESTAURANT
The name says it all: everything is cooked with ginger ranging from spicy shrimps to ginger ice cream as a dessert. A historical location in a museum. *Jew Town Mattancherry, Kochi-2 | tel. 0484 2 211145 | www.gingerhousecochin.com | Moderate*

KASHI ART CAFÉ
You will be served with a small dose of art alongside French toast with fresh fruit and homemade cakes. There are temporary exhibitions displayed in the room adjacent to the idyllic inner courtyard with its sculptures. *Fort Kochi | Burgher Street | tel. 0484 2 215769 | www.kashi artgallery.com | Budget*

ENTERTAINMENT

KATHAKALI ★ ●
Famous, colourful dance-dramas from Kerala performed in keeping with ancient traditions. Originally presented in or outside a temple. The voluminous costumes and the thickly applied, colourful make-up make performances extremely hard work for the dancers whose demanding training lasts several years. It is well worth watching the dancers being made up. Content and symbols are usually explained before each performance. Brief performances of the dance-dramas that originally went on for several nights are held for tourists. Traditional dance-dramas have been performed by the *See India Foundation Kathakali Theatre* for more than 30 years under the direction of its principal, Devan. *Every evening | Kalathi Parambil Lane | between Chittor Road and South Ernakulam Junction Railway Station | Ernakulam | tel. 0484 2 376471*

WHERE TO STAY

THE BRUNTON BOATYARD ●
This hotel on Mattancherry promontory is careful not to waste the valuable fresh water without cutting any corners with

regard to comfort. Pool, garden and restaurants. *24 rooms | Fort Kochi | tel. for reservations 0484 2 21 54 61 | www. cghearth.com | Expensive*

INSIDER TIP ▶ THE MALABAR HOUSE

Highly acclaimed designer hotel with garden, pool, works of art, restaurant serving Kerala food with a western touch. *17 rooms | 1/269, Parade Road | tel. 0484 2 21 66 66 | www.malabar house.com | Expensive*

OLD COURTYARD

Traditional rooms of character. Friendly atmosphere, good value for money. *8 rooms | Fort Kochi | 1/371 Princess Street | tel. 0484 2 21 50 35 | www.old courtyard.com | Moderate*

THE SPENCER HOME

This is a family-run hotel in the colonial style with a garden for relaxation. *8 rooms | 1/298, Parade Road | Fort Kochi | tel. 0484 22 10 49 | www.hotelspencer homes.com | Budget*

INFORMATION

GOVERNMENT OF INDIA TOURIST OFFICE

Next to the Taj Malabar Hotel | Willingdon Island | tel. 0484 26 6 91 35

INSIDER TIP ▶ TOURIST DESK

Here, you get reliable information, also for Kathakali performances. *Main boat jetty | Ernakulam | tel. 0484 2 37 17 61*

WHERE TO GO

LAKSHADWEEP (0) (𝄐 C–D 15–17)

You can only reach Lakshadweep and the coral reefs, which lie some 200–300 km/124–186 mi from the coast, from Kochi. Formerly known as the Lacca-

dive, Minicoy and Amindivi Islands, they can only be visited with a special permit so as to protect the tropical environment and its inhabitants. Three of the total of 36 islands – Bangaram, Agatti and Kadmat – are open to those who do not hold an Indian passport. Package tours organised by the official organisations *SPORTS (www.lakshadweeptourism.com)* include such permits. If you are planning your trip yourself, a confirmed booking by a private organisation is a prerequisite for a permit being granted. Applications must be made at least one month before the date of your planned journey. Basic accommodation can be found in the *Agatti Island Beach Resort (19 cottages | short.travel/ind14 | Moderate)*.

MADURAI

(195 D4) (𝄐 G16) The third-largest city in Tamil Nadu (pop. 1 million) has always been a centre for textiles, but is primarily an ancient temple location still visited by millions of pilgrims to honour the goddess Meenakshi.

A number of dynasties have left their mark here such as the Vijayanagaras and Nayaks. One of the exemplary buildings of Dravidian architecture is the *Shri Meenakshi Temple*, but the *Thirumalai Nayakkar Palace* is equally impressive. The Old Town of Madurai is constructed in the form of a mandala with concentric circles surrounding the Shri Meenakshi Temple – apparently due to sacred forces.

SIGHTSEEING

SHRI MEENAKSHI TEMPLE

The extensive, almost square temple site lies in the centre of the Old City. The nine, steep-sided, stepped towers with their flourish of colour and figures of

Meenakshi Amman temple – the nine towers are covered with countless sculptures

bright red, acidic yellow, bilious green and virbrant turquoise gods, animals, demons and strongmen made of granite and plaster, come as a surprise. ✴ It is now possible to climb up the inside of the highest tower (48 m/157.5 ft). Non-Hindus are not allowed to enter the innermost holy site with the shrine of the goddess.

Meenakshi was reputedly the daughter of a king of Pandya and was born with three breasts. It was prophesied that she would gain a normal appearance when her future husband saw her. That was Sundareshwarar, an incarnation of the god Shiva, and the cult of a mother goddess thus entered the patriarchal Hindu religion. The present appearance of the temple dates from the 17th century although its origins stretch back more than 2,000 years. The **INSIDER TIP** *Aayiram Kaal Mandapam*, the "Thousand Pillar Hall", contains the temple's art treasures. *Daily approx. 5am–1.30pm and 4pm–9.30pm | entrance at the south end of the complex*

TAMUKKAM-PALACE

The palace built for Queen Mangammal in the 17th century today houses the *Gandhi Memorial Museum* which tells the story of Gandhi and Indian Independence. *Open daily 10am–1pm and 2pm–5.30pm | Thangaraj Road*

FOOD & DRINK

SURYA ✴

In Hotel *Supreme* you can chose between the restaurant on the ground floor and one on the roof. The fantastic view over the city and the vegetarian food will soon make you forget the heat. You can then chill out in the Apollo 96 bar. *110, West Perumal Maistry Street | tel. 0452 2 34 31 51 | Moderate*

TAJ RESTAURANT

Southern Indian specialities, delicious thalis, excellent meat dishes. The biryani is not too hot. Friendly service. *55/10, Town Hall Road | tel. 0452 2 34 36 50 | Budget*

WHERE TO STAY

PARK PLAZA
Comfortable, close to the station and temple. Roof-top garden. *55 rooms | 114, W Perumal Maistry Road | tel. 0452 4 51 11 11 | www.hotelparkplaza.in | Budget*

THE GATEWAY HOTEL PASUMALAI ❄
You won't find anything better than this in Madurai: with a park, pool and a distant view of the city. *50 rooms | 40, TPK Road | Pasumalai Hill | tel. 0452 6 63 30 00 | www.thegatewayhotels.com | Expensive*

INFORMATION

TOURIST DEPARTMENT MAIN OFFICE
Hotel Tamil Nadu | West Veli St. | tel. 0452 2 33 47 57 | www.tamilnadutourism.org

WHERE TO GO

INSIDER TIP **PERIYAR TIGER RESERVE**
(194 C4) (*Ω F16*)
The wildlife sanctuary covers some 300 mi² – a fine bit of jungle. It was established in 1934 to protect elephants, tigers, panthers and buffalo in their natural habitat. If you take a boat trip across *Periyar* Lake you al-most always see animals on the banks. There are also guided hikes to the elephants and along Tiger Trail, also with tented accommodation for the night. Information: *Wildlife Information Centre in the Aranya Nivas Hotel. The hotel (30 rooms | tel. 04869 22 20 23 | www.ktdc.com/aranyanivas | Moderate– Expensive)* is just above the lake. *150 km/93 mi west*

MAMALLA-PURAM (MAHABALI-PURAM)

(195 E2) (*Ω H14*) **What looks more or less like any other resort (pop. 15,000) with dozens of hotels and restaurants was in fact the flourishing port of the powerful Pallava dynasty between the 6th and 9th centuries AD.**

Through the Pallavas Hindu culture spread as far as Indonesia. Some impressive religious sites dating from this time have survived. Artistic reliefs capture scenes from Indian mythology – some are carved from natural rock faces.

READING: LITERATURE FESTIVALS

The country with the highest rate of illiteracy is simultaneously one of the largest book markets in the world with at least 9,000 publishing houses. Literature festivals are sprouting up everywhere. International Pulitzer and Nobel prize-winners appear alongside new younger authors with critical social texts at the *Jaipur Literature Festival*. Other festivals to note include the *Kolkata Literature Festival* (January), the *Hyderabad Literary Festival* (January), the *Times Literary Carnival in Mumbai* (December) and the *Chandigarh Literature Festival* (November).

SIGHTSEEING

ARJUNA'S PENANCE ⭐

This huge relief (some 30 × 12 m/ 98.4 × 39.4 ft) has been chiselled out of two massive rocks. The gap between

The elephants at Arjuna's Penance are almost life size

them forms part of the composition as it represents the Ganges that was sent to thirsting India from the skies. All the figures of gods and humans in this masterpiece refer to this event. There are some 400 figures – groups of monkeys and elephants, gods and humans. The relief gained its name from the belief that Arjuna from the epic "Mahabharata" is also shown here asking the gods for a divine weapon that would make him invincible. *Arjuna's Penance | at the western end of Shore Temple Road*

SHORE TEMPLE

The main temple next to the sea dates from the 7th century. It is not carved from the cliff face but built of blocks of stone. Once there were seven such temples here. This one is dedicated to Shiva and Vishnu.

MAHISHAMARDINI SHRINE

There are ten cave temples behind the Arjuna relief. The most famous is dedicated to the goddess Mahishamardini (Durga) who is depicted riding a lion and fighting two demons.

PANCHA (PANDAVA) RATHAS

Five (pancha) temples from the 7th century. Each one was carved out of one single stone block in the shape of a chariot (ratha). Their names – Arjuna, Bhima, Nakula, Sahadeva and Yudhi shti-ra – come from the epic "Mahabharata". *South of the town*

FOOD & DRINK/ WHERE TO STAY

INSIDER TIP ▶ FISHERMAN'S COVE

Luxurious resort with a large garden and swimming pool, sports facilities and activities for children where you can really relax. *50 rooms and 38 cottages | 8 km/5 mi) north on Covelong Beach | Kanchipuram District | tel. 044 67 41 33 33 | www.vivantabytaj.com | www.idealresort.com | Expensive*

IDEAL BEACH RESORT

Located right on the beach, this resort also has a pool and garden. *40 rooms | Covelong Road | tel. 044 27 44 22 40 | Moderate*

INDECO MAHABALIPURAM ●

Steve Borgia operates this individually planned resort near Shore Temple, with ayurveda and yoga, pool, multi-cuisine

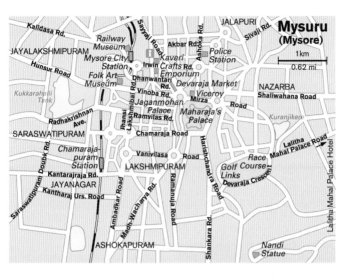

Mysuru (Mysore)

restaurant and museum with British legacies. *30 rooms and suites | Shore Temple Road | tel. 09444 41 03 94 | www.indecohotels.com | Moderate*

MOONRAKERS
This restaurant offers deliciously prepared seafood and serves chilled beer. *34, Othavadai Street | tel. 044 27 44 31 15 | Budget*

INFORMATION

TOURIST OFFICE
Kovalam Road | tel. 044 27 44 22 32 | www.tamilnadutourism.org

MYSORE

⬚⬚ **MAP ON P. 141**
(194 C2) (*ω F15*) **With its wide avenues, palaces and parks, Mysore (pop. 900,000) has preserved something of its old charm as a former royal city.**

However, Bangalore has long since assumed the position of the former Maharaja city as the capital of the state of Karnataka. The "city of sandalwood" is nevertheless a perfect base for trips to the temple sites of *Belur*, *Halebidu* and *Shravanabelagola*. *Chamundi Hill*, its temples and the city's museums are also worth visiting.

SIGHTSEEING

MYSORE PALACE (AMBA VILAS)
When the Maharaja of Mysore's wooden palace was completely destroyed in a devastating fire in 1897, he had an ornate fairytale palace constructed in its place completed by the British architect Henry Irwin in 1912. During festivals and every Sunday evening, the arches, turrets and domes are INSIDERTIP lit up by thousands of lights. The *Kalyana Mantapa,* the royal "marriage hall", is aglow with cut-glass chandeliers of Bohemian glass, Belgian glass mosaics and English floor tiles with peacock motifs; in the

ancillary rooms there are heavy chairs of silver and crystal. The pillars in the *Durbar Hall* (for audiences with the king) on the first floor are painted and ornately gilded. White marble, decorated with pietra dura work with semi-precious stones, heightens the magnificent pomp. The solid silver doors to the *private audience chamber* came from the previous palace that burned down and are therefore much older than everything else. The *museum* of the royal family at the back of the building includes miniature paintings from Tanjore and Kerala as well as private objects and curiosities. *Daily 10.30am–5.30pm*

FOOD & DRINK

PARK LANE HOTEL & RESTAURANT
Local inhabitants also like to come to the restaurant with its roofed beer garden to have a drink. There is a barbecue at the weekend. *Hasha Road | near the palace | tel. 09900 08 2117 | Moderate*

SHILPA SHRI
Tasty meals, also for the European palate, as well as cold beer. With roof terrace. *Gandhi Square | tel. 0824 2 58 97 38 | Budget*

WHERE TO STAY

THE GREEN HOTEL ✪
Stay in a *Chittaranjan palace* set in a park with its own library and a modern, cheaper wing. The hotel is environmentally friendly and its proprietors socially committed. *31 rooms | 2270, Vinoba Road | 5 km/3.1 mi west of the city centre | tel. 0821 4 25 50 00 | www.greenhotel india.com | Budget–Moderate*

LALITHA MAHAL PALACE HOTEL
Nostalgic luxury in the Maharaja's former guesthouse, dining room built in the Classicist style. Pool, large garden. *54 rooms | Sidharta Nagar | 5 km/3.1 mi from the city centre | tel. 0821 2 52 6100 | short.travel/ind15 | Expensive*

The illuminated palace of Mysore – a magnificent background for a group photo

MYSORE BED & BREAKFAST

This B&B is managed with great commitment by Stephen and Manjula: the large dining room where guests meet in the evening to enjoy delicious south Indian food is full of antiques. There is plenty of room to relax either on the roof terrace amidst lots of plants or in the living room. *4 rooms | 163, Moksha Marga, Siddhartha Layout | tel. 09886 70 5179 | www.man julasmysore.in/mysore-bed-and-break fast | Moderate*

INFORMATION

TOURISM OFFICE

Old Exhibition Building | Irwin Road | tel. 0821 2 42 20 96 and 242 36 52

WHERE TO GO

CHAMUNDI HILL (194 C2) (*W F15*)

The Durga temple, *Shri Chamundeshwari*, is on the top of a hill. Its 40 m/131.2 ft high tower is in the characteristic southern Indian style and decorated with a plethora of coloured sculptures. *7 km/4.4 mi south-west*

SOMNATHPUR (194 C2) (*W F15*)

13th-century Chennakesava Temple, which has a star-shaped plan, houses three shrines for Vishnu's different incarnations. Artistic reliefs adorn the external walls. *33 km/20.5 mi south-east*

INSIDER TIP SRIRANGAPATNAM (194 C2) (*W F15*)

The river island has a memorial to Tipu Sultan and his fight against the British – his opponent was none other than the Duke of Wellington who later defeated Napoleon at Waterloo. Fortress, summer palace with a *museum (Sat–Thu 9am–5pm)*, mausoleum, village atmosphere and Hindu sites. *12 km/7.5 mi north*

PONDICHERRY

(195 E2) (*W H15*) The "ville blanche" has a nostalgically French air to it. The "white town" on the coast has a number of colonial buildings, some French street names, churches and museums.

Pondicherry (or Puducherry: pop. 1.2 million) was a French colony until 1965. A canal that has since been filled in, divides the city into two. On one side, Pondicherry has a French feel to it; on the other side, the street scene is Indian through and through.

SIGHTSEEING

AUROBINDO ASHRAM

The politician and philosopher Sri Aurobindo founded his spiritual centre in 1926. He tried to fuse Indian culture with western rationality. After his death in 1950, Mira Richard (1878–1973) – the wife of a French diplomat and soon called "The Mother" in the ashram – took over the management. The graves of both Sri Aurobindo and The Mother are in the ashram courtyard. *Tel. 0413 2 33 63 96 | www.sriaurobindoashram.org*

FOOD & DRINK/ WHERE TO STAY

DUNE DE L'ORIENT

A heritage hotel in colonial building dating from 1760 with a garden and delicious food. *14 rooms and suites | 17, Rue Romain Rolland | tel. 0413 2 65 02 00 | www.dunewellnessgroup.com | Moderate– Expensive*

LE DUPLEIX

As soon as you enter the inner courtyard through the gateway, you can vividly imagine how the former French governor

Dupleix rounded off his evening after an extensive dinner with a glass of red wine. The building is 190 years old and the beautiful rooms with four poster beds are decorated with wooden carvings. *5, Rue De La Caserne | Le Dupleix | tel. 04 13 2 22 60 01 | www.sarovarhotels.com/le-dupleix-pondicherry | Moderate*

WHERE TO GO

AUROVILLE (195 E3) *(⩢ H15)*
Mira Richard founded the town of Auroville, 12 km/7.5 mi from Pondicherry, in 1968 as a project working towards peace and harmony and as a place of experimental coexistence for people who settled here. By now, more than 2,500 people from 52 countries live here. The town was originally designed for 50,000. The community, housed in widely scattered settlements in the forest and extending down to the sea, does not see itself as an object of interest as such. More and more visitors however are coming here now, also to see the architecture of the 30 m/98.4 ft high *Central Globe of Matrimandir*. There are a number of guesthouses, some of which are on the beach. Information in the visitor centre *(www.auroville.org)*.

INSIDER TIP CHIDAMBARAM
(195 E3) *(⩢ H15)*
The large *Nataraja Temple* with its four towers *(daily sunrise–noon and 4pm–9pm)* is impressive. Two of these are covered with figures that depict the 108 positions of the cosmic dance. The god Shiva, to whom the 10th-century temple is dedicated, embodies the dynamic power of fire. There are singing and drum rituals.
Accommodation available in peaceful Ramanathan Mansions *(28 rooms | 127, Bazar Street | tel. 041 44 22 24 11 | Budget)*.

Tourist office in Hotel Tamil Nadu | Railway Feeder Road | tel. 04144 23 87 39). 60 km/37.3 mi south

THANJAVUR (TANJORE)

(195 D3) *(⩢ G16)* **Thanjavur (pop. 220,000) lies at the centre of a huge agricultural area in the delta of the river Kaveri (Cauvery). Until 14th century it was the capital of the Chola dynasty that ruled large areas of southern India.**
Much-admired *Brihadisvara Temple (generally closed from 1pm–3pm)* is decorated with depictions of dancers. 250 Shiva *lingams* (fertility symbols) have survived in shrines on the outer walls. 1,100 years ago, the top portion of the shrine made of one single, 81-tonne block of stone was added. North-east of the temple in the middle of the Old Town is the *palace of the Nayaks (daily 9am–6pm)* dating from the 16th century. Have a look inside *Saraswathi Mahal Library (Thu–Tue 10am–1pm and 1.30pm–5.30pm)* with more than 40,000 books and 8,000 palm leaf manuscripts. The *Art Gallery* has a collection of bronze sculptures from the 9th–12th centuries; the *Royal Museum* houses exhibits from the 19th and 20th centuries. Lovely views can be enjoyed from the ☆ *Bell Tower*.
Low-priced rooms and a friendly atmosphere can be found in the hotel *Valli (20 rooms | 2948 M.K.M Road | not far from the station | tel. 0436 2 23 15 80 | Budget*. The roof terrace and restaurant compensate for the less than inviting impression you have from the street.
Information available in the *TTDC Tourist Office (in Hotel Tamil Nadu | Gandhiji Rd. | tel. 0436 2 23 09 84)*. 35 km/21.8 mi north-east, near Kumbakonam, is the

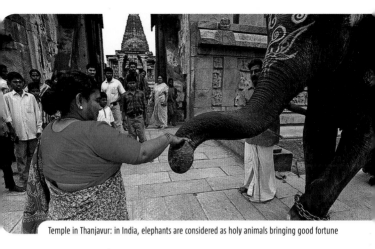

Temple in Thanjavur: in India, elephants are considered as holy animals bringing good fortune

small town of INSIDER TIP *Swamimalai* in a park-like setting. It is famous for the thousand-year-old tradition of making bronze icons. This is a good starting point for trips to the temples of the Chola dynasty and the villages in the Cauvery delta, one of the rice and grain belts in India. Stay the night in the idyllically situated *Indeco Hotel Anandham Swamimalai (24 rooms | tel. 09444 41 03 94 | www.indecohotels.com | Budget–Moderate)*, with bungalows, Ayurveda, musical and cultural events and excellent food.

THIRUVANAN-THAPURAM (TRIVANDRUM)

(194 C5) (*M F17*) **The capital of the state of Kerala (pop. 750,000) in south India is characterised by modern architecture and expanses of green.**
260-year-old *Padmanabhaswamy Temple*, in which jewels and gold valued at more than two billion dollars were found

in the cellar in 2011, is only open to Hindus. The colourful bazaar, the exquisite collection of bronzes in the *Napier Museum (Tue, Thu–Sun 10am–5pm, Wed 1pm–5pm | Museum Road, near the zoo)* and the Kalaripayattu Centre *CVN Kalari Sangham (tel. 0471 2 47 41 82)* for the ancient INSIDER TIP acrobatic martial art of Kerala, are all well worth a visit. The nearby beaches are tempting too – such as *Kovalam Beach*.

FOOD & DRINK

INSIDER TIP INDIAN COFFEE HOUSE
The scent of hot *dosas* (south Indian pancakes) and coffee rises up through the spiral room in the café. The striking brick-red house in helical form was designed by the British-Indian architect Laurie Baker MBE. *Maveli Café | at the KSRTC bus station | tel. 0471 3 21 45 05 | Budget*

WHERE TO STAY

AMBADI GUEST HOUSE
Homely atmosphere, excellent south Indian cooking. Siddhà centre (pre-Ayurve

da medicine and spa). *12 rooms | Poozhi-kunnu Ind. Estate | edge of town | tel. 0471 2 49 37 12 | Budget*

ARYA NIWAS

Its central location near the train and bus station, the cleanliness of the rooms and the restaurant, all speak in favour of this hotel. *24 rooms | Aristo Junction | tel. 0471 2 33 07 89 | Budget*

INSIDER TIP NIKKI'S NEST ⊘ ≥≤

The beautiful resort with cottages, chalets and rooms in the main building lies on a slope above the wide expanse of beach at Kovalam some 15 km/9.3 mi from Thiru-vananthapuram. Very good food, Ayurveda, yoga and meditation. The Duke's Forest Lodge in Anappara also belongs. *47 rooms | Azhimala Shiva Temple Road | Pulinkudi, Chowara | tel. 0471 26 78 22 | www.nikkisnest.com | Expensive*

SOMATHEERAM

Beach resort with attractive bungalows built in typical Kerala style. Find relaxation with Ayurveda treatments or Yoga classes. *46 rooms | Chowara | tel. 0471 2 26 81 01 | www.somatheeram.in | Moderate–Expensive*

INFORMATION

TOURIST OFFICES

*1. Park View | opposite the museum | also at airport | tel. 0471 2 32 11 32;
2. KTDC | Mascot Square | tel. 0471 2 72 12 43 | www.keralatoursim.org*

WHERE TO GO

KANYAKUMARI ★ (194 C5) (ɰ F17)

The subcontinent ends to the south, and there is nothing between you and the Antarctic except the ocean. Highly venerated religious sites were established in Kanyakumari. Even the numerous hotels and busloads of pilgrim tourists cannot spoil the special atmosphere of this site. The temple dedicated to the virgin (kanya) goddess Kumari is at the southern-most point (only accessible to Hindus). Even though it is perhaps not very reassuring to see the lifejackets being repaired on the pier: A boat trip to one of the rocks off shore where Swami Vivekananda (1863–1902), the Indian who revived the status of Hinduism, meditated and has been given an impressive sacred monument, can be recommended. *Approx. 100 km/62 mi south-east*

PADMANABHAPURAM PALACE (194 C5) (ɰ F17)

This ancient palace of the Travancore rulers is well worth a visit to see the richly carved architecture, the mural art and the picturesque halls and courtyards. *Tue–Sun 9am–5pm | 65 km/40.4 mi south*

TIRUCHIRAP-PALLI (TRICHY)

(195 D3) (ɰ G15–16) Most of the diamonds produced in India come from this busy city at the heart of Tamil Nadu (pop. 850,000), but Trichy is first and foremost one of the most significant temple sites in south India.

SIGHTSEEING

ROCK FORT TEMPLE ≥≤

437 steps lead to the top of the site from where you have a wonderful view. For a small donation, visitors are sometimes even allowed inside *Tayumanasvami Temple* half way up and in *Vinayaka Temple* at the top. Both are dedicated to Shiva. The fort was built around 1660.

The cave temples from the Pallava dynasty with their beautiful stone carvings are about 1,000 years older.

SRIRANGAM TEMPLE

This extensive site (700 × 900 m / 2,297 × 2,953 ft) is a temple city 4 km/2.5 mi from Tiruchirappalli dating from the 14th–17th centuries. It is dedicated to Vishnu but its decorative ornamentation depicts many different gods and heroes. The highest tower (73 m/239.5 ft) above the south entrance was restored in 1987 to its former very colourful glory with funding from Unesco. 21 temple towers rise above the site; a festive hall with 904 pillars is impressive. The neighbouring site with the smaller Jambukeshvara (Shiva) temple is just as old.

FOOD & DRINK

Simple, cheap restaurants can be found near the bus stop on *Rockin's Road*.

WHERE TO STAY

KVM HOTEL

This hotel has modern furnished rooms with attractive decorative elements as well as a restaurant, which offers south Indian specialities. *36 rooms | 140, Amma Mandapam, Srirangam | 500 m/1,640 ft from the temple | tel. 0431 4 03 62 22 | www.kvmhotels.com | Budget*

SANGAM

The best hotel in town with a swimming pool and a multi-cuisine restaurant. *90 rooms | Collector's Office rd. | tel. 0431 4 24 45 55 | www.hotelsangam.com | Moderate*

INFORMATION

TOURIST OFFICE

101, Williams Road | tel. 0431 2 46 01 36 (also at the station and airport)

In Kanyakumari the sub-continent ends at the most southern tip of India

DISCOVERY TOURS

① INDIA AT A GLANCE

START: ① Mumbai
END: ㉒ Varanasi

Distance:
🔁 approx. 9,200 km/5,717 mi

28 days
Actual driving time
156 hours (incl. 48 hours on a houseboat)

COSTS: approx. 324,000 INR per person (not in the high season, incl. flights, train tickets, meals, entrance fees, additional travelling costs, excluding car rental)

WHAT TO PACK: Clothes for warm and cold temperatures, sun protection, light and stable footwear, swimming gear, mosquito repellant, earplugs for night travel and food supplies

IMPORTANT TIPS: Allow plenty of time while travelling. Flights from Khajuraho to Varanasi only operate on Mon, Wed and Sun. If not otherwise specified, travel by taxi to the next starting point on the tour. Several journeys are undertaken on night trains.

Would you like to explore the places that are unique to this region? Then the Discovery Tours are just the thing for you – they include terrific tips for stops worth making, breathtaking places to visit, selected restaurants and fun activities. It's even easier with the Touring App: download the tour with map and route to your smartphone using the QR Code on pages 2/3 or from the website address in the footer below – and you'll never get lost again even when you're offline.

TOURING APP

→ p. 2/3

This route will take you through the whole of India place by place and each stage of your tour will additionally provide an insight into the history of the country and offer you highly diverse impressions of the sub-continent while still giving you time to relax and discover cultural highlights.

The tour begins in ❶ Mumbai → p. 92, where the Gateway of India was built in honour of Queen Mary and King George V who first set foot on Indian soil here in 1911. **From Chhatrapati Shivaji Terminus**, the majestic railway terminus built during the colonial period in the economic

DAY 1–5

❶ Mumbai 🏛 🚉

602 km / 374 mi

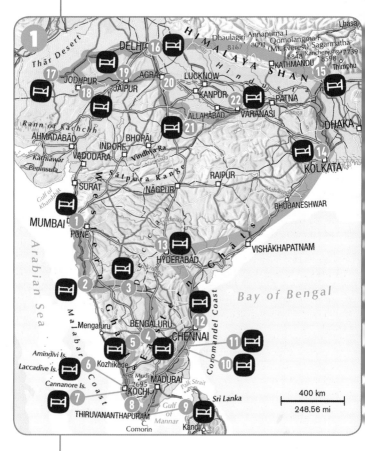

hub, d**ay 2 continues by rail in approx. 9 to 14 hours via Goa's main station in Magadon to** ② **Panaji** → p. 129 in Goa. On day 3, you can relax on the beaches to the north and south and enjoy the Portuguese-influenced lifestyle of Goa. **The journey continues on the night train to the small town of Hospet with a journey time of approx. ten hours. Here you will take an auto rickshaw (13 km/8.1 mi)** to visit ③ **Hampi** → p. 132. Explore the ruined city of the fallen empire of Vijayanagara situated in a unique landscape. On day 5, you return to the modern era: **an approx. 10-hour train journey will take you to the metropolis** ④ **Bangalore** → p. 119, one of India's high technology centres. Back in the colonial era, the British enjoyed the

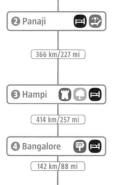

② Panaji

366 km / 227 mi

③ Hampi

414 km / 257 mi

④ Bangalore

142 km / 88 mi

pleasant climate of this city. **On day 6, you will take a comfortable three-hour train journey to ⑤ Mysore →** p. 141. This is a great place to buy sandalwood souvenirs. **On day 7, the journey continues by bus (approx. 8 hr) to ⑥ Kochi →** p. 134 where you will experience an evening performance given by the dance theatre **Kathakali**. **On day 8, you will take a taxi south (1 hr). At Alappuzha, you arrive in the ⑦ backwaters →** p. 135. Here the mode of travel takes central stage: let yourself be taken past green river banks in a *kettuvalam*, a knotted houseboat, for up to three days. **On day 11, you will be driven in a rented car with a driver via Kollam and Thiruvananthapuram on a four-hour journey to Kanyakumari with an intermediate stop at ⑧ INSIDER TIP Varkala Beach. ⑨ Kanyakumari →** p. 146 is the southernmost tip of the sub-continent where the waters of the Arabian Sea and the Gulf of Bengal meet the Indian Ocean on the cape.

Now you will explore the eastern coast of India. **On day 12, a train will take you on an approx. 13-hour journey to the former French colony ⑩ Pondicherry →** p. 143. Here the police still wear uniforms with a French type of helmet: the *kepi*. On day 13, you will be taken by taxi (45 min.) to nearby ⑪ **Auroville →** p. 144 where there is a long-term experiment in alternative living which has been running for over 45 years – for two days, you will be part of this community. Once you have regained your strength through meditation, you continue on day 15 **with a four-to five-hour train journey** to the chili centre of ⑫ **Chennai →** p. 123, the fourth-largest city in the country. Take a stroll on Marina Beach, one of the longest municipal beaches in the world. **The next day, you will fly to the predominently Muslim city of ⑬ Hyderabad →** p. 90 which is today known as "Cyberabad" and strives for the title of high-technology metropolis alongside its competitor Bangalore. **On day 17, you will fly to ⑭ Kolkata →** p. 108, the former British-Indian colonial capital city, now a boomtown and destination of a growing number of immigrants.

On the next stage of the trip, **taking the train is compulsory** – you will arrive in ⑮ **Darjeeling →** p. 106 after around 20 hours where you will also spend the next day. Watch the harvesting of the famous tea at an altitude of over 2,000 m/6,562 ft and experience the amazing dimensions of the mountains: the panorama of the Himalayas is simply breathtaking. **From the nearest airport, Bagdogra**

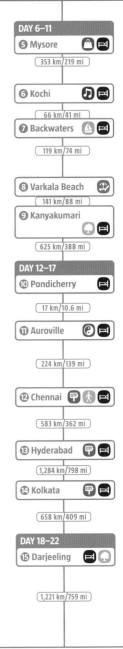

DAY 6–11
⑤ Mysore
───── 353 km/219 mi ─────
⑥ Kochi
───── 66 km/41 mi ─────
⑦ Backwaters
───── 119 km/74 mi ─────
⑧ Varkala Beach
───── 141 km/88 mi ─────
⑨ Kanyakumari
───── 625 km/388 mi ─────
DAY 12–17
⑩ Pondicherry
───── 17 km/10.6 mi ─────
⑪ Auroville
───── 224 km/139 mi ─────
⑫ Chennai
───── 583 km/362 mi ─────
⑬ Hyderabad
───── 1,284 km/798 mi ─────
⑭ Kolkata
───── 658 km/409 mi ─────
DAY 18–22
⑮ Darjeeling
───── 1,221 km/759 mi ─────

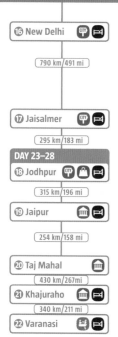

16 New Delhi

790 km/491 mi

17 Jaisalmer

295 km/183 mi

DAY 23–28

18 Jodhpur

315 km/196 mi

19 Jaipur

254 km/158 mi

20 Taj Mahal

430 km/267mi

21 Khajuraho

340 km/211 mi

22 Varanasi

Airport 70 km/43.5 mi to the south, you will take a two-hour flight on day 20 to 16 New Delhi → p. 44, the city of the Hindu rulers, Moslem moghuls and seat of government during the British colonial period. Nowadays, India's capital is a symbol of the fight for independence. Here you will also spend the next day before boarding the night train on the eve of day 22 **for an overnight journey to 17 Jaisalmer → p. 79,** situated in the foothills of the the Silk Road through the Thar desert.

On **day 23, you will be back on the train on a 3.5-hour journey to the "blue city" of 18 Jodhpur →p. 80** where you can wander through the bazaar with its multitude of spice stalls. **The four-hour train journey through Rajasthan culminates in a visit to the "pink city" 19 Jaipur → p. 75** with its open-air observatory Jantar Mantar. A journey through India would however not be perfect without travelling **by train for 3.5 hr to Agra → p. 35,** to visit the 20 Taj Mahal **on day 25.** In Agra, you take the train on **day 26 (9–10 hr)** to 21 Khajuraho → p. 52 where you will visit the unique Hindu temple with its erotic sculptures. **A one-hour flight will bring you to 22 Varanasi → p. 62** where you stay overnight and can take a boat trip on the Ganges the next morning, watching the sun rise over the ghats in the holy city.

2 RAJASTHAN, LAND OF THE RAJPUTS AND TIGERS

START: ❶ Jaipur END: ❶ Jaipur	6 days Actual driving time 23 hours
Distance: 🚗 1,280 km/795 mi	

COSTS: car rental with driver: 29,000 INR, accommodation 30,000 INR, meals 12,000 INR
WHAT TO PACK: sun protection, light and stable footwear, binoculars, food

IMPORTANT TIIPS: The most comfortable way to travel is in a rented car with a driver and air conditioning. Travelling is still strenuous however due to the long individual stages of the journey with only a few short breaks.
In Bundi, the monkeys are free to run around! Make sure that you keep any food, cameras, sunglasses etc. in a bag during your visit.

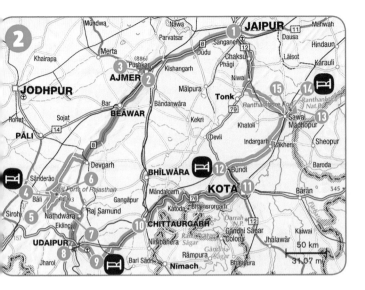

This tour through the desert region in the west of India leads you from one palace to the next and shows you one architectural, artistic and natural highlight after another. You can recover from the long stages of the journey in wonderfully romantic and reasonably priced heritage hotels.

Bevore leaving ❶ **Jaipur** → **p. 75**, make sure that you have time to wander round the city with its pink walls. **The drive along Highway No. 8 will take you through the outskirts of the Thar Desert → p. 80**. **Your first intermediate stop is** ❷ **Ajmer**, a city with half a million inhabitants containing both Moslem and Jain sacred sites. Not far away is ❸ **Pushkar** → **p. 83** with its holy lake, devotional kitsch and small restaurants. Further south, Rajasthan is much greener: **you cross the river Luni which is also known here as Sagarmati, and follow the NH8.** In the evening, you arrive at your first hotel where you will spend two nights: ❹ **Maharani Bagh** → **p. 85** near Ranakpur certainly lives up to its name – "queens' garden". The natural landscape is highly diverse: dry forests interspersed with rocky terrain and wherever water springs up from the soil, it is soon surrounded by lush greenery.

From the hotel, you will make a day trip to ❺ **Ranakpur** → **p. 85** with its **Jain temples,** also visiting the magnificent Rajput fortifications ❻ **Kumbhalgarh** → **p. 85**

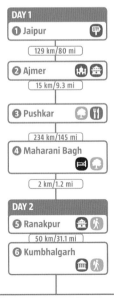

DAY 1

❶ Jaipur

129 km/80 mi

❷ Ajmer

15 km/9.3 mi

❸ Pushkar

234 km/145 mi

❹ Maharani Bagh

2 km/1.2 mi

DAY 2

❺ Ranakpur

50 km/31.1 mi

❻ Kumbhalgarh

(approx. 1 hr by car). Both sites are ideal for hikes – information is available in Maharani Bagh.

Delicately decorated facade of the city palace of Udaipur

In the morning of day 3, **you leave the hotel and travel around two hours in the direction of Udaipur to ⑦ Molela**. In this village of ceramicists, you can see highly skilled craftmanship: sculptures of deities and animals are made here and sold throughout Rajasthan. **After another 60 km/37.3 mi, you will arrive at ⑧ Udaipur → p. 83**. The old town centre and the bazaars in the northen district are full of tempations to buy. You can find peace and original purity **south-east of Udaipur** in the heritage hotel ⑨ **Karni Fort Bambora** *(32 rooms and Suites | Bambora | tel. 9983 33 61 57 | www.karni hotels.com | Moderate–Expensive)*, located in an age-old fort which has been lovingly restored by the princely family.

You leave the hotel, travelling towards the north-east, and after an approx. three-hour journey (99 km/61.5 mi) arrive at the ruins on the high plateau of ⑩ Chittorgarh → p. 84, the medieval residence of the rulers of Mewar where you stop for a visit. **The journey continues for another 193 km/120 mi to the Maharajah city seldom visited by tourists: ⑪ Kota**. The former residence **Garh Palace** now houses a museum. Kota's closest town ⑫ **Bundi** is more picturesque and only around 40 km/24.9 mi away – do not miss a visit to the mighty **Palace** above the town with its colourful frescos before continuing to your hotel: **Haveli Braj Bhushanjee** *(24 rooms| opposite the Ayurvedic Hospital | tel. 0747 2 44 23 22 | www.kiplingsbundi.com | Moderate)*.

Around halfway between Bundi and Jaipur (approx. 3 hr journey) you will arrive in Sawai Madhopur at the ⑬ National Park Ranthambore with an area of around 154 mi² *(circular tour 2.5 hr | book in advance at the Forest and Project Tiger Office | around 500 m/1,640 ft from the station Sawai Madhopur | tel. 0921 2 77 72 23 | www. ranthamborenationalpark.com)* with wild animals including tigers. You will stay the night in a former hunting lodge: ⑭ **Jhoomar Baori Castle** *(12 rooms and 2 Suites | Ranthambhore Road | Sawai Madhopur | tel. 0746 2 22 04 95 | www.tourism.rajasthan.gov.in | Moderate)*.

The **villages around Sawai Madhopur** are well-known for their handmade carpets. It is fascinating INSIDER TIP watching the weavers at work. Ask about a visit in advance at the ⑮ **Village Women Craft** *(behind the Hotel Ranthambore Bagh (Ranthambore Road) | Sawai Madhopur | tel. 0941 4 07 81 81 | www.villagewomencraft.com)*. They will tell you which village to visit and provide you directions. **After this final stop, you return north on the NH12, arriving at the starting point ① Jaipur after around 3.5 hr.**

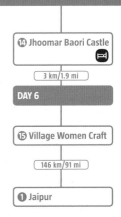

③ BEACH LIFE AND JAIN TEMPLES IN KATHIAWAR

START: ① Ahmedabad END: ① Ahmedabad	6 days Actual driving time 26 hours
Distance: 🚗 922 km/573 mi	

COSTS: rented car with driver 24,300 INR, overnight stays 21,000 INR, meals 5,600 INR, bicycle rent in Diu 285 INR/day
WHAT TO PACK: swimming gear, binoculars, sturdy shoes, sun protection, food

IMPORTANT TIPS: Gujarat is a dry state, meaning that the sale, serving and consumption of alcohol are prohibited. There are exceptions for bars and superior hotels. Street vendors frequently offer dubious alcohol from potentially dangerous sources filled in bottles with well-known brand labels.
In many Jain sacred sites, all forms of leather (belt, camera and phone cases etc.) are prohibited.

Kathiawar, the peninsula in the national state of Gujarat, is home to several jewels among India's holiday destinations. Discover the predominently Muslim Ahmedabad, millenia-old cultural monuments and a wonderful national park and spend some time at the beach in the former Portuguese colony Diu.

You arrive in Kathiawar through the *Gateway of Gujarat*, ① **Ahmedabad** → p. 66. Here you can go on a **heritage walk** organised by the Ahmedabad Municipal Corpora-

tion *(tel. 079 25 39 18 11 | heritagewalkahmedabad.com)*, taking you through the old town and also showing you round the richly decorated courtyards of grand old manor houses. In the **Sabarmati Ashram → p. 68,** you will follow in the footsteps of Gandhi, tracing the extraordinary path of India towards independence. In the evening, you will make your way to the noble boutique heritage hotel **The House of MG → p. 69** for your overnight stay.

DAY 2

332 km/206 mi

2 Junagadh
🚶 🏛 ⛱ 🛏 🚶

91 km/56.6 mi

On the Highway 8A, you drive via Rajkot to 2 Junagadh. Around 2 km/1.2 mi west of Damodar Kund, the ascent begins to the holy mountain Girnar of the Jain. Once you have ascended the 10,000 steps, you will be rewarded by a fantastic view and caves decorated with ornamentation dating from the 3rd to 4th century. Visit the magnificent mausoleum of the former rulers of the town of Junagadh. You will stay overnight in the **Relief Hotel** *(14 rooms | Chitta Khana Chawk | tel. 0285 2 62 02 80 | www.reliefhotel.com | Budget)*.

DAY 3

3 Gir National Park
🌳 🚙 🛏

91 km/56.6 mi

The route continues to the 3 Gir National Park where the last lions in Asia live in the wild. A certain amount of luck is however needed to actually espy one of the around 300 remaining animals. You will spend the night at the **Gateway Hotel Gir Forest** *(28 rooms | tel. 02877 28 55 51 | www.thegatewayhotels.com | Expensive)*.

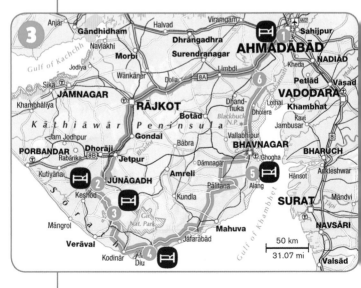

The Gir National Park is the home of the last remaining Asian lions living in the wild

90 km/55.9 mi outside of Gujarat at the southern end of Kathiawar lies the island of ④ Diu → p. 73. Which was was an important settlement of the portuguese colonial empire from the 16th century on, nowadays captivates with a romantic old town with its white churches and cafés. For an overnight stay the hotel **Samrat** is recommended.

Rent a bike or a moped for the morning to get around the only 13 km/8.1 mi long island. There are several sandy beaches where you can go swimming. **The return journey in the evening takes you back in the direction of Ahmedabad to the small town of ⑤ Palitana → p. 70** where you will stay overnight in the **GTDC Hotel Sumeru**.

The next day, you have to get up very early and climb a lot of steps: the **Jain temple hill** of Palitana awaits you at an altitude of 600 m/1,969 ft with its seemingly infinite number of white marble shrines. This location is particularly magical in the silence of daybreak. **Once you have returned to the town, you travel in a north-westerly direction towards Ahmedabad (3 hr), stopping off on the way at** ⑥ INSIDER TIP **Lothal** (site open daily from sunrise to sunset / Museum Sat–Thu 10am–5pm). Over 4,000 years ago in the era of the Indus culture, this was a harbour situated close to the mouth of the river Sabarmati and is now one of the most important excavations sites in the sub-continent.

A further journey of 79 km/49.1 mi brings you back to ① **Ahmedabad**.

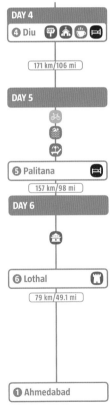

DAY 4

④ Diu

171 km/106 mi

DAY 5

⑤ Palitana

157 km/98 mi

DAY 6

⑥ Lothal

79 km/49.1 mi

① Ahmedabad

SACRED HINDU AND BUDDHIST SITES

START: ❶ Varanasi
END: ❶ Varanasi

10 days
Actual driving time
20 hours

Distance:
🚗 1,383 km/859 mi

COSTS: approx. 145,800 INR incl. rental car with driver, accommodation, meals, entrance fees and other expenses
WHAT TO PACK: sun protection and food

This tour will take you from Varanasi via the Buddhist sites north and south of the Ganges to temple groves and banana plantations, continuing with great contrasts ranging from the foothills of the Himalayas close to the border with Nepal to the megacities of Lucknow and Allahabad which are seldom visited by tourists.

DAY 1–2
❶ Varanasi 🏙️ 🛏️
⎯⎯ 10 km/6.2 mi ⎯⎯
❷ Sarnath 🏛️ 🗼
⎯⎯ 256 km/159 mi ⎯⎯

DAY 3
❸ Bodh Gaya 🎪 🛏️
⎯⎯ 69 km/42.9 mi ⎯⎯

DAY 4–5
❹ Rajgir 🏛️ 🏞️
⎯⎯ 22 km/13.7 mi ⎯⎯
❺ Nalanda 🏰
⎯⎯ 80 km/49.7 mi ⎯⎯
❻ Patna 🏰 🛏️
⎯⎯ 43 km/26.7 mi ⎯⎯

You have not seen India properly if you have not been to ❶ **Varanasi** → p. 62, the pilgrimage site of all devout Hindus and tourists interested in Indian culture – although many will shudder at the thought of the open-air cremation sites. Plan two overnight stops here as Buddha preached only **10 km/6.2 mi north of Varanasi in** ❷ **Sarnath** → **p. 65** which you can visit on the second day.

On day 3, take the Grand Trunk Road, the national road No. 2 towards Kolkata, which brings you after around 250 km/155 mi to ❸ **Bodh Gaya** → p. 105, the site of Buddha's enlightenment. You will stay overnight here and therefore have plenty of time to look around the temples and sacred sites.

On the following day, leave Bodh Gaya and continue to Patna. First pay a visit to the sites of ❹ **Rajgir** – including the tree park **Venu Vana** where Buddha lived with his pupils, visited by Hindus from all round the world. **Your next stop is** ❺ **Nalanda** → **p. 105** where you will find the ruins of one of the most important Buddhist universities from medieval times. **After this stop, continue to** ❻ **Patna, the capital of Bihar where you will be based for two nights in the **Hotel Windsor** *(79 rooms | Exhibition Road | tel. 06122 20 32 50 | www.hotelwindsorpatna | Budget)*. On day 5, you can visit the **palace ruins of Kumrahar** in Patna on the Ganges which are attributed to the Maurya emperor Ashoka, the great promoter of Buddhism who ruled over a large part of India in the 3rd century BCE.

After crossing the Ganges bridge in Patna, one of the longest bridges in India with a length of 5,575 m/18,291 ft, you reach a lush tropical landscape with banana and mango groves. **After around an hour travelling in a northerly direction, you will arrive in ➐ Vaishali** where you can visit several Buddhist stupas, an Ashoka pillar with the symbol of a lion and an ancient Shiva lingam with four faces. According to the ancient myth *Ramayana*, the first ever Indian parliament convened in Vaishali. **In the late afternoon, 217 km/135 mi further north-east close to the border with Nepal, you will arrive in ➑ Kushinagar,** where Buddha is said to have entered Nirvana. The **Nirvana Temple** containing a gigantic statue of Buddha reclining and the **Mukta Bandhana statue** are well worth seeing. You can stay overnight in the moderately-priced **Imperial Kushinagar** (*44 rooms | Buddha Marg | tel. 05564 2730 96 | www.hoteltheimperial.com | Moderate*) in the town, but simpler accommodation is also available in Gorakhpur, 50 km/31.1 mi west of Kushinagar.

The next day, you travel west on the National Highway 28 towards Lucknow. Just 6 km/3.7 mi away from Faizabad,

DAY 6

➐ Vaishali

217 km / 135 mi

➑ Kushinagar

189 km / 117 mi

DAY 7–8

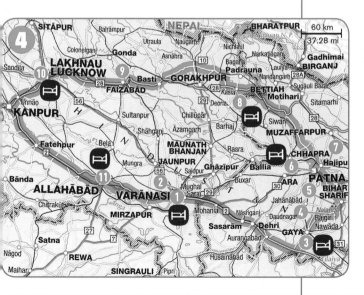

On the occasion of the pilgrim festival *Kumbh Mela* the believers take a bath in the *Sangam* in Allahabad

⑨ Ayodhya 🏛

135 km/84 mi

⑩ Lucknow 🏨 🛏 🍽

201 km/125 mi

DAY 9–10

you will reach ⑨ Ayodhya which is according to legend the birthplace of the heroic deity Rama and now one of the seven holiest pilgrimage sites in India. Ayodhya provides an example of the role of religion in social and political life in India: a mosque erected at the supposed site of the birth was destroyed in 1992 by radical Hindus. Renewed unrest broke out in 2002, also in Gujarat, during which hundreds of Muslims who had previously lived in a peaceful coexistence with their Hindu neghbours were massacred. By the time the police intervened, it was too late. India's Prime Minister Narendra Modi, then Prime Minister of Gujarat, has remained the focus of criticism due to these riots. **The destination of today's journey is 130 km/81 mi away from Faizabad: ⑩ Lucknow → p. 57**, where you will be based for the next two nights. The city with over a million inhabitants is seldom visited by tourists although it is one of the especially interesting cities in the north of India. It was the residence of the rich Nawabs of Oudh (Avadh) and site of the rebellion against the British colonialists in 1857. Take a stroll through the **Janpath Market** *(MG Marg | Hazratganj)* and look out for the local typical goods for sale: richly embroidered *Chikan* shirts and the sweet scent of *Attar* (oil refined with distilled petals).

The next morning, you set off in the direction of Varanasi. The road crosses the Ganges at Kanpur and reconnects to the **Grand Trunk Road, taking you around 200 km/124 mi to ⑪** INSIDER TIP **Allahabad**. The Yamuna flows into the Ganges close to the city. As both rivers are considered sacred, millions of Hindus flock to Allahabad to bathe in the Sangam (translation: confluence or also community). Even if you are not in Allahabad during a pilgrim festival, the city is still well worth a visit: pay a visit to the temple, home of the Nehru family (Anand Bhavan), which Indira Gandhi gifted to the state in 1970. There are also gardens and museums to look round. Stay overnight in Allahabad, e.g. in the **Hotel Kanha Shyam** *(102 rooms | Civil Lines | tel. 05322 56 01 23 | www.hotelkanhashyam.com | Moderate–Expensive)* to give yourself plenty of time for sightseeing and travel the remaining 136 km/85 mi of your journey back to ① **Varanasi** on day 10.

⑪ Allahabad

136 km/85 mi

① Varanasi

⑤ GOA'S GREEN HINTERLAND

START: ① Panaji (Panjim) END: ① Panaji (Panjim)	**2 days** Actual driving time 6 hours, approx. 1 hour waiting time at the ferries
Distance: ⏱ 102 km/63 mi	

COSTS: scooter 970 INR, meals 2,430 INR, accommodation 2,000 INR, entrance fees, pedalo rental and ferry tickets 1,215 INR
WHAT TO PACK: swimming gear, sun protection, mosquito repellant, sturdy footwear and food supplies

IMPORTANT TIP: the flea market in Anjuna is only held on Wednesdays.
The condition of the roads in Goa is good, but only ride on a scooter if you are familiar with Indian road traffic. Alternatively, you can rent a car with driver (costs: 8,100 INR).

Enjoy the relaxed lifestyle in Goa: spend time on the beach, purchase attractive souvenirs and take walks along idyllic lakes and to waterfalls. This trip is simultaneously a journey through time – from ancient Hindu temples to the colonial architecture originating during the 400 years of Goa's Indo-Portuguese history.

① **Panaji (Panjim)** → p. 129 **is the starting point of this route.** You should spend a few hours here to explore Goa's capital. Take a walk around the old district of **Fontainhas** and discover its most charming corners on foot. You can take a break in the roof restaurant *(Budget–Moderate)* of the **Hotel Manvin's** → p. 131 and enjoy a beautiful view

DAY 1
① Panaji (Panjim)

23 km/14.3 mi

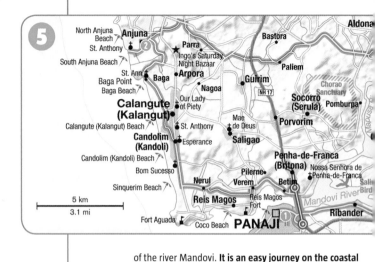

5

North Anjuna Beach — **Anjuna**
St. Anthony
South Anjuna Beach
St. Ann — **Baga**
Baga Point
Baga Beach
Calangute (Kalangut)
Calangute (Kalangut) Beach
Candolim (Kandoli)
Candolim (Kandoli) Beach
Bom Sucesso
Sinquerim Beach
Fort Aguada
Coco Beach
Parra
Ingo's Saturday Night Bazaar
Arpora
Nagoa
Our Lady of Piety
St. Anthony
Esperance
Nerul
Reis Magos
Bastora
Guirim
NH 17
Mae de Deus
Saligao
Pilerne
Verem
Reis Magos Fort
PANAJI
Paliem
Chorao Sanctuary
Socorro (Serula) Pomburpa
Porvorim
Penha-de-Franca (Britona) Nossa Senhora de Penha-de-Franca
Betim
Mandovi River
Bird
Ribander
Aldona

5 km
3.1 mi

❷ Anjuna

28 km/17.4 mi

❸ Mayem Lake

DAY 2

10 km/6.2 mi

❹ Temple site Sanquelim

4 km/2.5 mi

❺ Waterfalls of Arvalem

2 km/1.2 mi

of the river Mandovi. **It is an easy journey on the coastal road to the north, past the beach resorts Candolim and Calangute, to ❷ Anjuna → p. 130.** The flea market in town is a great institution. Formerly a last resort income for the hippies, it has now become a real crowd-puller. You are certain to find souvenirs here. Also find some time to spend on one of the nearby beaches. If you have always dreamed of riding a plastic banana in a warm sea, now is the time to do it. Other activities include windsurfing and paragliding *(large selection of offers in the beach resorts | www.watersportscenter.com.* You can either purchase supplies for a picnic at the flea market or buy food from the vendors on the beach.

The next stop on the trip is 28 km/17.4 mi to the east in the hinterland: 5 km/3.1 mi before Bicholim, you will arrive at ❸ Mayem Lake surrounded by ancient trees. Here you can stay overnight in the **Mayem Lake View Resort** *(17 rooms | tel. 0832 2 36 21 44 | www.goa-tourism.com | Budget)*, but first bring the day to a quiet end with a pedalo trip.

On the second day, you continue travelling to the east for 10 km/6.2 mi to the ❹ temple site Sanquelim. The **Vithalla Temple** with clear characteristics of north Indian architecture is situated on a high promontory above the lake. The temple was built by a ruling family with roots in Rajasthan. **A few miles further, you will reach the easternmost point of the route: the ❺ INSIDER TIP Water-**

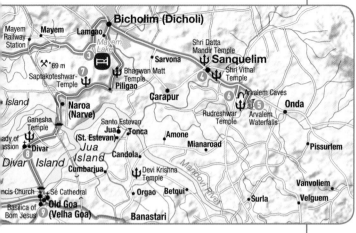

falls of Arvalem cascading from a height of 25 m/82 ft. You can take a swim in the water at the foot of the falls. A further location of cultural significance can be found **around 2 km/1.2 mi to the west:** the ❻ **Temple Grottos which were carved from the** rocks during the 7th and 8th century.

The return journey begins on the NH1, turning off at Bicholim to reach the valley of Naroa (Narwe). Here you will find the ❼ **Saptakoteshwar Temple**, a favourite destination for Hindu pilgrims, built in 1668 by the Marathan ruler Shivaji (Sanskrit Inscription above the entrance). The Shiva lingam inside dates from much further back.

Continue on the same road to the banks of the Mandovi and take the ferry to the island ❽ **Divar**. You will pass many fields and natural landscapes, two white churches along the wayside and some attractive houses in the village of Divar. **Then continue across the idyllic island, drive round the village and then again take the ferry across the river to get to** ❾ **Velha Goa (Old Goa)** → p. 129. Take a stroll through ruins and churches dating from the former Portuguese colonial capital **before returning down the road along the banks of the Mandovi and across the Ponte de Linhares to** ❶ **Panaji (11 km/7.5 mi).** Reward yourself at the end of the trip with a Punjabi festive dinner at the **Sher-e-Punjab** *(12/84 Kudlip Plaza | 18th June Road | tel. 0832 2 22 79 75 | Moderate)*.

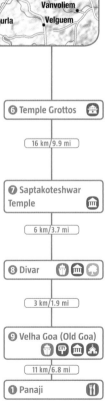

❻ Temple Grottos

16 km/9.9 mi

❼ Saptakoteshwar Temple

6 km/3.7 mi

❽ Divar

3 km/1.9 mi

❾ Velha Goa (Old Goa)

11 km/6.8 mi

❶ Panaji

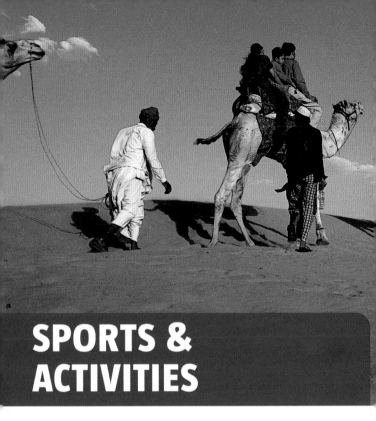

SPORTS & ACTIVITIES

Sports play a different role in India than in western countries, mainly due to the climatic particularities of the country, but have become a status symbol for the upwardly mobile middle classes. Jogging is popular despite the fact that the smog in the large cities makes breathing in itself a real challenge.

Wellness tourism is nothing new for the land of yoga, ayurveda and meditation: guests from Europe and the USA have been coming here for decades to the ashrams to improve their health and find relief from stress and everyday life. Nowadays, the majority of offers within this sector do not have a spiritual component at their core. Hotels, resorts and spas are frequently established precisely for this market, attracting guests with concepts such as balanced eating, holistic health, affinity with nature, fitness, stress management and of course yoga and meditation.

Cricket is almost a religion in India: it is a genuine catastrophe if the national team loses. Polo was invented as a riders' equivalent of hockey in 600 BCE and spread to India where it became a sport for the nobility. Many maharajahs were considered the best polo players in the country. Today, Jaipur and Delhi still remain firm polo strongholds.

Western sports such as football and tennis have now become as popular in India as paragliding. Suitable areas for this sport can be found in the Himalayas, the mountain range of the Western Ghats and Nilgiri mountains in the south.

Experience India through sports: riding on the back of a camel through the desert or paragliding above the Himalayas.

CAMEL RIDES

A special treat in *Thar Desert* in Rajasthan. Trips lasting several days are available and include visits to desert villages, tented accommodation, meals and campfires. It is absolutely essential to wear something on your head, long-sleeved clothing and take suncream with you. Between September and April you will also need warm clothes and a blanket for the very cold nights. Starting points: *Jaisalmer (Real Desert Man Safari | near National Handloom | tel. 09649 86 55 00 | www.realdesert mansafarijaisalmer.com) and Bikaner (* INSIDER TIP *Rajasthan Safaris and Treks | Bassai House Purani Gianni | tel. 08946 96 44 79)*. State-run tourist offices also arrange camel rides.

RAFTING

You'll get absolutely soaked on one of these inflatable boat trips down one of the wild mountain rivers in the Himalayas!

The better-organised rafting companies have life-jackets and helmets at the ready for participants. The best information about degrees of difficulty can best be obtained locally.

Rafting on the young *Ganges* in *Rishikesh* (*Himalayan River Runners* | *March–May and Sept–Oct* | *www.hrrindia.com*) can be recommended. In Sikkim, the mountain rivers *Teesta* and *Ranjit* are popular. Beginners should plump for the scenic stretch of countryside near Pemayantse (2 hr). Information in *Gangtok* at *Sikkim Tourism Development Corporation* (*Hotel Mayur* | *tel. 03592 20 13 72* | *www.sik-kimstdc.com*

RIDING SAFARIS

Horseriders can enjoy "safaris" in *Rajasthan* in particular, e.g. in *Nawalgarh* in the Shekawati region as organised by *Roop Niwas Kothi* (*tel. 015954 22 20 08* | *www.roopniwaskothi.com*). *Rohet Garh Heritage Hotel* (*tel. 08448 28 53 49* | *www.houseofrohet.com*), 50 km/31.1 mi south of Jodhpur also offers riding safaris.

TREKKING

The Himalaya regions Darjeeling, Sikkim, Himachal Pradesh, Ladakh and Uttarakhand are an eldorado for guided trekking and hiking tours. Some of the best trekking tours in India go through the INSIDER TIP *Valley of the Flowers* in Uttarakhand. A virtually intact ecological system can be discovered at an altitude of almost 400 m/1.312 ft. You pass thundering waterfalls, wade through rivers and are constantly accompanied on your tour by the impressive panorama of the Himalayas

A trekking tour in the Himalayas should only be tackled with a guide

and the valley with its carpet of rare exotic flowering plants. *(Best time for trekking: March to October | www.uttarakhandtourism.gov.in).* Time to acclimatise is essential at high altitudes. Trekking off your own bat is difficult as there is no infrastructure (e.g. no signposts). For this reason you are strongly advised not to go hiking without a guide. Bearers can be hired in villages where expeditions start. They will also put up the tents and get a fire going. Organised tours with guide can be booked at local agencies. Information is available from: *Garhwal Mandal (Shail Vihar Vikas Nigam | Rishikesh | tel. 01352 2 43 17 93 | Himalayan Mountaineering Institute (HMI) | (on the premises of the Zoological Park Darjeeling | tel. 03542 25 40 87 | www.hmidarjeeling.com) and Nainital Mountaineering Club (Mallital | Naini Tal | tel. 05942 23 50 51).*

WATER SPORTS

Swimming is possible at many beaches but it is not safe everywhere. On the east coast especially, near *Puri*, there are dangerous currents. There are also powerful undercurrents in the south in Kerala and Tamil Nadu. Make sure you heed local warnings.

Diving is very popular in several bays in *Goa* (Vainguinim and Bogmalo) and around the Lakshadweep (Bangaram) and Andaman Islands (Havelock Island and Marine National Park) thanks to their unpolluted, crystal-clear water. Information on diving courses is available through the Professional Association of Diving Instructors (PADI) *(The Pavilions, Bridgwater Road, Bristol, England | tel. 0044 11 73 00 72 34 | www2.padi.com)* In Kerala, Goa and a few other beaches, you can accompany the fishermen out to sea during the season.

It is no surprise that India can offer good surfing conditions with a coast of more than 7,000 km/4,350 mi, but many locations are hard to reach. During the past years, surfing businesses have sprung up on certain beaches e.g. in Arambol in Goa, Covelong in Tamil Nadu and Varkala in Kerala which also rent out surfboards. In 2004, Surfing Swami, aka Jack Hebnar, of Boston USA, founded the *Ashram Surf Retreat (4 rooms | 6-64, Kolachikambla | Mulki, Mangalore | tel. 09663 14 11 46 | www.surfingindia.net)* where certified surfing teachers give lessons. Guests do not consume alcohol and meat or smoke cigarettes and daily life in the ashram focuses on yoga, meditation, good food, surfing – and other watersports ranging from snorkeling to stand-up paddling.

YOGA

Yoga is more than physical training – it is a form of mental concentration, is spiritually uplifting and ultimately leads to being able to master one's body and organs completely.

According to Buddhist tradition and the vadas, yoga can be based on an eight-branched "path to Enlightenment".

Lots of ashrams, yoga centres and hotels in both larger cities and smaller towns offer courses that can last anywhere from a few days to weeks or even months. Anyone looking for a way to make their body more supple will probably find the answer in a classic Hatha yoga course.

Rishikesh is a place to note for yoga and meditation. Every year at the beginning of February, an international yoga week is held with courses in the open air. Many hotels however also offer yoga lessons throughout the year.

TRAVEL WITH KIDS

Some people who know India well generally advise not to take children to the subcontinent. That does not have to be the case but you should we aware of certain things. The climate, dust and bacteria can cause infections that are much worse for small children than for adults. Coming face to face with poverty, seeing sick people on the streets and an everyday life that is so very different to back home can be very disturbing. India's tourist infrastructure does not always cater for small children either. Although hotels in the lower to middle categories may have folding beds as extras, they will not have cots with high sides. Childminders and children's clubs are rare and generally only found in top-notch hotels. Ecologically-aware hotels, for example, such as the 🌀 *cgh Earth Group* in Kerala with spacious, comfortable rooms and the use of natural materials can be recommended and a perfect for families.

PREPARING FOR YOUR TRIP

None of this needs actually stop anyone from making a trip to India with children – in fact, quite the opposite. India can seem like a fairyland to children with its vivid colours, national parks, elephants and donkeys on the street and palaces and forts. It is however a big plus point if you, as parents, have already travelled around the country and have some idea of the conditions to expect.

Intensive preparations are recommended to be made well in advance which should also include explaining things to children and practicing how to deal with certain situations, such as beggars for example. You would not necessarily undertake long journeys in rickety old country buses and stay in cheap hotels with your children. Plan your time and budget accordingly. You can however undertake everything described in this book with children over the age of ten.

HEALTH

Your family doctor or a institute for hygiene and tropical medicine will be able to help you choose the best regions to visit and advise you what to put in your first-aid kit. Vaccinations well in advance for diphtheria, hepatitis A and B, polio, typhoid fever, tetanus, rabies

Travelling with children to India takes a certain amount of planning so that the tigers and forts don't lose their magic

and Japanese encephalitis are essential. Ensure that your child's sensitive skin is always well protected from the sun. Apart from sun-blocker with a high protection factor, long-sleeves and trousers give added protection against insect bites. Sandals should not be open-toed and must fit properly.

Children must drink a lot of water in the hot climate of India but only out of bottles that have their original seals intact. See that their finger nails are short and properly wash or disinfect their hands every time before they touch anything to eat.

TRAVELLING AROUND

Hour-long bus trips along pot-holed roads are totally out of the question for small children. But anyone landing in Delhi and taking a comfortable car to Jaipur on the properly surfaced motorway, for example, can certainly travel around Rajasthan with a three-year old,

providing you stay in one place and the day trips are not too tiring. The same goes for a holiday on one of India's beaches, such as in Diu in the northwest, Kerala and Goa in the south.

Hill stations such Ooty, Mount Abu, Shimla or Darjeeling, established by the British due to their pleasantly mild climate and wonderful scenery, are suitable for children for the same reasons and are generally much more relaxing than major cities.

WHAT'S ON

Delhi and other large Indian cities have a wide – if irregular – selection of activities that are also suitable for children. Up-to-date information on what's on and places to visit can be found for example in *Time Out Delhi (www.time out.com/delhi)* that also has a seperate children's section.

FESTIVALS & EVENTS

Colourful, loud and entertaining – there is probably nowhere in the entire world with as many festivals as India. Most of these have a religious basis and are celebrated over several days with fireworks and processions with magnificently ornamented elephants. The dates are calculated according to the lunar calendar and differ from year to year. You can obtain the exact dates from the Indian tourist information office *(www.incredibleindia.org)*.

PUBLIC HOLIDAYS AND FESTIVALS

JANUARY

Pongal (Makar Sankranti) – 3-day harvest festival celebrated everywhere, especially in Tamil Nadu, Karnataka and Andhra Pradesh. Freshly harvested rice is cooked with sugar, milk and *dal*. Wonderfully decorated cows also get a taste.

FEBRUARY/MARCH

● *Desert Fair Festival, Jaisalmer* – 3-day desert festival with camel polo, acrobatics and sword dancing
Vasant Panchami – spring festival with singing and dancing (esp. in eastern India).
Carnival – unique spectacle in Goa: carnival procession with brightly decorated floats

Shivaratri – commemorating Shiva's cosmic dance, music and singing all night long, esp. impressive in Mumbai and Khajuraho
⭐ *Holi* – India's most colourful festival: the Hindus welcome in the spring by throwing small packets filled with bright colour pigments at each other.

APRIL

Gangaur Festival – the festival of women in Rajasthan. To honour Parvati, Shiva's wife, unmarried women pray that they will find Mr. Right; married women fast for a happy marriage. The festival begins one day after Holi and lasts 18 days. Tip: the Gauri procession in Jaipur

MAY/JUNE

Id-ul-Fitr – the Muslim festival celebrating the end of Ramadan, the month of fasting

JULY/AUGUST

Teej – another women's festival in Rajasthan. The beginning of the monsoon is celebrated with dance. Women hang up swings in the garden and receive presents.

AUGUST/SEPTEMBER

Onam – colourful Kerala festival with snake boat races, elephant processions and dancing

Ganesh Chaturthi – celebrated throughout India, esp. in Maharashtra, with fireworks and clay statues of Ganesh which are then submerged in water

Jammashtami – the birthday of the womaniser Krishna is particularly celebrated in Agra, Mathura, Vrindavan and Mumbai

SEPTEMBER/OCTOBER

Muharram – commemoration of the violent death of the Imam Hussain, grandson of Mohammed: processions are organised by the Schiites, especially in Hyderabad and Lucknow, and decorated images of the grave are displayed.

★ **Dussehra/Durga Puja** – brightly painted papier-mâché statues of gods and demons are burnt at the end of the 10-day festival or submerged. In Bengal, the mighty Durga, the goddess of victory, is honoured

OCTOBER/NOVEMBER

Diwali – the festival of light is for Indians almost like Christmas and New Year's Eve in one. Relatives visit each other, presents are exchanged, lights are strung up and the victory of light over darkness is celebrated.

NOVEMBER/DECEMBER

Pushkar Fair – huge camel and cattle market in Pushkar/Rajasthan, with camel races

Nanak Jayanti – the birthday of Guru Nanak, the founder of the Sikh religion is celebrated by Sikhs with processions and displays of the martial art Gatka.

Hornbill Festival – In Kohima in northeast India, the ethnic group Naga presents its culture that has a strong affinity with nature. Simultaneously, the Hornbill Festival is India's largest rock music competition.

PUBLIC HOLIDAYS

Here is a list of nationally valid official public holidays with fixed dates. All other public holidays are either not Indian national holidays or are oriented to other calendars such as the Hindu or lunar calendar.

26. Jan	Republic Day
15. Aug	Independence Day
2. Oct	*Gandhi Jayanti* (Mahatma Gandhi's birthday)

LINKS, BLOGS, APPS & MORE

LINKS & BLOGS

short.travel/IND1 Explore the the ghats in Varanasi online as a 360 degree panorama. Links to other Google Earth panoramas

www.tourism-of-india.com Perfect complete package to start off with which will supply you with information on different regions, the people and their culture, accommodation tips, tours and special events

www.outlookindia.com/outlooktraveller The number 1 among Indian travel magazines featuring colourful reports and the presentation of new hotels and restaurants

www.seat61.com/India.htm A beginners guide to train travel in India. The "man in seat 61" is actually Mark Smith and lives in England. He calls himself a "career railwayman" and provides reliable and independent information for anyone intending to travel by train

www.indiawildliferesorts.com Mowgli, Shir Khan and Balu send their greetings. This is a good access point on the internet if you are planning to go on safari through the Indian national parks

www.bollywood.com With interactive Bollywood reviews, celebrity news and interviews, trailers and gossip. Prepare yourself for a real Indian experience!

www.indiamike.com Every conceivable question about a trip to India seems to have been posted sometime on indiamike

www.realbikaner.com/recreation/camel-safarirealbikanercom Bikaner is one of the best places in Rajasthan for camel safaris through the Thar Desert. Useful addresses

thrillophilia.com/blog "Travel Experiences of Lifetime" is the subtitle of this blog by an Indian tour operator with best-of lists for the entire country. Danger of "wanderlust"!

Regardless of whether you are still researching your trip or already in India: these addresses will provide you with more information, videos and networks to make your holiday

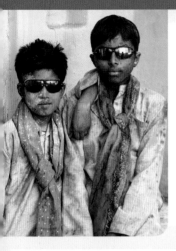

www.news18 news18 blogs by CNN-IBN anchors, presenters and reporters, incl. latest news blogs, current affairs, politics, business, sports and much more

www.expat-blog.com/en/directory/asia/india All sorts of expats writing about all sorts of things they have experienced on the subcontinent

http://indianbloggers.org Directory of top blogs in India and most widely-read Indian bloggers, covering virtually every conceivable topic of interest

VIDEOS & MUSIC

www.bringhomestories.com Here you will find videos, photo essays and reports on life In the metropolises Delhi and Mumbai.The web site is a real treasure trove, not just for its own inhabitants, for all topics ranging from exhibitions, shopping locations to cafés

short.travel/ind5 The Beatles in India. Slightly zany and rather superficial, but certainly entertaining

www.indiavideo.org Lots of videos covering all sorts of different aspects of India, from Ayurveda to village life in Zainabad. The project went online in 2007 with the support of Unesco

APPS

Zomato Reviews, menus, addresses and phone numbers of restaurants, bars and clubs in major metropolises. Arranged according to location and the style of food offered. Generally expensive venues. Practical link to GPS module for all smartphones

Navfree GPS Live India Free navigation for iOS and Android. An online link is needed when entering target location; no roaming costs when in use. Maps provided by OpenMaps

Indian Rail Info for planning journeys by train: you can find immediate Information on seat availability, train numbers and delays with the inofficial app for iOS and Android

TRAVEL TIPS

ARRIVAL

Direct flights from London to Mumbai, Delhi and several other major cities are operated by a number of national airlines. Flight time: approx. 9½ hr. Some charter flights also go to Goa. Prices vary considerably depending on when you book, availability and the season. Shop around! Return flights must ben confirmed 72 hours before departure.

BANKS & CREDIT CARDS

In addition to the customary credit cards (Mastercard, Visa, Maestro), you should have sufficient cash with you. The best way to get rupees is at ATMs. Check if there are additional charges. In rural areas, the ATMs are often not filled with sufficient cash. The State Bank of India is a reliable option for exchange with no extra charges, or you change money in larger hotels. Do not accept any torn notes! Superior restaurants and hotels accept credit cards; you can also use your credit card to withdraw cash in private exchanges and travel agencies. You are not officially permitted to take out or bring in rupees to the country, but nobody makes checks.

BUSES

Some services are efficient, but travelling with them can also become tedious or even dangerous: overland buses. The quality of the state-run bus companies depends on the region of the country – e.g. the *KSRTC* in Kerala is particularly good. The advantage of the state buses is their punctuality and the possibility of reserving seats well in advance. Privately-run buses are often cheaper, but are said to take risks. "Super Deluxe Video Coach" often means Hindi pop music played throughout the journey – don't forget your earplugs!

CAR HIRE

It is usual to hire a car with a driver as most tourists cannot cope with the traffic. Reliable companies offer a good standard of service at very reasonable prices – in the country from £13/US$17.50, in major cities (if you can haggle well) from £44/US$58 per day and 200 km/124 mi, including all extras. You have to pay tolls, parking fees and also the return of the car to the starting point if you are not making a round trip. Make sure that the driver speaks English and ask your hotel to recommend a rental firm. The *Metropole Tourist Service (224, Defence Colony Flyover Market | New Delhi | tel. 011 24 31 03 13 | www.metrovista.co.in)* has proved very reliable for decades.

RESPONSIBLE TRAVEL

It doesn't take a lot to be environmentally friendly whilst travelling. Don't just think about your carbon footprint whilst flying to and from your holiday destination but also about how you can protect nature and culture abroad. As a tourist it is especially important to respect nature, look out for local products, cycle instead of driving, save water and much more. If you would like to find out more about eco-tourism please visit: *www.ecotourism.org*

From arrival to weather

Your holiday from start to finish: the most important addresses and information for your trip to India

CLIMATE, WHEN TO GO

Southern India has a tropical climate, northern India is subtropical, the Himalayas alpine — albeit with hotter summers and more snow in winter. In the west (Rajasthan) the afternoon heat is already scorching in April, but the nights are cold. The monsoon begins in June with heavy rain in the south and works its way northwards week by week. It is dry and cooler in October with first frosts in the Himalayas. The best time to travel is October–March.

CONSULATES & EMBASSIES

BRITISH HIGH COMMISSION

Shantipath, Chanakyapuri | New Delhi 110021 | tel. 009111 2419 2100 | for British Deputy High Commissions in other cities see: www.gov.uk/government/world/india

U.S. EMBASSY NEW DELHI

Shantipath, Chanakyapuri | New Delhi 110021 | tel. 009111 2419 8000 | for other Consulates and American Centers see: newdelhi.usembassy.gov

HIGH COMMISSION OF CANADA

7/8 Shantipath, Chanakyapuri | New Delhi 110 021 | tel. 009111 4178 2000 | www.canadainternational.gc.ca/india-inde/

CUSTOMS

All standard items for personal use may be taken into the country. In addition, anyone over 17 is allowed 200 cigarettes (or 250 g/0.55 lbs tobacco), a "reasonable" amount of perfume and 2 litres of alcohol over 22 %, as well as goods to the value of approx. £210/US$325. The export of items more than 100 years old is not permitted. If returning to the UK check under: *www.hmrc.gov.uk/customs/arriving/arrivingnoneu.htm*

BUDGETING

Bananas	from 2p/US¢2–3 *each in southern India*
Tea	from 13p/US¢17 *per cup*
Beer	£1.25–1.75/US$1.65–2.30 *for a bottle (0.7 l)*
Cinema	50–80p/US¢70–US$1.05 *for a ticket*
Taxi	60p–£1/US¢80–US$1.30 *for 3 km/1.9 mi in a threewheeler*
Rail travel	£8.40/US$11 *Delhi–Bangalore in a couchette*

ELECTRICITY

There is 220 V/50 Hz alternating electrical current. Sockets mostly have a round form with three holes and take Euro plugs: Schuko plugs sometimes only with slight pressure. An adapter is not necessary, but helps to avoid loose connections in old sockets. There are periodical power failures, cuts and fluctuations. Spare batteries and power bars for vital electronic equipment help to bridge gaps when electricity is not running.

ENTRANCE FEES

The entrance fees for museums and archaeological sites for foreigners have

CURRENCY CONVERTER

£	INR	INR	£
1	88	10	0.11
3	264	30	0.33
5	440	50	0.55
13	1,144	130	1.433
40	3,520	400	4.40
75	6,600	750	8.25
120	10,560	1,200	13.20
250	22,000	2,500	27.50
500	44,000	5,000	55

$	INR	INR	$
1	70	10	0.14
3	210	30	0.42
5	350	50	0.70
13	910	130	1.82
40	2,800	400	5.60
75	5,250	750	10.50
120	8,400	1,200	16.80
250	17,500	2,500	35
500	35,000	5,000	70
500	35,000	5,000	70

For current exchange rates see www.xe.com

10 days you may be a little more seasoned and will be able to stomach peeled fruit and raw vegetables.

Inoculations against diphtheria, hepatitis A and B, typhus, rabies and Asian meningitis are recommended. The risk of malaria is low in most areas and it is sufficient to pack emergency medication. Protection against mosquitos is however compulsory as there are repeatedly individual cases of Dengue fever.

Protect your head from the sun at all times. Take plasters, disinfectant for cuts, insect bites and sunburn, mild pain-killers and tablets for stomach upsets with you. A syringe in its original packaging is also advisable. Better hotels can give you the names of doctors, even if you're not a guest there. There are good private hospitals in the larger cities of India and doctors speak English. Public hospitals are not so well supplied. Private clinics are often better equipped than public hospitals. International health insurance coverage is absolutely essential.

been brought in line with international standards. They must be paid in rupees and mostly cost £0.90–7/US$1.15–9.30. The Taj Mahal costs about £10.50/US$14.

HEALTH

Caution is needed especially initially. Only eat and drink in trustworthy restaurants. Do not eat anything which has not been cooked or peeled. Only drink mineral water from bottles with intact caps. Clean your teeth with mineral water too and do not use filtered water in hotels and restaurants. Drink a lot, more than just quenches your thirst. Salty food helps replace lost minerals. Absolutely essential: always wash your hands. After around

HOTELS & ACCOMMODATION

Taxes of varying amounts (depending on the state you are in) are added to hotel prices. Countless Maharajas have converted their palaces into hotels and many combine international standards of comfort with the atmosphere of the Orient. But not all so-called "heritage hotels" are luxury accommodations by any means. Some are basic and correspondingly cheaper. The number of modern medium standard hotels is growing, e.g. the *Trident* hotels belonging to the Oberoi Group and the *cgh Earth* Hotels in the south. It is always best to have a look at cheap hotel rooms or dormitory accommodation before checking in. Homestays and, in larger cities, Airbnb are highly recommended.

IMMIGRATION

You require a visa to enter India. If your stay is under 60 days, you can apply for an electronic tourist visa *(www.indianvisa online.gov.in)* up to four days prior to travel. Your application must include a scan of your passport and a passport photo.

To procure a regular tourist visa (valid for six months), you must fill in an online application which you then print and either send by post or hand in personally to the visa centre responsible for your place of residence. The office address can be found at *www.indianembassy.com.*

INFORMATION

Tourism Offices Directory – India: *www. towd.com/search.php?country=India*

INLAND FLIGHTS

Alongside Air India, there are now a large number of private airlines with budget inland flights such as Indigo, Spice Jet and Jet Airways. Aircraft are of the same standard as in Europe and delays are rare. It is best to book online: special offers are frequently available.

INTERNET & WIFI

There are countless Internet cafés and "cyber centres". They are very cheap but the computers usually slow, the cabins tiny and power cuts common. Big hotels and travel agents are better alternatives. WiFi is available with increasing frequency, also in cafés. Some airports and stations have free hotspots. A mobile phone is often needed to register. Access in hotels can be expensive (approx. £4.40/US$5.80 for 30 mins.). WiFi is seldom found in Internet cafés and where it does exist, it is not reliable.

OPENING HOURS

Temples, museums, shops and offices open between 8am and 10am. The midday break is usually from noon or 1pm until 4pm or 5pm. Museums open in the afternoon can be visited from 1pm or 2pm until 4pm or 5pm. Temples are usually open until sunset, shops until 8pm or later. Some restaurants open around noon and close for several hours in the afternoon. Many however are open from mornings until well into the night.

PERSONAL SAFETY

Tourists are seldom the victims of criminal attacks. Nevertheless you should always be careful. Use money belts hidden under your clothing to protect yourself from pickpockets and to carry money around when travelling at night on trains or in similar situations. Safes in good hotels are the right place to store valuables. You should scan and save in the cloud your passport, visa and travellers cheques. Take photocopies of these with you too. Steer well clear of dubious offers to consume, buy or transport drugs. Checks are thorough and penalties draconian (at least several years in prison). It can also be dangerous accepting food or drink from strangers. The authorities give out warnings about narcotics – after falling into a deep sleep, victims awake to find their baggage and valuables have disappeared. Women holidaying alone should travel in groups, utilise offers such as women's carriages in trains and enquire locally whether particular locations are risky. Reserved behaviour in public is recommended.

PHONE & MOBILE PHONE

Phoning, except for Whatsapp, Skype and others, both inland and abroad, is best done from private telephone agencies. These are however becoming progressively rare in the face of the "mobile revolution". Many travellers buy a special Indian SIM card for their European mobile. The registration process is complicated (form to fill in, provision of a local address and passport copy), but you can also purchase data volume at a budget price. Fast and cheap is Airtel, located in the arrival hall at Delhi airport. Phone numbers change constantly due to the ever-growing networks. The international dialing code to the UK is *0044*, US/Canada *001*. The code for India is *0091*.

POST

Opening times: Mon–Fri 10am–5pm, Sat 10am–1pm, main post offices often around the clock. Post to Europe takes around a week (from major cities) to several months.

TAXIS

Alongside normal taxi cabs, there are auto rickshaws, also known as *three-wheelers* or *tuk-tuks*. It is best to hire a taxi at a stand or flag one down. At airports and railway stations, it is better to organise a taxi at a prepaid counter to save tedious haggling or unpleasant surprises. Private taxi firms such as *Uber* or *Ola* can be called via app, but are not available everywhere in India. Rickshaws and taxi cabs have compulsory taximeters, but there are wide differences in how these are employed. Before you get in, check that the taximeter is functioning and has been switched on. In case of difficulties,

WEATHER IN MUMBAI

	Jan	Feb	March	April	May	June	July	Aug	Sept	Oct	Nov	Dec
Daytime temperatures in °C/°F	28/82	28/82	30/86	32/90	33/91	31/88	30/86	29/84	30/86	32/90	32/90	30/86
Nighttime temperatures in °C/°F	19/66	20/68	22/72	24/75	27/81	26/79	25/77	24/75	24/75	24/75	23/73	21/70
Sunshine hours/day	9	9	9	9	9	5	3	2	5	8	10	10
Precipitation days/month	0	0	0	0	0	16	26	20	14	3	1	0
Water temperature in °C/°F	25/77	26/79	26/79	27/81	28/82	29/84	28/82	27/81	27/81	27/81	27/81	26/79

taxi companies mostly have complaint hotlines which are free of charge. Extra charges are frequent for large pieces of luggage or night fares. If there is no taximeter, you have to agree on a price before the journey – patience and skill are necessary when haggling.

TIME

The UK is 4½ hours behind India in the summer; New York 9½ hours behind.

TIPPING

Workers rely on tips. A tip of around 40 rupees is usual in India.

TRAIN TRAVEL

Travelling by train is the cheapest alternative when travelling from A to B in India. The simplest seating class *Second Sitting* is a non-air-conditioned adventure, whereas travelling in *AC First Class* is relatively comfortable. As long-distance trains are frequently booked out months ahead, it is best to reserve tickets online on the Indian Railways web site *(www.indianrail.gov.in)* or via Cleartrip *(www.cleartrip.com)*. You first have to register online with Indian Rail *(100 rupees)*. Alongside so-called Tatkal tickets with which remaining seats are sold on the day before travel, there is a contingent of seats for tourists. Larger stations such as in Delhi and Bangalore have a special tourist counter, but online booking saves time and nerves.

WHAT TO WEAR

Light, loose-fitting clothes made of cotton or modern sportswear materials are best. You also need warmer things to put on in air-conditioned rooms and cooler regions in the winter months.

USEFUL PHRASES HINDI

Many of the following words used among Hindus and may not be suitable when speaking to Muslims.

Yes/No	Jee haan/Jee nahin	जी हाँ / जी नहीं
Yes (good; alright; understood)	Accha	अच्छा.
Please/Thank you	Krpaya/Dhanyavad	कृपया. / धन्यवाद.
Pardon me/Sorry	Mafa kijiye	मुझे खेद है!
Hello/Goodbye (north)	Namaste!	नमस्ते!
Hello/Goodbye (south)	Namaskar!	नमस्ते!
My name is ...	Mera naam ... hai	मेरा नाम ... है.
I'm from ...	Mein ... se hoon	मैं...
How much is it?	Yeh kitne paisse hai?	ये कितने पैसे हैं?
Excuse me, where can I find ...?	Jee, ... kahaan hai?	जी, कहाँ ... है?

1	ek	१ (एक)	5	paanch	५ (पाँच)	9	noh	८ (नौ)
2	doh	२ (दो)	6	chah	६ (छह)	10	das	१० (दस)
3	teen	३ (तीन)	7	saat	७ (सात)	20	beess	२० (बीस)
4	char	४ (चार)	8	aath	८ (आठ)	100	soh	१०० (सौ)

ROAD ATLAS

The green line indicates the Discovery Tour "India at a glance"
The blue line indicates the other Discovery Tours

All tours are also marked on the pull-out map

Photo: View to the Indus valley from the Thikse monastery

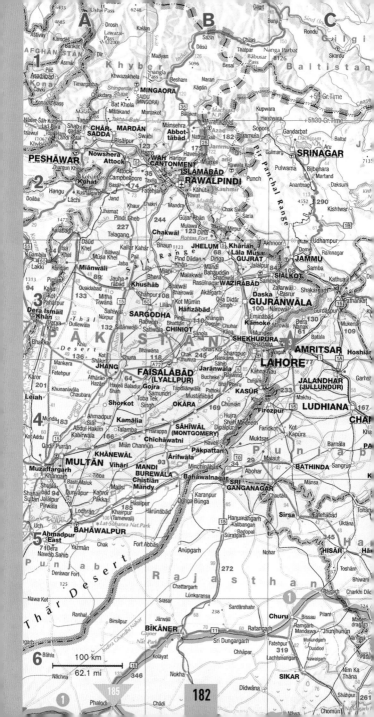

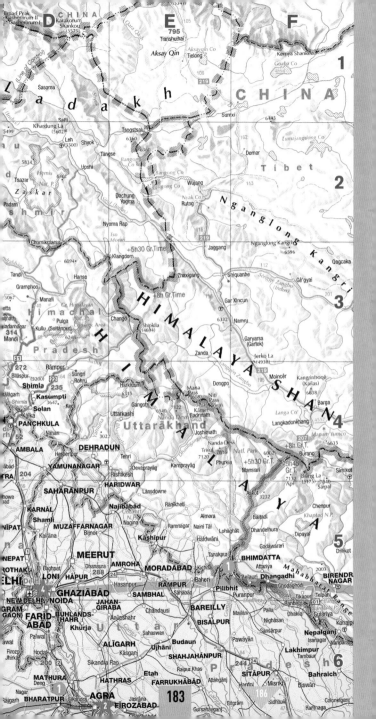

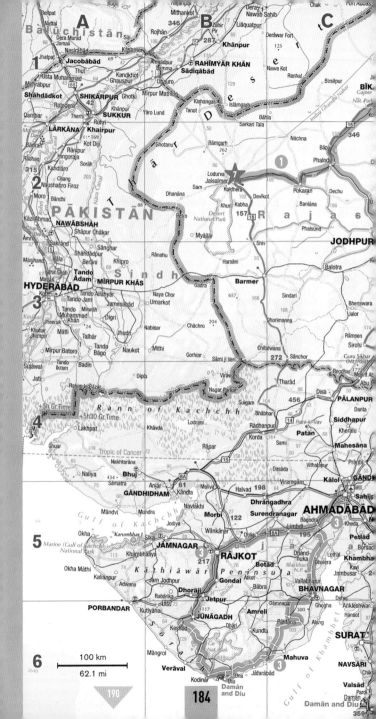

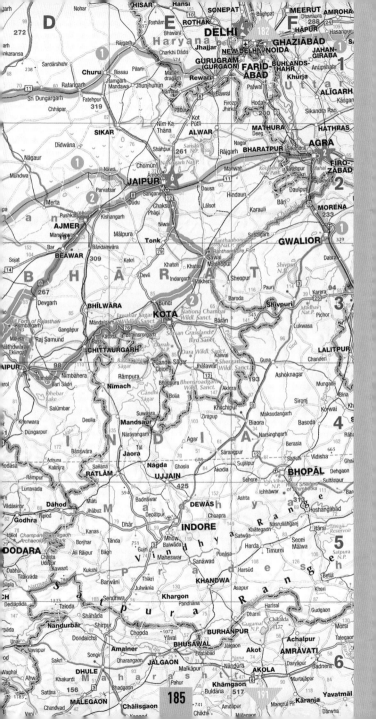

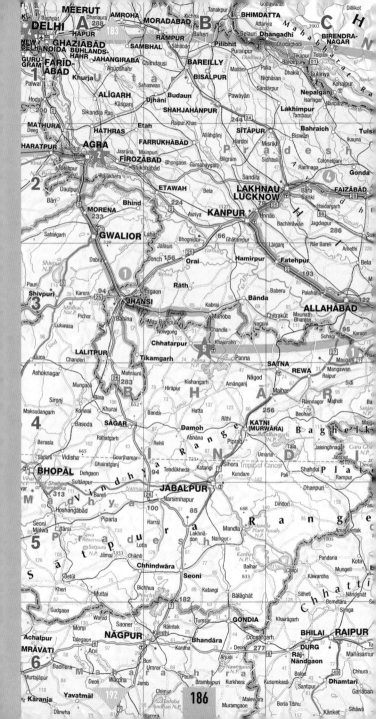

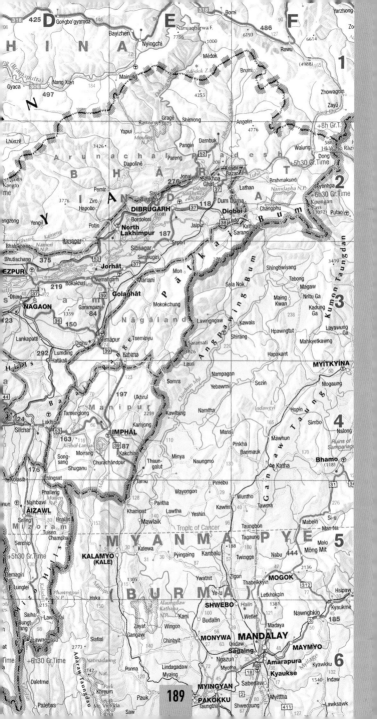

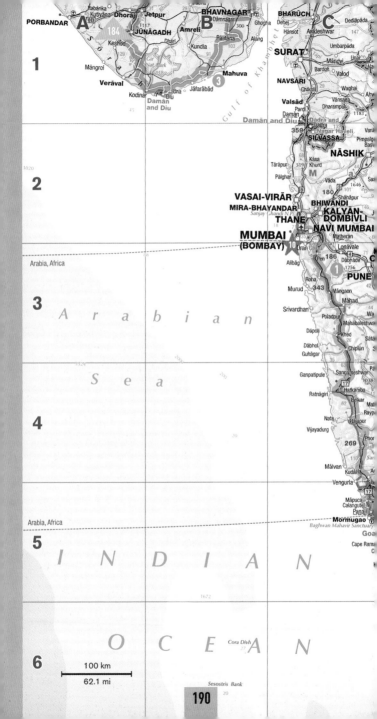

PORBANDAR

A
Rabārika Kutiyāna **Dhorāji** **Jetpur**
JUNĀGADH 1117 **Dhāri**
Keshod
Mängrol
Verāval
Kodinār Una
Diu
**Damān
and Diu**
45

B
Dāmnagar
Amreli
Pālitāna
Kundla
103
Jāfarābād
Gir
Nat. Park 448

BHAVNAGAR
Ghogha
300
Mahuva
Aliang

BHARŪCH
C
Dediāpāda
Dehej
Hānsot **Ankleshwar**
Umbarpāda 147
SURAT
Māndvi
Bardoli Una
NAVSĀRI Waghai
Chikhli
Valsād Vānsada
Pardi **Dharampur**
Damān 1183
Damān and Diu

1

Dādra and
Nagar Haveli
359 Vāni
SILVASSA Pimpalg
Basv
NĀSHIK
Kāsa
Khurd
Tārāpur 519 Vāda
Pālghar 668 Vāda 1646 Sāi
31 101
VASAI-VIRĀR 180 Shāhpur
MIRA-BHAYANDAR Sanjay Ghandi N.P. **BHIWANDI**
THANE **KALYAN-**
18 **DOMBIVLI**
MUMBAI **NAVI MUMBAI**
(BOMBAY) Matheran
Uran Gaon Lonāvale
Pen 186 Dābhāde
Alibāg 1256
PUNE
Roha 42
Murud 343 Māngaon
Srivardhan Māhad
Poladpur Mahābaleshwar
Dāpoli Khed Sāta
Dābhol Chiplūn
Guhāgar 35

2

Arabia, Africa

3

A r a b i a n

S *e a*

Ganpatipule Sangameshwar
17 1038
Ratnāgiri Hatkāmba
Belkar
Nate Raypu
Rājapur
Vijayadurg 269 Phor
Sān
Mālvan 110
Kudāl
Vengurla
Māpuca
Calangute 17
Panaji
Mormugao
Baghwan Mahavir Sanctuary
Goa
Cape Rama
C

4

Arabia, Africa

5

I N D I A N

6

O C E Cora Divh *A N*

100 km
62.1 mi

Sesostris Bank

190

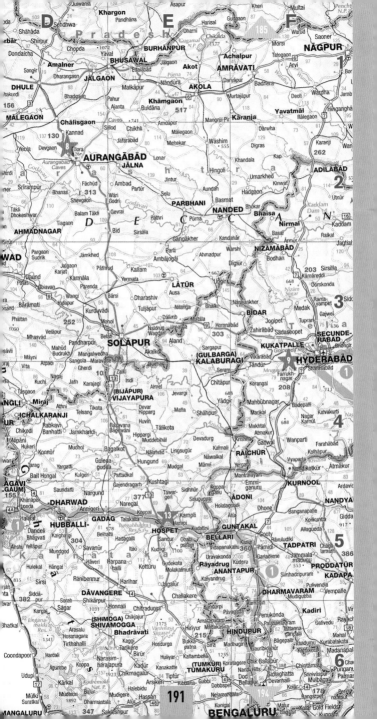

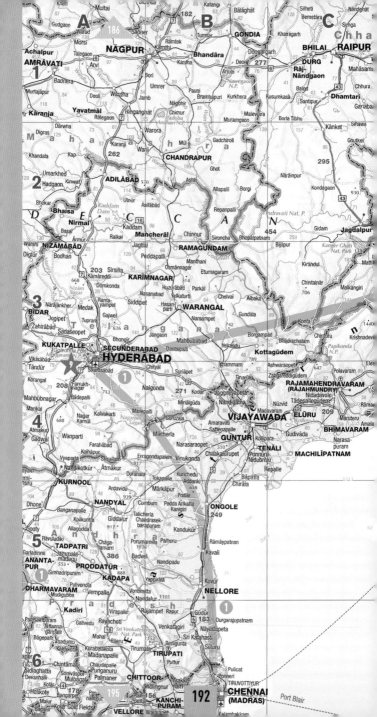

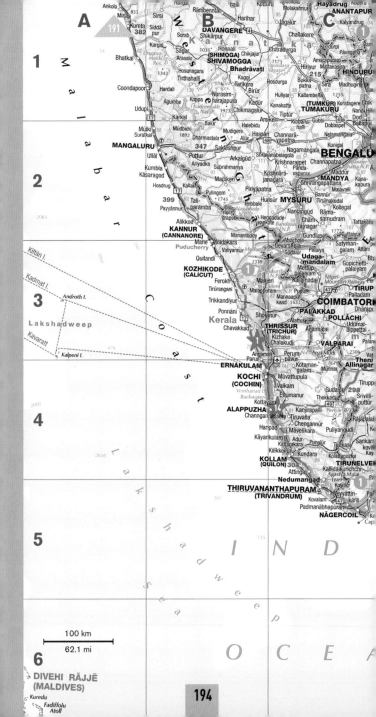

KEY TO ROAD ATLAS

Autobahn, mehrspurige Straße - in Bau Highway, multilane divided road - under construction	════ ═ ═ ═ ═	Autoroute, route à plusieurs voies - en construction Autosnelweg, weg met meer rijstroken - in aanleg
Fernverkehrsstraße - in Bau Trunk road - under construction	──── ─ ─ ─ ─	Route à grande circulation - en construction Weg voor interlokaal verkeer - in aanleg
Hauptstraße Principal highway		Route principale Hoofdweg
Nebenstraße Secondary road		Route secondaire Overige verharde wegen
Fahrweg, Piste Practicable road, track		Chemin carrossable, piste Weg, piste
Straßennummerierung Road numbering	E20 11 70 26 5 40 9	Numérotage des routes Wegnummering
Entfernungen in Kilometer Distances in kilometers	● **259** ● 130 129	Distances en kilomètres Afstand in kilometers
Höhe in Meter - Pass Height in meters - Pass	1365 •	Altitude en mètres - Col Hoogte in meters - Pas
Eisenbahn - Eisenbahnfähre Railway - Railway ferry	─────── ··········	Chemin de fer - Ferry-boat Spoorweg - Spoorpont
Autofähre - Schifffahrtslinie Car ferry - Shipping route		Bac autos - Ligne maritime Autoveer - Scheepvaartlijn
Wichtiger internationaler Flughafen - Flughafen Major international airport - Airport	✈ ✈	Aéroport importante international - Aéroport Belangrijke internationale luchthaven - Luchthaven
Internationale Grenze - Provinzgrenze International boundary - Province boundary		Frontière internationale - Limite de Province Internationale grens - Provinciale grens
Unbestimmte Grenze Undefined boundary		Frontière d'Etat non définie Rijksgrens onbepaalt
Zeitzonengrenze Time zone boundary	-4h Greenwich Time ••••••••• -3h Greenwich Time	Limite de fuseau horaire Tijdzone-grens
Hauptstadt eines souveränen Staates National capital	**MANILA**	Capitale nationale Hoofdstad van een souvereine staat
Hauptstadt eines Bundesstaates Federal capital	**Kuching**	Capitale d'un état fédéral Hoofdstad van een deelstat
Sperrgebiet Restricted area		Zone interdite Verboden gebied
Nationalpark National park		Parc national Nationaal park
Antikes Baudenkmal Ancient monument	∴	Monument antiques Antiek monument
Sehenswertes Kulturdenkmal Interesting cultural monument	* Angkor Wat	Monument culturel intéréssant Bezienswaardig cultuurmonument
Sehenswertes Naturdenkmal Interesting natural monument	* Ha Long Bay	Monument naturel intéressant Bezienswaardig natuurmonument
Brunnen Well	⌣	Puits Bron
MARCO POLO Erlebnistour 1 MARCO POLO Discovery Tour 1		MARCO POLO Tour d'aventure 1 MARCO POLO Avontuurlijke Routes 1
MARCO POLO Erlebnistouren MARCO POLO Discovery Tours		MARCO POLO Tours d'aventure MARCO POLO Avontuurlijke Routes
MARCO POLO Highlight	★	MARCO POLO Highlight

INDEX

This index lists all places, federal states and sights as well as key words featured in this guide. Numbers in bold indicate a main entry.

CREDITS

WRITE TO US

e-mail: info@marcopologuides.co.uk
Did you have a great holiday?
Is there something on your mind?
Whatever it is, let us know!
Whether you want to praise, alert us to errors or give us a personal tip – MARCO POLO would be pleased to hear from you.
We do everything we can to provide the very latest information for your trip.

Nevertheless, despite all of our authors' thorough research, errors can creep in. MARCO POLO does not accept any liability for this. Please contact us by e-mail or post.
MARCO POLO Travel Publishing Ltd
Pinewood, Chineham Business Park
Crockford Lane, Chineham
Basingstoke, Hampshire RG24 8AL
United Kingdom

CREDITS

Cover photograph: Holi festival (Look/age Fotostock)

Photos: DuMont Bildarchiv: Huber (26, 96, 138, 170/171, 171), Krüger (51), Modrow (30 left, 48); J. Holz (7, 66/67, 81, 85, 154, 164/165, 170); huber- images: G. Cozzi (184/185); huber-images: J. Banks (65), U. Bernhart (172 top), G. Cipriani (109), G. Cozzi (34/35, 55), Gräfenhain (flap right, 12/13, 38, 98), B. Mitchell (173), T. & B. Morandi (72, 74), B. Pipe (43), Schmid (118/119, 128, 131), R. Schmid (45); G. Jung (56); O. Krüger (flap left, 5, 17, 19, 22/23, 24, 32/33, 36, 41, 53, 59, 61, 76, 78, 94, 100/101, 102, 107, 111, 116, 123, 136, 140, 145, 148/149, 166, 168, 168/169, 169, 172 bottom); Laif: Huber (4), Jonkmanns (120), D. Kruell (14), Modrow (32, 82); Look/age Fotostock (1); K. Maeritz (28/29, 46, 63, 68, 70, 104, 124, 133, 134/135); mauritius images: D. Delimont (147), M. Harker (2), Kugler (33), J. Warburton-Lee (86/87); mauritius images/age (112); mauritius images/Alamy (6, 8, 9, 10, 21 bottom, 30 right, 31, 91, 93, 114, 127, 160), S. Abraham (21 top), J. Benninghofen (20 bottom), A. Ghawana (20 centre); mauritius images/Axiom Photographic (142); mauritius images/Imagebroker: F B Dolczewski (20 top); mauritius images/Pixtal (157); mauritius images/Prisma (11); mauritius images/Rubberball (3); D. Renckhoff (88)

2nd edition – fully revised and updated 2020

Worldwide Distribution: Marco Polo Travel Publishing Ltd, Pinewood, Chineham Business Park, Crockford Lane, Basingstoke, Hampshire RG24 8AL, United Kingdom. Email: sales@marcopolouk.com
© MAIRDUMONT GmbH & Co. KG, Ostfildern
Chief editor: Stefanie Penck
Authors: Edda and Michael Neumann-Adrian, Gabriel A. Neumann; reviser: Alexandra Lattek
editor: Christin Ullmann
Cartography road atlas: © MAIRDUMONT, Ostfildern; cartography pull-out map: © MAIRDUMONT, Ostfildern
Cover design, p. 1, pull-out map cover: Karl Anders – Studio für Brand Profiling, Hamburg; design inside: milchhof:atelier, Berlin; design p. 2/ 3, Discovery Tours: Susan Chaaban Dipl.-Des. (FH)
Translated from German by Christopher Wynne and Lindsay Chalmers-Gerbracht
Editorial office: SAW Communications, Redaktionsbüro Dr. Sabine A. Werner, Mainz: Julia Gilcher, Cosima Talhouni, Dr. Sabine A. Werner; prepress: SAW Communications, Mainz, in cooperation with alles mit Medien, Mainz

MIX
Paper from
responsible sources
FSC® C018236

DOS & DON'TS ☞

A few things you should bear in mind when travelling in India

DO OBSERVE THE NO-SHOE RULE

Do not enter a temple with your shoes on. Taking your shoes off is a fundamental requirement. The same applies when invited to an Indian house.

DO NOT TAKE PHOTOGRAPHS OF EVERYTHING

Not everything that is colourful or bizarre can simply be photographed. Private individuals should always be asked first. Taking pictures of the holy of holies in temples and cremation ceremonies is absolutely taboo.

DO NOT SMOOCH IN PUBLIC

Kissing, walking arm in arm and other signs of affection in public are not appropriate and are seen as offensive. (Sun)bathing in the nude is not tolerated. Plain clothes police patrol beaches.

DO NOT BE TAKEN ANYWHERE BY ANYONE

Do not be lured into offers to take you to a cheap shop run by someone's uncle, brother or other relative. The "commission" for the "guide's" services is added to the price. Not everyone who pretends to be a guide is qualified to do so. At least make sure his English is good and work out a price before going on a tour.

DO NOT GIVE MONEY

Never give begging children money as this just aggravates the situation. Instead, give them something to eat, crayons or even soap.

DO AVOID MISUNDERSTANDINGS

Female tourists should not flirt with Indians if they do not want friendliness to be mistaken as an invitation for more. Men ask men for directions, for example, not female passers-by (and vice versa).

DO NOT BE CAUGHT OUT BY DRUG DEALERS

Indian authorities do not have any sympathy with drug dealers or addicts and Indian prisons are notoriously atrocious. The consumption or possession of cannabis is illegal and can easily lead to 6-months in prison. Alcohol is legal but drunks are sometimes arrested and can not expect any sympathy either.

DO NOT SHOW THE BARE SOLES OF YOUR FEET

While being bare-footed is normal in India, if you put your feet on a bench or even a table this is seen as offensive. It is absolutely taboo to point your bare feet at a religious icon or the Indian flag.